The Sense of Place in Contemporary Cinema

The Sense of Place
in Contemporary Cinema

Corinne Maury

Translated by Francis Guévremont

EDINBURGH
University Press

Edinburgh University Press is one of the leading university presses in the UK. We publish academic books and journals in our selected subject areas across the humanities and social sciences, combining cutting-edge scholarship with high editorial and production values to produce academic works of lasting importance. For more information visit our website: edinburghuniversitypress.com

© Corinne Maury, 2022, 2024
English language translation © Francis Guévremont, 2022, 2024

Edinburgh University Press Ltd
The Tun – Holyrood Road
12 (2f) Jackson's Entry
Edinburgh EH8 8PJ

First published in hardback by Edinburgh University Press 2022

Typeset in Garamond MT Pro by
Cheshire Typesetting Ltd, Cuddington, Cheshire
A CIP record for this book is available from the British Library

ISBN 978 1 3995 0139 2 (hardback)
ISBN 978 1 3995 0140 8 (paperback)
ISBN 978 1 3995 0141 5 (webready PDF)
ISBN 978 1 3995 0142 2 (epub)

The right of Corinne Maury to be identified as author of this work has been asserted in accordance with the Copyright, Designs and Patents Act 1988 and the Copyright and Related Rights Regulations 2003 (SI No. 2498).

Originally published in French as *Du parti pris des lieux dans le cinéma contemporain* by Éditions Hermann, Paris, 2018.

Contents

List of Figures — vii
Acknowledgements — ix

Introduction — 1

Part 1: Chantal Akerman: Cloistered Nomadism — 13
1. *Blow Up My Town*: Everyday Rowdiness — 17
2. *Jeanne Dielman*: Neurotic Seclusion — 22
3. From Cities to Walls: A Local Change of Scenery — 29

Part 2: The House as a Place of Declarations and Meditations — 43
4. Avi Mograbi: The Political Workshop — 45
5. A Moving Inwardness: Alexander Sokurov's *A Humble Life* — 61

Part 3: The Forest: From Sensory Environment to Economic Site — 73
6. Philippe Grandrieux's Forest-matter: A Multisensory Place — 75
7. Naomi Kawase's *The Mourning Forest*: The March of Bodies, the Spiritual Journey — 83
8. Danièle Huillet and Jean-Marie Straub: The 'Sacred Sobriety' of the Undergrowth — 90
9. Lisandro Alonso's *La Libertad* and *Los Muertos*: The Dual Forest — 103

Part 4: The *Banlieue:* Off-centred, Isolated — 111
10. Pasolini's Wastelands — 115
11. Pedro Costa's *Colossal Youth*: From the Slums to the Sanitised Apartment — 124
12. Tariq Teguia and the Algerian *Banlieue*: A Field of Ruins — 134

Part 5: The Strangeness of Places and the Solitude of Men   **145**
13. Bruno Dumont's Hamlets: Cursed and Isolated Places   147
14. Béla Tarr: Waiting behind Barricades   159
15. Sharunas Bartas's Undergrounds   167

Epilogue   **177**

Bibliography   180
Index   188

Figures

1.1	*Blow Up My Town* (1968)	20
1.2	*Blow Up My Town* (1968)	20
2.1	*Jeanne Dielman, 23, quai du commerce, 1080 Bruxelles* (1975)	26
2.2	*Jeanne Dielman, 23, quai du commerce, 1080 Bruxelles* (1975)	26
2.3	*Jeanne Dielman, 23, quai du commerce, 1080 Bruxelles* (1975)	27
2.4	*Jeanne Dielman, 23, quai du commerce, 1080 Bruxelles* (1975)	27
3.1	*News from Home* (1976)	38
3.2	*News from Home* (1976)	38
3.3	*Down There* (2006)	39
3.4	*Down There* (2006)	39
3.5	*No Home Movie* (2015)	40
3.6	*No Home Movie* (2015)	40
4.1	*August: A Moment Before the Eruption* (2002)	57
4.2	*August: A Moment Before the Eruption* (2002)	57
4.3	*How I Learned to Overcome My Fear and Love Arik Sharon* (1997)	58
4.4	*Avenge But One of My Two Eyes* (2005)	58
5.1	*A Humble Life* (1997)	68
5.2	*A Humble Life* (1997)	69
5.3	*A Humble Life* (1997)	69
5.4	*A Humble Life* (1997)	70
6.1	*Un Lac* (2008)	80
6.2	*Un Lac* (2008)	80
6.3	*Un Lac* (2008)	81
6.4	*Un Lac* (2008)	81
7.1	*The Mourning Forest* (2007)	87
7.2	*The Mourning Forest* (2007)	87
7.3	*The Mourning Forest* (2007)	88
7.4	*The Mourning Forest* (2007)	88
8.1	*Workers, Peasants* (2001)	99
8.2	*Workers, Peasants* (2001)	100
8.3	*Le Genou d'Artémide* (2008)	100
8.4	*Le Genou d'Artémide* (2008)	101

9.1	*La Libertad* (2001)	107
9.2	*La Libertad* (2001)	107
9.3	*La Libertad* (2001)	108
9.4	*La Libertad* (2001)	108
10.1	*Mamma Roma* (1962)	120
10.2	*Mamma Roma* (1962)	120
10.3	*Mamma Roma* (1962)	121
10.4	*Mamma Roma* (1962)	121
11.1	*Colossal Youth* (2006)	131
11.2	*Colossal Youth* (2006)	131
11.3	*Colossal Youth* (2006)	132
11.4	*Colossal Youth* (2006)	132
12.1	*La Clôture* (2003)	141
12.2	*Rome Rather Than You* (2006)	141
12.3	*Rome Rather Than You* (2006)	141
12.4	*Rome Rather Than You* (2006)	142
13.1	*Hors Satan* (2011)	155
13.2	*Hors Satan* (2011)	156
13.3	*Hors Satan* (2011)	156
13.4	*Hors Satan* (2011)	156
13.5	*Hors Satan* (2011)	156
13.6	*P'tit Quinquin* (2014)	157
14.1	*Damnation* (1988)	163
14.2	*Damnation* (1988)	164
14.3	*Sátántangó* (1994)	164
14.4	*Sátántangó* (1994)	164
14.5	*The Turin Horse* (2011)	165
14.6	*The Turin Horse* (2011)	165
15.1	*Three Days* (1991)	172
15.2	*Three Days* (1991)	173
15.3	*Three Days* (1991)	173
15.4	*Three Days* (1991)	174
15.5	*The Corridor* (1995)	174
15.6	*The Corridor* (1995)	175

Acknowledgements

I would like to thank:

- José Moure, for his kindness and the dialogue that went on all through the writing of this book
- Sylvie Rollet, for her meaningful remarks and her unwavering ardour
- David Faroult, Camille Gendrault, Jessie Martin and Guillaume Sibertin-Blanc, for their friendly support
- Joëlle Hauzer, for her much-appreciated proofreading
- Olivier Zuchuat, for his care, every day and everywhere
- Claire Atherton, Philippe Avril (Les Films de l'étranger), Lore Gablier (Paradise Films), Nicola Mazzanti and Arianna Turci (Royal Film Archive of Belgium), Avi Mograbi, Boris Pollet, Jean-Marie Straub and Barbara Ulrich (BELVA Film), Gaël Teicher (Éditions de l'œil) and Tariq Teguia.

The French version was completed with the financial support of PLH/ELH (Université de Toulouse – Jean Jaurès) and Films du Mélangeur.

The English version was completed with the financial support of Films du Mélangeur.

The section of Chapter IV titled 'Sharunas Bartas's Undergrounds' is an extended version of the following publication: '*Trois jours* et *Corridor*, de Sharunas Bartas. Entre lieux marginalisés et silence agité des visages', in Robert Bonamy (ed.), *Sharunas Bartas ou les hautes solitudes*, De l'incidence Éditeur/Centre Georges-Pompidou, 2016, pp. 157–68. It was included here with the consent of De l'incidence Éditeur and Robert Bonamy, whom I wish to thank.

Introduction

In *The Man Without a Past* (2002), Aki Kaurismäki continues with biting irony his study of the excluded, the abused and the losers, which he began in *Drifting Clouds* (1996). A man gets off the train in Helsinki, hoping to find work. Just outside the station, he is savagely beaten. He is taken to the hospital and pronounced dead. However, he leaves his room mysteriously. At this point, Kaurismäki inserts a view of the port, with symphonic music, in a slow high-angle shot that reveals gradually the body of the 'dead' man, lying on the rocky soil. This is followed by a wide shot of a black and pink sky. A tramp comes along and takes the boots off the prone body, then two blond children, carrying a water can, see it and run off. The next image, a fixed long shot, shows powder blue and rust-coloured metal containers. In front of the biggest container, on top of which lies a water tank, a fire is burning. The two children run up to their father to tell him of their discovery. The audience then understands suddenly that a poor family lives in that container. The polished colorimetry of the shot (the red sky, the blue and yellow containers) produces an affected optical lyricism, which in turn resonates with the orchestral music playing through these shots. The rusted vats and jerrycans, the old containers and the various bits of scrap iron lying about, are carefully and geometrically arranged in this lot near the port, as if chaos was more structure than dislocation. This sophisticated dereliction gives off a feeling of artificiality, of exoticism. In this parable-movie, this harbour rubbish dump is more celestial than terrestrial. It seems one must resort to using the term 'scenery' to describe this sundry spatial arrangement, in which poverty is a form of decoration.

In *Damnation* (1988), Béla Tarr shows the wanderings of Karrer, a disillusioned and dissatisfied man, in an isolated and muddy town on the great Hungarian plains. Having been abruptly thrown out of his flat by his lover, Karrer remains seated on the floor, leaning on the door frame. In the following shot, we see a wet street stretching across the screen. On the kerb, a rubbish bin lies on its side, having rolled up against a concrete post, presumably pushed there by the wind. Starting from a pylon, wires cross the grey sky. At the foot of a building with sagging walls, a dog is nosing around, looking for food or a scent. We hear footsteps: Karrer walks across the shot then disappears in an alley, followed by another dog. His modest silhouette scurries along walls, which basically means that Karrer, from a cinematic point of view, is equal to the dogs. He exits the screen, and the street goes back to its rainy sleepiness. The last dog turns into a side street and the main street returns to its 'obsessive wallness'.[1] Béla Tarr allows the shot to continue, with no characters in it, as if suspended, paralysed, sent back to a time that seems unchanging. The shot started before Karrer entered it; it continues after he left it. Throughout *Damnation*, Béla Tarr expresses within the frames the repeated experiences of a daily life filled with rainy landscapes. Men are just ordinary bodies, anonymous minor figures that walk through the world while disintegrating. Yet Karrer is not foreign to this network of streets through which he wanders tirelessly. He is an integral part of this muddy environment that is both his habitat and the space of his disintegration, of his dissolution. On the screen, Karrer and the city are joined, and the urban space becomes a pivot that reveals the scars left by time and the breaking-down of beings. How, then, should one describe this process of spatial sinking and of gradual erosion that simultaneously ties the character to space and space to the character?

The words *space, territory, scenery* are unable to apprehend the *dwelling* relationship (in a phenomenological sense) between the character and the muddy alleys of the city. The notion of *place* seemed to me more fertile as a way to point out the types of spaces that, in film, are associated with presence, intimacy, inhabitation, *habitus*, nearness and being-here. Filmmakers such as Chantal Akerman, Lisandro Alonso, Pedro Costa, Bruno Dumont, Naomi Kawase, Avi Mograbi, Béla Tarr, Tariq Teguia or Sharunas Bartas choose not to focus solely on the cinematic narration of the fate of their characters. They send them 'off centre' so they stop being the only pole of the film. These filmmakers thus offer immersive *topo-stories*. The all-powerful *pathos* is stifled, the invasive sovereignty of narration is thwarted, the rhythm of the story is slowed because it is dotted with moments of silent apnoeas, of injunctive revolts. These filmmakers show mundane, trivial events, and therefore shift the emphasis on to the *topoi*. They create what we shall call from now on 'place' – inhabited territories, existential matrices where ways of doing and of living are mobilised, where modes of production are built, where resistances are improvised. Places witness the frantic transformations of the world, its apathetic forces, its political or economic tensions. These filmmakers give place a temporal depth, an aesthetic plasticity. Thus, they give it – paradoxically – the possibility of being 'embodied' on screen. In a sense, place in film is complex, it is welcoming, but it is also a territory where active and constraining forces are liberated. Singular rhythmicities, vital or destructive powers are established and help unveil the state of the world. What purpose does *place* serve in films, when it is not just a background to actions, or is indistinguishable from the landscape, or, worse, a simple space to walk through, a kind of neutral territory? How do the *different forms of places* manifest themselves on screen? What are their different aspects, their matric potentialities?

As opposed to the notions of space, of scenery, of landscape, place has rarely been investigated by film studies. For the founders of semio-narratology, place is 'the text of [cinematic] space.'[2] The construction of a narrative world is based as much on place as on characters because place represents space in a way that can become 'a true meaning-producing system'. Three types of places are defined: *referential places* (whose main purpose is to be a realistic anchor); *incipient places* (locations that are favourable to the creation of speech, such as restaurants, offices, tribunals); and *anaphoric places* (where networks of calls and recalls are set up in order to increase narrative cohesion). From this standpoint, place is a narrative agent and produces social meaning. Using the word 'place' to describe these narratological functions seems simplistic to me because it does not fully exploit the polysemic density with which it has been applied in the social sciences.

Since the 1970s, the social sciences, geography, sociology, ethnography, architecture and literature have been intermittently interested in the 'science of place'. The debates about the notion have essentially attempted to conceptualise it and simultaneously distance it from closely related notions such as territory and space: from Michel de Certeau's 'practice of place'[3] to Marc Augé's 'non-place'[4] – and, of course, Pierre Nora's 'memory space'.[5] Writers and poets have often perceived place as a space that is already out of the way, where one can hide, seek solace, in a sort of creative withdrawal: 'Place is what takes place, without possession – place has nothing but it is not nothing, it is a receptacle, an area that welcomes and collects, that exists before the mark and waits for it,' write Jean-Christophe Bailly.[6] Place is there *before*, it precedes but does not exceed, it is a matrix waiting for the future, for what is to come. Michel Butor suggested using the term 'genius of place' to show the hold that certain places have over humans. He claims they have a great ascendancy which sets them apart from unequivocal, lifeless space, perhaps makes them opposites:

> Certain places are particularly active and reveal parts of ourselves that we did not know: that's what I would call their 'genius', based on the Latin tradition. It is often because they were made by men, because they are the materialization of a culture or of an era.[7]

However, as Anne Cauquelin pointed out, 'we mix indiscriminately *space, place, site, locale, here, there, spot, territory, area, length, environment, milieu, nature, landscape, location* ...'[8] There are many expressions using the word 'place' – 'take place', 'all over the place', 'in the first place', 'in last place', 'this is not the place to discuss it' – that refer both to space and to time, that make them coextensive.[9] And, as Patrick Prado suggests quite rightly:

> To go from space to place is to go from a category to a modality, from theoretical categories of the understanding of space-time to the practical modalities of accomplishment, that is, to the specific qualities of place that were conferred over time by agents, individuals or social groups, that came through it or dwelled in it.[10]

Dwelling is thus central to the notion of place – places are structured by complex ties, ever renewed, between subjects and space. But dwelling, in this case, can have two meanings: architectural (housing, buildings) and phenomenological (dwelling as 'being-in-the-world'). Benoît Goetz, a philosopher, says that places are linked to the senses, which form the basis of any phenomenological perception of the world:

> Places are, in general, a sensible space, that is appropriate to the senses (an appropriate space, a perceptible space), but also an oriented and orienting space (which provides an answer to the question: 'where are we?'), and finally a space that makes sense, that has good sense, that is sensible. Thus, place is also poetical, in the sense that 'poetically men dwell on this earth' but also because it was made (*poiein*), fabricated, structured. It was not only made to dwell, but also because people dwelled in it. Places are inhabited or inhabitable places. It is dwelling that defines them.[11]

Place is therefore, in part, housing, a building that protects. In Book IV of *The Physics*, Aristotle defined place (*topos*) in this way:

> Just, in fact, as the vessel is transportable place, so place is a non-portable vessel. So, when what is within a thing which is moved, is moved and changes, as a boat on a river, what contains it plays the part of a vessel rather than that of place. Place on the other hand is rather what is motionless: so it is rather the whole river that is place, because as a whole it is motionless. Hence the place of a thing is the innermost motionless boundary of what contains it.[12]

Place is often linked to architecture, to what is built, as if it needed some sort of outer layer to separate portions of space and become inhabitable. Martin Heidegger thinks place can only be built:

> Man's relation to locations, and through locations to spaces, inheres in his dwelling. The relationship between man and space is none other than dwelling, strictly thought and spoken. When we speak, in the manner just attempted, about the relation between location and space, but also about the relation of man and space, a light falls on the nature of the things that are locations and that we call buildings.[13]

Architecture creates a space (*einräumen*), then builds and structures a *where* in it (*bauen*), so as to make it an inhabitable place (*Ort*).[14] Henri Maldiney, a poet who was a great reader of Heidegger, asks: 'Space is openness, born of tension, so to speak, made by it. What relation between space and place? What links them is man. As being in the world, man is a spatial being and he is a founder of places.'[15]

Geographers are more attached to the notion of territory, with its implications of administration and politics, of a spatiality bound by rules. In physical geography, territories are spaces that have been topographically measured; they are often defined by their legal affiliation. But human geography defines territory as 'an organization of material and symbolic resources that structure the practical means of existence of an individual or a community and that in return help this individual or this community apprehend their own identity'.[16] The notion of territory – the subject of much debate because it is unable to account for globalisation, for the structure of networks or for lives that are more and more polytopic – would thus be more complex and more extensive than that of place. Jean-Luc Piveteau, a geographer, has defined place, as opposed to territory, by three adjectives: 'localized, unitary and remarkable'.[17] *Localized* because, according to him, place 'can be understood immediately, as an immediate datum of consciousness'. Territories can be broken up and become archipelagos, but place is 'practically indivisible', likened to 'an idea of *autonomy*'. It is therefore also *unitary*. Finally, place is a remarkable space because it serves as a landmark, it is fixed. Jean-Luc Piveteau adds: 'Place implies permanence, stability, duration, continuity, transmission in time.' This definition resonates with the idea of place in film that we intend to use here. In his documentary essay *The Man with No Name* (2009), Wang Bing shows a poor man trying to organise his daily life while living in a hollowed-out space in a wasteland. The filmmaker looks upon this marginal reality patiently, directly, frankly, and soon the audience begins to view this hole in the ground not as an ephemeral shelter, but as an atypical and intimate lair where new ways, new approaches to daily life are invented. The wasted landscape around the hole seems at first, to use a phrase coined by Gilles Clément, a 'third-landscape'.[18] Gradually, as the film progresses, this cavity becomes 'a place of silent hospitality', and then 'the place that retrieves the exhausted and rejected body and gives it refuge'.[19]

Neither *space* nor *territory*, place is altogether different from *landscape*, the celebrated *topos* of film studies. The classical notion of landscape that appeared in fifteenth-century painting is often associated with an 'essentialist' belief that landscapes are "Nature"'.[20] Landscape stands 'before us', it 'goes without saying', it grants the viewer a 'pictorial', harmonious and framed access to the elements of nature, ontologically speaking. But as Cauquelin explains, this is a delusion:

> Nature is an 'idea that only appears fully dressed', i.e. as everchanging perspectivistic profiles. It appears as a kind of ornamental 'thing', in language and in the construct of specific forms that are themselves historically constructed. However, it is possible to distinguish between these cultural preconceptions through reflection and analysis. As their unity is in a constant state of flux, the differences blur and coalesce into the feeling of a lone presence: the self as datum.

From a phenomenological standpoint, the perception of the landscape by the subject is a composite process. According to Michel Collot,

> landscape, for such a subject, is not a spectacle to watch from the outside, but an environment to which ek-sistence is closely linked: it is not in front of the subject, but all around. Therefore, it is not always clearly perceived, but globally and confusedly apprehended. It is felt without being seen. But even when landscape is not at the centre of attention, it is constantly present, on the horizon, forming a background to the consciousness of the subject's situation in the world.[21]

In film, landscape can be perceived in two ways, one being within the other: the character is watching the landscape while being watched by the audience. Wide shots are generally fixed, even if, in editing, a series of fragmentary wide shots can be assembled to form a compounded, unified landscaped composition, thus modifying the various horizons shown. Tracking shots can open space up, unwind it like Chinese landscapes painted on rolls of paper. Sometimes, cinema and art come together, and shots are like paintings. In *Mother and Son* (1997), Alexander Sokurov shows harmonious Friedrichian landscapes with two characters; the balance of the composition, where the two (bodies/landscape) cannot be dissociated, the geometric structures, the colours[22] are all borrowed from Romantic painting. Landscapes are sublime, blinding, a harmonious elevation that changes with the seasons. They become the scene of an unconscious outpouring, of a spiritual meditation where doubts and contemplations are projected, an atmospheric mirror of emotional bursts. In other words, landscapes reflect what the audience sees in them, puts into them – an abundance of feelings, at once experienced and fantasised. They are also a living, dynamic tableau in which the weather and the passing of time are part of the same dramatic unit, where the story, intermittently, finds its rhythm.

Films have often used landscapes as narrative moments that must be thought of 'as a construct that calls to itself the eyes of the audience, a part of a strategy of discourse that includes it'.[23] As such, wide shots have been mostly used in films as crude tools of narration, aids to action and editing: brief contemplative, suspensive pauses, when the action is suspended; establishing shots that give *context*; point of view shots (that follow a close-up of a character 'looking' far away); ellipses (one night, one season …); markers of motion or of distances covered (shot from a train, a car and so on). André Gardies categorised in detail the narrative functions of landscapes: background, exposition, expression, catalyst, dramatic.[24] But usually, landscapes are 'something atmospheric', to quote Dominique Château, whether there are characters in them or not, whether they are just a background to the action, whether they are looked at or only recognised without really being seen.

This notion of 'atmospheric landscapes' can nevertheless be quite productive. Phenomenologically, landscapes are both 'in front of' and 'inside', resonating in the depths of one's being:

> But even if landscapes are not the centre of attention of the subject, they are constantly there, on the horizon, in the background of the subject's consciousness of his or her situation in the world. To describe this 'consciousness of situation', Heidegger used the term *Stimmung*.[25]

Thus, wide shots influence films in two ways: intimate emotions are projected on to the world and, conversely, the 'sensible echoes' of this external world are territorialised in the subject.

However, landscapes in film often remind people of the humble dimensions of their bodies, of the awesome power of the immense land that surrounds, encloses, exceeds and overwhelms them. The canonical example of this monumentality of landscape is the importance of Monument Valley in John Ford's films. Ford places characters and animals in a majestic emptiness where man is crushed, dominated by the monumental power of the region, and the red colour of the rocks only seems to underline nature's eccentricity. The audience is set apart; the spectators are not incorporated into the landscape, but rather forced into a sort of dazed contemplation. Both glorified and hostile, Ford's landscapes, his 'trap canyons', are a place of struggle, and white men can only trek across them warily. José Moure wrote, about *The Searchers* (1956):

> the territory of Monument Valley, a passive landscape, void of any human presence, serves as a sort of solemn and almost abstract scenery, for this initiatory journey into emptiness. It functions, just like all-encompassing space, as a sound box to all things; in it, characters hear an echo to their own solitude and powerlessness. It appears mainly as a 'tomb-space', haunted by the presence of the dead that are buried there and by an ancient past that left an indelible mark.[26]

Of course, this desert, with its rocky outcrops, its immense *uninhabitable* spaces, its high ridges from which the Indian menace descends, has not played a big part in the conquest of the Wild West: the wars against the natives, the fights over territories took place in the more central (and more fertile) regions of the United States.[27] This barren scenery symbolises the empty and virgin lands that had to be conquered (since even vegetation hardly grows there) and thus represents the perfect landscape for the great story of the American nation, the backdrop to a carefully maintained mythology.

There are other filmmakers who film wanderlust, who show bodies measured against vast and uninhabited spaces, sometimes absorbed by them, lost in them. The road is for these bodies in flight a space to run through,[28] to overcome. To wander is to follow roads and paths, to try to orient oneself, or to experience unlimited spaces. In these movies, the horizon is constantly out of reach but is a central element of the picture. Vast areas, unending roads form the structure of spatial entities that cannot be located nor restricted.

The sense of place that interests us does not correspond to a space that is travelled, a mythified place or a fantasised zone; it is a telluric spatiality, a territorial concreteness that describes the state of the world. Place can also acknowledge difference, legitimise strangeness, respect what is *apart*. It is made into a single unit through the presence of bodies who dwell in it, explore it, haunt it. The most notable and substantial quality of place is, we believe, its capacity to host events, to condense the experiences produced by bodies. Within these spaces, forces of emancipation and existential adynamy are at play. Place is a spatial and temporal refuge where daily practices are stored, exposed, experimented with, but are not exclusively related to forms of stability, regularity or norms. Sometimes, insecurities and vulnerabilities can hide in it and spread.

For contemporary filmmakers such as Béla Tarr, Pedro Costa, Chantal Akerman or Tariq Teguia, place is a spatiality where the perceptible is welcomed, where corporal commitments and failures, vocal rhythms and gestural strengths and fragilities are played out. These filmmakers try to unfold in places the ways of living which link a body (and, thus, a subject) to space. They become in turn precarious shelters, tired corners, inhabited recesses, monumental openings; they defy anonymity, indifference, triviality, and give character, energy and limits to gestures and words of the (non-)actors. In films that intermingle documentary reality and fictional construct, these contemporary filmmakers often call on men and women with no acting experience in order to create an immediate churning effect, a 'being-in-reality' that is outside the bounds of 'controlled, professional acting'. They radically refuse to see the actors rely on a system of virtuoso performance. They seek to destroy the anthropocentric hierarchy of the classical age to create images in which reality quivers, in which are exposed fragments of existence, slivers of life, rather than homogenised scenarios, well-wrought narrations and excessive theatrics.

The point of this book is not to offer a classification, a typology of the different kinds of places in contemporary cinema; nor is it to present an erudite journey leading from place to non-place.[29] We will suggest analytical paths in films that make use of the expressive power of place and that invent new ways of existing, of testifying, of protesting. This journey through place in contemporary cinema will begin with houses in the films of Chantal Akerman (Part 1, 'Cloistered Nomadism'), Avi Mograbi and Alexander Sokurov (Part 2, 'The House as a Place of Declarations and Meditations'). For these filmmakers, houses are not really a sheltered space where one can discover a more serene way to relate to the world, but rather a lair in which to question the entropy of the outside world, a permeable home where 'begins the utopia in which the *I* meditates while staying home',[30] as Emmanuel Levinas put it.

Often presented on screen as a landscape to contemplate or scenery on which a phantasmagoria of life is projected, the forest becomes, in the films of Philippe Grandrieux, Naomi Kawase, Danièle Huillet and Jean-Marie Straub, or Lisandro Alonso (Part 3, 'The Forest: From Sensory Environment to Economic Site'), a tactile place that gives new strength and new energy to a lost self, a minor place where literary texts can be celebrated, a modest production site where one can exist ephemerally.

In 'The Banlieue: Off-centred and Isolated' (Part 4), we will explore unusual, marginal places – intractable zones, areas often considered by the collective unconscious as subservient territories. Tariq Teguia, Pedro Costa and Pier Paolo Pasolini all attempt to rehabilitate, both creatively and politically, these 'debased' places. Part 5 ('The Strangeness of Places and the Solitude of Men') continues this reflection on 'solitary' places in the films of Bruno Dumont, Béla Tarr and Sharunas Bartas – where, in heavy silence, exhausted worlds converge.

Notes

1. Corinne Maury, 'De l'habitat d'état à l'errance damnée', in Corinne Maury and Sylvie Rollet (eds), *Béla Tarr: de la colère au tourment*. Crisnée: Yellow Now, 2016, p. 44.
2. André Gardies, *L'Espace au cinéma*. Paris: Méridiens Klincksieck, 1993, p. 71 (and pp. 78–80 for the following quotations).
3. Michel de Certeau, 'Pratiques d'espace', in *L'Invention du quotidien. 1. Arts de faire*, ed. Luce Giard. Paris: Gallimard, 1990, p. 173.

4. Marc Augé, *Non-places: Introduction to an Anthropology of Supermodernity*, trans. John Howe. London: Verso, 1995.
5. See Pierre Nora (ed.), *Rethinking France: Les Lieux de mémoire*. Chicago: University of Chicago Press, 1999–2010.
6. Jean-Christophe Bailly, *Le Propre du langage: voyage au pays des noms communs*. Paris: Seuil, 1997, p. 109.
7. Michel Butor, 'Alphabet d'un apprenti', in *Michel Butor par Michel Butor*. Paris: Seghers, 2003, p. 98. See also Michel Butor, *Le Génie du lieu* [1958]. Paris: Grasset, 2015.
8. Anne Cauquelin, *Le Site et le paysage*. Paris: PUF, 2002, p. 74.
9. Cf. Aline Brochot and Martin de la Soudière (eds), 'Pourquoi le lieu', *Communications*, 87 (2010), p. 9.
10. Patrick Prado, 'Lieux et "délieux"', *Communications*, 87 (2010), p. 126.
11. Benoît Goetz, 'La Dislocation: critique des lieux', in Chris Younès et Michel Mangematin (eds), *Lieux contemporains*. Paris: Descartes & Cie, 1997, pp. 98–9.
12. Aristotle, *Physics*, *The Complete Works of Aristotle, The Revised Oxford Translation*, vol. 1, ed. Jonathan Barnes. Princeton: Princeton University Press, 1991 (IV, 212a 15).
13. Martin Heidegger, 'Building Dwelling Thinking', in *Poetry, Language, Thought*, trans. Albert Hofstadter. New York: Harper Colophon Books, 1971.
14. For Heidegger, space *is determined by place*. But it is not space as pure spatiality (*spatium*). Space (*Raum*) is, according to Heidegger, that which has been cleared.
15. Henri Maldiney, 'Topos–Logos–Aisthèsis', in Michel Mangematin, Philippe Nys and Chris Younès (eds), *Le Sens du lieu*. Brussels: Ousia, 1996, p. 17.
16. Bernard Debarbieux, 'Territoire', in Jacques Lévy and Michel Lussault (eds), *Dictionnaire de la géographie et de l'espace des sociétés*. Paris: Belin, 2013, p. 999.
17. Jean-Luc Piveteau, 'Lieu et territoire: une consanguinité dialectique?', *Communications*, 87 (2010), pp. 152–3.
18. Gilles Clément, 'Le Tiers-Paysage'. Available at: <http://www.gillesclement.com/cat-tierspaysage-tit-le-Tiers-Paysage> (last accessed 14 February 2017).
19. Corinne Maury, 'Du sol refuge à la friche nourricière', in Caroline Renard, Isabelle Anselme and François Amy de La Bretèque (eds), *Wang Bing*. Aix-en-Provence: Presses Universitaires de Provence, 2014, p. 129.
20. Cauquelin, *L'Invention du paysage*, p. 20 (and pp. 53, 75, 11 for the following quotations).
21. Michel Collot, 'Paysages en movement: l'image-émotion', *Vertigo*, 31 (2007), p. 9.
22. An optical and photochemical treatment reduced the perception of depth, which gives the impression that the images are made of a field of colours, just like in a painting.
23. André Gardies, 'Le Paysage comme moment narratif', in Jean Mottet (ed.), *Les Paysages du cinéma*. Seyssel: Champ Vallon, 1999, p. 143.
24. Ibid., pp. 144–9.
25. Michel Collot, *La Pensée-paysage*. Arles: Actes Sud/ENSP, 2011, p. 155.
26. José Moure, *Vers une esthétique du vide au cinéma*. Paris: L'Harmattan, 1997, p. 69.

27. Cf. Yves Lacoste, 'Westerns et géopolitique', in Mottet (ed.), *Les Paysages du cinéma*, p. 163; Jean-Louis Rieupeyrout, *La Grande Aventure du western, 1894–1964*. Paris: Cerf, 1964: and Michel Foucher, 'Du désert, paysage de western', in Alain Roger (ed.), *La Théorie du paysage en France (1974–1994)*. Seyssel: Champ Vallon, 1995, p. 75.
28. Antoine Gaudin coined the term 'film-parcours' (journey movies). These are films in which 'the main agents of classic narration have disappeared, and therefore, it is the journey of the characters through landscapes, shot on location, that becomes the principal issue' (Antoine Gaudin, *L'Image-espace: pour une géopoétique du cinéma*. PhD dissertation, Université de Paris-III, 2011, p. 293).
29. Marc Augé defines non-place in this way: 'a person entering the space of non-place is relieved of his usual determinants. He becomes no more than what he does or experiences in the role of passenger, customer or driver' (Augé, *Non-places*, p. 103).
30. Emmanuel Levinas, *Totalité et infini, essai sur l'extériorité*. The Hague: M. Nijhoff, 1961, p. 130.

Part 1

Chantal Akerman: Cloistered Nomadism

In *Poetics of Space*, Gaston Bachelard praises the native home, that first 'matricial' place that welcomes the movement of childhood and institutes – between reverie and boredom – a 'topography of our intimate being'.[1] Bachelard's home is a maternal figure, which, 'even more than the landscape, is "a state of mind"'. It is an autonomous space, protected from the outside, where the voices of the unconscious are expressed and where the manners and materials of dreams unfold. Disconnected from the dark rumours of the world, the house is, according to the philosopher, a 'primitive hut' that protects from conflictual agitation and centrifugal forces, a shell conducive to withdrawal. *To dwell*, then, is to remain temporarily, to exist *in* and *through* the imagination, and it means to seek relief from the weight of everyday domestic life, to minimise the burden of the commonplace, to abbreviate and compress the intrusive and cataclysmic forces of the outside world, and to prefer contemplative states of reverie.

However, houses[2] 'in films' are not necessarily Bachelardian in inspiration: they are, in turn, primordial settings, spaces of passage and circulation, or even shelters; they are the natural spaces of cinematographic scenarios, from the most classic to the most adventurous. Houses are the privileged scenic and scenographic tools where the sometimes intimate, sometimes collective psychological journey of the characters unfolds. Often, they are projected before the spectator's eyes as the catalysts, and as the crystallising environments of suspended or forthcoming dramas. The fact that houses are the privileged spaces of reception and collection of dialogues and confidences does not imply that they are 'seen', or even that they are inhabited. In fact, houses 'in films' are most often either beautiful, deserving of contemplation, or disgraceful and repellent: they have the virtues of social identification – ensuring close and intimate relationships or creating separations between the characters. They find their place in films as elementary architectural garments, and they are framed as empty vessels despite the stature that scenarios frequently attempt to confer upon them. In this sense, the representations of houses 'in films' mostly draw facades, technical settings where the characters' movements are organised. The home is thus limited to being a building that houses the characters, a building that is nonetheless absent since it has no real presence on screen, as it is limited to being a contextualising space. Thus, the house exists more as a stage set, where life is interpreted, than as a place of habitation, where existence is fixed, a home.

In contrast, Chantal Akerman's living spaces are often tempestuous rather than calm, dynamic rather than static, conflicted rather than peaceful, real rather than illusory, ordinary rather than fantastic. For the filmmaker, a house is not a closed space in which to invest a fictional drama, in which to deploy an amusing phantasmagoria, but rather a place of habitation where the prosaic dramas of daily life are exhausted, related, thought about and dispelled. Through this connection to outside life, the house loses its private dimension and becomes a place of vision. As Benoît Goetz correctly writes,

> a house is not an image (any more than a face is an image). On the contrary, it is from the house that the world proposes itself to be contemplated in a vision. But it is not the house that is in view, it is the house that is an instrument of vision[3].

In Chantal Akerman's films, the apartment is an alcove, a retreat, within which the cloistered powers of the quotidian are revealed, as well as its alienating flaws. We will analyse in this part of the book the indirectly political critique of daily life offered, with a sort of dislocated enthusiasm, by the filmmaker, even in her early films. Akerman creates images of reclusion that unveil, with determined clarity, her complex relationship with daily chores, her immense love for her mother, her painful questions about exile and illness. A great number of her films show confinement: cameras are continuously secluded within various interiors. Chantal Akerman uses words and bodies, her own and those of others, to express the heaviness and emptiness of everyday time, the different ways of being walled in, of rushing into those spaces, of becoming breathless in them, of being restored by them ... In other words, a sort of cloistered nomadism underlies her films. Caught up in the stifling resignation of time, the walls and rooms of the flats in the films are no longer anonymous surfaces and insignificant barriers; indeed, they define and create a 'daily place', a jewellery box within which tiny lives are stored.

Notes

1. Gaston Bachelard, *Poetics of Space* [1957]. Paris: PUF, 1961, p. 34 (and pp. 57, 77, 47 for the following quotations).
2. The term 'house' here refers to the '*domus*', which thus includes flat, for example.
3. Benoît Goetz, *Théorie des maisons: l'habitation, la surprise* [A Theory of Houses: Dwelling and Surprises]. Lagrasse: Verdier, 2011, p. 50.

CHAPTER 1

Blow Up My Town: *Everyday Rowdiness*

In *Blow Up My Town* (1968), the young Chantal Akerman upsets domestic life and skilfully disrupts it. As she is the only actor in this debut short,[1] we see her rushing up a staircase, entering a tiny kitchen and, by quick, nervous gestures, simultaneously humming and moaning, endeavouring with great tenacity to dismember daily life, to destroy it, to break it down and, ultimately, to make it explode. This is not hysterical violence, but rather a manifestation of feverish obsessions about daily life, a pathological goofiness. The kitchen in *Blow Up My Town* becomes a sort of laboratory, where destructive impulses proliferate, thus emphasising the intolerable situation, the hermetically sealed anonymity in which endlessly repeated chores ensnare individuals. The film brings to mind the words of Maurice Blanchot:

> the quotidian is the movement by which men remain, unknowingly, in human anonymity. In our daily life, we have no name, little personal reality, we barely have a face, just like we do not have a social class that sustains or restrains us.[2]

Blow Up My Town stages what could be called *reversed domesticity*; the point is to overthrow the established order, to get rid of the tasks imposed by daily life and thus to throw everything into chaos. Through gentle madness and charming unsteadiness, the *I* rebels against space, against objects, against anything that implies and symbolises domestic repetition. This urge to put an end to domestic seclusion borrows from comedic aesthetics and philosophy: that is, according to Petr Kràl, that the only interesting world is 'a world that doesn't quite work right, a world where things and people refuse to do their jobs, where they destroy one another, where they rebel, where they go on strike'.[3] By reversing the order of things, by destroying household items and kitchen utensils, Chantal Akerman emphasises the alienating, devitalising dimension of daily existence. Just like a comic hero shows 'his inability to adapt',[4] the filmmaker/actor uses concrete acts to destroy the unbearably material burdens of daily life.

As Bruce Bégout points out, everyday life is about 'the regular flow of things. It is what happens usually, it is that which poses no problem at all and for this reason is accepted without question.'[5] Yet, because the screenplay of *Blow Up My Town* does not bother with psychological dross, it reverses this proposition. It disturbs with unnerving gusto the smooth process of being 'our ordinary selves'.[6] The radical and peculiar notion of taping the kitchen door in order to block the way out literally transforms the room into a domestic jail. In *Blow Up My Town*, the female body does not tidy up, it upsets; it does not clean, it dirties; it does not create harmony, it dismantles. Chantal Akerman bounces about restlessly, like a broken machine: she does everything backwards, makes incoherent gestures, spills boxes and objects on the floor, hurls a mop, brutally knocks over a bucket full of water, cleans excessively, covers her calves with shoe polish … These gestures signify simultaneously a loss of control and an explosive consciousness; the point is to break down and degrade (conscientiously and meticulously) all that must be redone and reused on a daily basis. Chantal Akerman unleashes her joyful rage upon daily chores, and she does not clean the kitchen up so as to 're-establish order',[7] but really to take everyday acts to a chaotic extreme and thus make them more intense – to make visible their stifling, gruelling characteristics. As she creates an excessive relationship with the familiar objects of 'her' kitchen, she breaks down the link to the trite, she condemns it through this volcanic staging of the body. The kitchen space is compromised, marred, yet the mood remains nervously cheerful because she takes full responsibility for these conscious destructive impulses. Daily life must not be organised or structured any more, but rather merrily demolished.

These acts of depredation and destruction are a way of nullifying any form of care given to the domestic space. According to Jean-Marc Besse, 'to clean means to make room in order to make time. Between men, and between men and the things that surround them. It is an action that has a very specific effect, temporally speaking.'[8]

In *Blow Up My Town*, the flat refusal to have anything to do with housekeeping means that time is 'on the loose'; it evaporates. Cinematographic temporality can be used to display the life of objects, in all their minute variations; here, on the contrary, time is constantly disrupted by impatient frenzy. In her later films, Chantal Akerman would employ a much more flexible and hypnotic temporality, as if to explore spaces better, whereas in *Blow Up My Town* the nervous impetuousness of her body turns time into an explosion, immediate and without depth. As the performance/film ends, the actor/director (frantically) lays her head on the gas stove, turns it on and blows everything up: a radical, uncompromising act that not only ends the character's life, but also breaks the cycle of daily, endless repetitions.

Chantal Akerman described her first shorts as 'teenage' films. However, *Blow Up My Town* is paradoxically a movie about a *mature revolt* against the established order, against the patriarchal domination that forces women to do all the daily chores. The director often said that seeing her mother move about the house when she was a child had a great influence on her movies. She states, in the documentary *I Don't Belong Anywhere: Le Cinéma de Chantal Akerman* (2015), directed by Marianne Lambert: 'I realised that my mother was, all things considered, at the centre of all my films, and that is why I am afraid now. My mother is not there any more – do I still have something to say?'

More than forty years before she made that declaration/confession, the feverish direction of *Blow Up My Town*, at once funny and indirectly political, celebrated the body's outbursts against daily chores, against the stifling tasks imposed on it, in a clear reference to the maternal body. Following unrestrained impulses, she does not bother with pointless modesty and describes daily life as a spatial structure that confines women's lives.

In *Blow Up My Town*, the young director hums constantly; her faint and raspy voice helps anchor the images, and the various vocal sounds heard off screen (shouts, groans, noises, chants) intermittently enter the frame, like a spasmodic racket. They introduce an imbalance, a malfunction symptomatic of psychological and physical distress. Akerman's body is driven by a nervous strength that fills up all functional space, that stifles it, that twists it up, and thus transforms it into a pure place, wild and liberated. In other words, it is the body that affects space, that exerts itself in it and against it – a sort of spatial abuse which, in its comic form, tends to show that the practical and technical space of the kitchen could be considered a psychological place, where a torrent of emotions and internal strife is felt. In this movie, the household is not just a backdrop, a place where the action takes places or a spectacular setting. In *Blow Up My Town*, the body takes priority over space, it *contradicts* it, disrupts reality and does not enter into a dialogue with it. As Gilles Deleuze said: 'It is through the body (and no longer through the intermediary of the body) that cinema forms its alliance with the spirit, with thought. "Give me a body then" is first to mount the camera on an everyday body.'[9]

Thus, the body, in *Blow Up My Town*, occupies domestic space, makes it into a target and a model, and then breaks it down and transforms it into an unconscious place. Daily life generates an anxiousness about the presence of the unconscious (the 'refuge of the being', as Jon Mills put it[10]) that weighs heavily upon the body: nervous pauses, shouts, gesticulations bring affects into concrete existence, brutalise space, make it visible, as if the familiar isolation became suddenly explosive. The mental processes of the unconscious shake up the household.

> Specifically, unconscious mental activity is a series of spacings out in space, each marked by temporal moments of chaos, symmetry, self-alienation,

self-recuperation and reconstitutions. [...] Unconscious spacing is a dislocation within differences socially arranged by its own deployment, a spacing out that must nevertheless be made safe.[11]

In all of Akerman's films, the state of seclusion is a recurring and obsessional motif. Her narrations take place within *sealed neurotic boxes*, where the commonplace and the philosophical meet, where nothingness and excess, conscious and unconscious intersect. This is just as true in her first (*Blow Up My Town*, 1968) as in her last film (*No Home Movie*, 2015). Paradoxically, she also believed in the value of clumsiness. Her first picture uses a comedic aesthetics, showing immediate impulsive states and well-controlled awkwardness. *No Home Movie* presents Akerman's mother at the end of her life, with a sort of tragic frenzy. Behind the old woman's illness, one can sense the

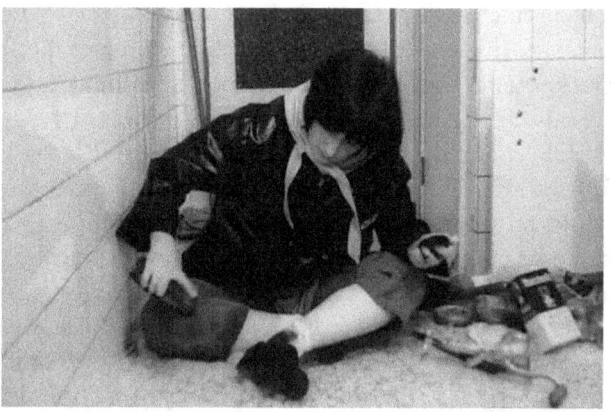

Figure 1.1   Blow Up My Town *(1968)*

Figure 1.2   Blow Up My Town *(1968)*

depressive disorder against which the director had to struggle – one of the subjects of a previous film, *Down There* (2006). Two bodies, together yet separately, must fight off different diseases.

Notes

1. Chantal Akerman studied at the INSAS (Institut National Supérieur des Arts du Spectacle, a Belgian film and drama school) but left before graduating. She was seventeen years old when she directed *Blow Up My Town*.
2. Maurice Blanchot, *L'Entretien infini*. Paris: Gallimard, 1969, p. 362.
3. Petr Kràl, *Le Burlesque ou la morale de la tarte à la crème* [Burlesque or the Cream Pie Morals] [1984]. Paris: Ramsay, 2007, p. 205.
4. Sarah Leperchey, *L'Esthétique de la maladresse au cinéma*. Paris: L'Harmattan, 2011, p. 99.
5. Bruce Bégout, *La Découverte du quotidien*. Paris: Allia, 2005, p. 38.
6. Blanchot, *L'Entretien infini*, p. 358.
7. Jean-Marc Besse, *Habiter un monde à mon image*. Paris: Flammarion, 2013, p. 17.
8. Ibid., p. 22.
9. Gilles Deleuze, *Cinema 2. The Time-Image*, trans. Hugh Tomlinson and Robert Galeta. London: The Athlone Press, 1989, p. 246.
10. Jon Mills, *L'Inconscient et son lieu: genèse de la réalité psychique* [Origins: On the Genesis of Psychic Reality], trans. Anne-Hélène Kerbiriou. Montreal: Liber, 2013, p. 95.
11. Ibid., pp. 94–5.

CHAPTER 2

Jeanne Dielman: *Neurotic Seclusion*

Chantal Akerman's *Jeanne Dielman, 23, quai du commerce, 1080 Bruxelles* (1975) carries out a kind of solemn purification. A young widow, Jeanne, walks around her flat, going from room to room (kitchen, bedroom, bathroom, corridors, living room); she prepares a meal, tidies up her room, prostitutes herself, does the laundry ... This housebound, secluded film takes places over three days. Daily activities are shot with impassive directness: making frequent use of medium shots, so as to put body and space on the same level, Akerman shows how her character (played by the beautiful and distant Delphine Seyrig) organises daily tasks with obsessive meticulousness. Babette Mangolte, the cinematographer, shows with merciless formality this compulsive, ritualised behaviour. From a narration perspective, nothing much happens: the fussy, mechanical gestures are the story. Even sex is 'automatised'. *Something is brewing, but it never boils over.* Daily life is over-organised, over-structured, but it appears as an 'unconscious act'[1]: Jeanne Dielman's automaton body projects on to domestic space its own pathologies, its unconscious chaotic marks. The frenzied body of *Blow Up My Town* becomes, in *Jeanne Dielman*, a body besieged by the anticipation and the over-organisation of the mundane. Chores (cooking, cleaning, washing) follow one another, their succession determined by Jeanne's neuroses and her need to feel protected from a life filled with inhibitions and prohibitions. According to Jacques Lacan, 'the compulsive person solves the problem of evanescence of their desire by making it into a prohibition. The Other becomes bearable precisely when the Other is forbidden.'[2] The filmmaker uses long, patient medium shots to display the mental cycle of a woman who prostitutes herself to earn a living. And when she feels pleasure with a client, when enjoyment overtakes her, her reaction is to murder that man: 'she kills because she wants to get order back'.[3]

Jeanne Dielman, 23, quai du Commerce, 1080 Bruxelles is more than a movie about home seclusion. Chantal Akerman explores the structure of an inner life that feels threatened, and she archives a mental disorder, hoping that by compulsively organising daily life, she might find a cure. Babette Mangolte's unmoving, frontal camera acts as a sort of hourglass: as time passes in each shot, the psychological pressure felt by Jeanne Dielman slowly increases. As soon as the second client leaves, she puts, as always, the money earned in the tureen on the living room table, and then goes back to the bedroom to remove the towel she invariably puts on the cover, makes the bed, goes to the bathroom to clean up, and finally arrives in the kitchen to check on the potatoes she has been cooking. When she realises that they are overdone, she goes back to the bathroom, walking with a stumbling impatience, the unwieldy pan in her hand, as a sort of preview of the great turmoil that is about to take over her life. She throws the overcooked potatoes away in the kitchen bin, looks nervously for more in the pantry, realises that there are few left. Tense and edgy, she leaves to buy more. When she gets back, she settles down at the kitchen table and starts peeling the newly acquired potatoes, slowly, almost drowsily. The strokes with the knife do not look like natural, precise motions, but forced, mechanical reflexes. The camera shows this directly, with 'dramatic simplicity', creating an iconic image of the neurotic subject. Chantal Akerman's own mother said: 'Chantal, that shot with the potatoes, everything is in there.'[4]

'Everything', says the director's mother, meaning all at once the endless repetition of daily chores, the impossible attempts to control and contain the emptiness of existence, and the slow unravelling of the character's being. The 'potato shot' possesses much more than a symbolic value; it is a *domestic cataclysm*, an exterior event that reveals the hidden psychological disaster. Jeanne Dielman's world is ordered and structured by the appropriation of spaces and of the objects in them, by regulating their use and disciplining their manipulation; *in fine*, by putting them away, she created a tidy 'order of things'. And when, in one brief instant, her control over the daily universe slips, all of life is suddenly altered and becomes a suspended fall. The lengthy potato shot is, aesthetically speaking, minimalistic, but Akerman manages to condense the disorder into a single symptom, while simultaneously spreading it out over time. The meal was being prepared, up until then, with energy, but after this psychological tipping point, everything slows down, becomes less intense, denotes depressed fatigue and sickly slowness.

> The body is never in the present [writes Gilles Deleuze]; it contains what came before and what will come after, the tiredness, the waiting. [...] Everyday behaviour puts the before and the after in the body, it puts time in the body, the body is a revelation of the end. [...] Fatigue may be the first and last of all attitudes, because it contains the before and the after [...].[5]

In *Jeanne Dielman*, Chantal Akerman films the daily experience of the exhausted body, the crystallisation of the temporalities of the far away and of the here and now. She documents, through the slow sedimentation of static shots, the collapse of an individual who tries to reattach daily life to the before that is past and the after that will come.

In his book *Théorie des maisons*, Benoît Goetz claims that 'undwelling', the opposite of dwelling, leads to 'the unbearable, the intolerable, the *foul*', which takes place in the 'non-space of the camp'.[6] By contrast, he defines the 'uninhabited' as 'a way of standing and living [...] without a house, without a home', which determines beings who say they are just 'passing through'.[7] Akerman's homes, on the contrary, are not 'undwellings', or even *uninhabitable*; they are tormented, exhausted, neurotic. As such, they prohibit any form of spatial *harmonia*, any fusion with the home, any domestic spaces favourable to daydreaming, as theorised by Gaston Bachelard in *The Poetics of Space*. In Chantal Akerman's films, houses and flats are restless epicentres, where the quotidian is perceived as a burden and where the soul's wounds are expressed. To dwell does not mean to celebrate of the forces of domestic space, but quite the opposite: it means to be constantly shaken by psychological states, by the body's agitation. The home, because of such rough treatment, breaks down. It is precisely the body's agitation, the confusion of the mind (the disturbances, the dysfunctions) that fix the subject in space, that immobilise them, and that sometimes make them want to desert, to leave, to go into temporary exile.

In her 1986 short *Portrait d'une paresseuse*, Akerman films an idle morning. Waking up is presented as a difficult moment: before the credits, Chantal Akerman is shown in a wide shot, lying on a bed. Suddenly, she looks up directly at the camera and says: 'Today is Saturday, and I'm making a film about laziness.' Later, while she is still sitting up on the bed, a woman's voice can be heard singing the following: 'Lazy girl, get up, lazy girl, get dressed, lazy girl, go and get washed!' The bed is not a neutral place, nor is it a purely decorative piece of furniture. It is a pedestal, an object that links existential philosophy and corporal intimacy.[8] It is, as Georges Perec put it in *Species of Spaces*, 'a space outside of desire, an improbably rooted place, a space for dreaming, for oedipal nostalgia'.[9]

The bed is all at once a protective shelter, a voluptuous island, a rooted, nomadic, tormented place. Lying in bed might be a way of being, an original and horizontal way of inhabiting a home, but it is also, for Chantal Akerman, a way to resist the demands of daily, vertical life, the internalised commands of powerful habits. In *Portrait d'une paresseuse*, she shows her own actions, as if to state her function better, on screen, as a conscious subject; she makes mandatory demands upon her own daily life. Paradoxically, through this, she gives new value to mechanical, demeaning chores. It is as if she asked herself: how do I get rid of the mechanical constraints of those ever-present habits? What strategies can I use to liberate myself from their legitimate, yet coercive chains? Akerman opens the door of the fridge and says: 'There is nothing in there, so I will just not eat, at least that's something. I'll smoke this cigarette and then I'll make the bed.' Later, seeing a table covered in leftovers and dirty dishes, she declares: 'I'll take some vitamins and then I'll clear this up.' Tasks that need to be done are considered as time lost for oneself. She wants to resist the mechanical repetition, the rhythmic, hurried time that social life and economic activity force upon her. As Alain Corbin points out:

> laziness [...] is becoming more and more connected to the autonomy of time only for myself. Not a time used to meditate, to pray, to worship, but a time to contemplate the world, a time for introspection or, more simply, a pause, a moment to catch my breath.[10]

Akerman grabs this *time for herself* because she wants to stir vague desires up, because she wants to stand up to the demands of profitable time forced upon her by society and its moral obligations. *Portrait d'une paresseuse* thus proclaims itself a work of art about moodiness and apathy in the midst of the fragile awakening that Akerman experiences. Unhurried time takes over from the acceleration that dominated *Blow Up My Town*. The passive motions of the filmmaker – smoking, lounging in bed, waiting, taking a long time to make a decision – stand in contradiction to the active, coordinated, anticipatory gestures of *Jeanne Dielman*. The short film presents a self-portrait of the filmmaker as reluctant to take care of the housekeeping; *Jeanne Dielman*, on the other hand, shows a sort of mirror image of a mother who does all of the housework with extreme fussiness. It is as if the daughter held, over the course of several films, a conversation with her mother and managed consequently to break the chains of habits. To stay in bed, to speak while lying in bed: these are ways of protesting, of freeing the forces of transgression and using them against the powers of rules and restrictions. However, one should not think of the unruly impulses of the filmmaker as a defensive posture or as simple oppositional tantrums meant to assert oneself, or as acts of transgressive creation. According to Michel Foucault,

> transgression does not seek to oppose one thing to another, nor does it achieve its purpose through mockery or by upsetting the solidity of foundations; it does not transform the other side of the mirror, beyond an invisible and uncrossable line, into a glittering expanse. Transgression is neither violence in a divided world (in an ethical world) nor a victory over limits (in a dialectical or revolutionary world); and exactly for this reason, its role is to measure the excessive distance that it opens at the heart of the limit and to trace the flashing line that causes the limit to arise.[11]

In all of her films, Akerman looks into the transgressive nature of mundane gestures: idling in bed, an orgasm with an ordinary customer, a disorderly kitchen – all of these can be seen as transgressions, planned or unplanned, wanted or endured, of normal domestic situations. But at the same time, the movies seem to dialogue with one another, and even to complement each other. In *Jeanne Dielman*, certain gestures reveal a kind a familial, educational memory, while *Portrait d'une paresseuse* and *Blow Up My Town* show a build-up, through excessive apathy or an overflow of energy, of odd surges of freedom. To dwell within a domestic space, for Chantal Akerman, means to go from neurotic gestures to apathetic postures, from excesses

Figure 2.1   Jeanne Dielman, 23, quai du commerce, 1080 Bruxelles *(1975)*

Figure 2.2   Jeanne Dielman, 23, quai du commerce, 1080 Bruxelles *(1975)*

of making to excesses of unmaking. Daily life, transgressive and repetitive, therefore becomes the central place in all her work. In these tangled family relationships, which Akerman alternatively tightens and loosens, she favours acts that go constantly from pause to repetition, from control to overflow, from loose intervals to well-organised time.

Figure 2.3   Jeanne Dielman, 23, quai du commerce, 1080 Bruxelles *(1975)*

Figure 2.4   Jeanne Dielman, 23, quai du commerce, 1080 Bruxelles *(1975)*

Notes

1. Mills, *L'Inconscient et son lieu*, p. 100.
2. Jacques Lacan, *Le Séminaire, livre V. Les Formations de l'inconscient (1957–1958)*. Paris: Seuil, 1998, p. 415.
3. Interview with Chantal Akerman, by Blandine Jeanson and Martine Storti, *Libération*, 9 February 1976; reproduced in Dominique Bax and Cyril Béghin (eds), *Chantal Akerman, Bande(s) à part*, vol. 25. Bobigny: Bande(s) à part Festival de Cinéma à Bobigny, Le Magic Cinema, 2014, p. 167.
4. Ibid.
5. Deleuze, *Cinéma 2. L'image-temps*, pp. 246–7.
6. Goetz, *Théorie des maisons*, p. 52.
7. Ibid., p. 53.
8. In her short *I, You, He, She* (1974), Chantal Akerman describes a bed as both a place of anxious meditation and the scene of exuberant sexuality; in *The Room* (1972), the camera turns upon itself and shows, in a 360-degree panorama, the director's bedroom; she is lying on the bed, with a sort of dynamic passivity, and sleeps, dreams, moves about and hides.
9. Georges Perec, *Espèces d'espace* [Species of Spaces] [1974]. Paris: Galilée, 2000, p. 35.
10. Alain Corbin, 'Conquérir la paresse' [Conquering Laziness], *Le Magazine littéraire*, 433 (July 2004), pp. 35–8.
11. Michel Foucault, 'Preface to Transgression', in *Language, Counter-Memory, Practice: Selected Essays and Interviews*, ed. Donald F. Bouchard, trans. Donald F. Bouchard and Sherry Simon. Ithaca, NY: Cornell University Press, 1977, p. 35.

CHAPTER 3

From Cities to Walls: A Local Change of Scenery

Chantal Akerman's *News from Home* (1976) weaves together a voice-over reading of letters that her mother sent from Brussels, and scenes of New York, where she resided at the time: streets, subways and squares. Natalia Akerman's letters are a link, a materialisation of geographical distance, and as they cross over the Atlantic and come to New York, they express the rhythm of her family's daily life back in Brussels. The one who is absent, who remained in Europe, becomes an integral part of the American city. These thoughtful missives, written by the mother, read by the daughter as she wanders about the streets, create a poetic connection: they roam around together, follow in the footsteps of anonymous passers-by. The words of the mother, affectionate and forceful, transform unknown silhouettes into familiar bodies, lessen the anonymity that predominates in major cities. Obviously, New York does not transform itself into Brussels, but the letters, as they are read, are superimposed over the images of the American city and establish a correspondence between exterior and interior, as if the world outside was invariably drawn towards the inner life. In other words, in *News from Home*, the daily life of New York City is permanently attached to the 'everyday privacy' of the flat in Brussels. The geographical gap between the ordinariness of the streets and the sentimentality of home exposes, within the frame of the cinematographic picture, a form of *sedentary nomadism*, a wavering between the here and the far away, the exterior and the interior, between reclusion and wandering. *News from Home* creates a *local change of scenery*, in a way that is reminiscent of Maurice Blanchot, who wrote that 'a change of scenery does not mean the loss of one's homeland, but rather a more authentic way of dwelling, of inhabiting without habits; exile is but a new way to relate with the Outside'.[1]

To travel, to relocate, to be in transit, all these expressions convey a sense of moving, of mobility. But these ways to exist, to 'inhabit without habits', also aim to look for and find an elusive *locus*. Akerman is at once taken away by perpetual motion, but also impeded by it: she needs to get away from her mother while remaining in close contact with her. The ghost of the family's home haunts Akerman's body and determines her state of mind.

Down There (2006) continues to ask the same questions about separation and distance; it is more a reclusion-movie, however, than a wandering-movie. Having come to Israel to work on a project, Akerman locks herself up in a Tel Aviv apartment and describes, in a voice-over, her daily life, the daily life of others, of her family. Confined within a space that is both familiar and foreign, she ambles about, using only *words*, while shutting herself away. The film uses a radical form of cinematography: the viewer is shown windows covered with venetian blinds and, thus, only sees fragmented images. The outside world is obscured by the stripes of the slats of the translucid blinds. A succession of static shots, framed by the windows, weave together the varying light of the passing days and the opening or closing of the blinds that cover the windows of the opposing buildings, thus creating a contemplative atmosphere.

The film begins with static shots of the windows; the buildings across the street can be seen through the blinds. A couple takes in the sun while sitting on a terrace and moving potted plants about … The phone rings and puts an end to this silence. The spectator hears the low and fragile voice of Chantal Akerman. 'No, I'm fine,' she says slowly. 'Yes, the weather is nice. No, really, I'm getting better. The beach, no, no, I haven't gone to the beach, I have to work …'

She hangs up. We hear her calm footsteps. She starts talking again. She reads an interrogative monologue – a series of fragmentary notes – about loss and the death of close friends and relatives.

> Why was the suicide linked to Tel Aviv – a rainy day – Amos's mother?[2] At more or less the same time, my aunt Ruth committed suicide, a day the sun was shining weakly in Brussels. Suicides everywhere. Was it, for both of them, a form of exile, wherever they are? Women who dreamt of something, of what? They didn't know themselves, probably, but couldn't sleep any more, not in Brussels, not in Jerusalem. Both had a son: one became a great writer, long, long after the death of his mother; the other didn't, even though his mother would have loved it.

Near the end of the film, as a sort of reminder of the beginning, Chantal Akerman says that 'a man from the university' came to see her and that she tried to get him to talk about Israel. She asks him if it was because she thought of herself as an exile in Israel that Amos Oz's mother committed suicide, if she had lost something of herself when she left Europe. Reversing the notion of *aliyah*,[3] Akerman wonders all through *Down There* if Israel should be considered a land of exile (rather than a land of welcome). Speaking very slowly, she tells the dreadful story of her family's attempts to flee across borders.[4] The suicides of mothers and aunts stand as statements of the impossibility of going on with life, as if the Shoah and the exiles that followed it had made the past unattainable and, thus, had made the future impossible. For Chantal Akerman, Israel is more than a land to which one is symbolically attached: it is a 'sick' country because of its unavoidable link to a traumatic History.

> Exile is always an exile of the mind inasmuch as experiences, before touching the displaced body, inscribe the psychological mark of the separation, of an exclusion that is first perceived in the mind. We feel it in our conscience before we live it as a condition,[5]

writes Alexis Nuselovici. Confined within her flat, Akerman moves around in a present that has been stopped by the past trauma of the Shoah. 'I cannot escape the yellow star. It is in me. It is engraved on me. Yesterday was a really bad day,' she says in the voice-over. Akerman's body is never completely where it speaks: she is always here and there, stuck between the hesitations of daily life and the problem of being rooted without habits. She goes on, with uncommon clarity:

> I don't feel like I belong, without any real suffering, without pride. Pride, it happens. I feel disconnected from almost everything. There are a few things that keep me anchored, but sometimes they let go of me, sometimes I let go of them, and then I just float about, adrift. This is what happens most of the time. Sometimes, I try to hang on, for a few days, minutes, seconds, and then I let go again. [...] And all of this has to do with all of that, with Israel or not Israel. Of course, not a real Israel, an Israel where I would suddenly belong. I also know that this is a mirage.

The problem of belonging is, for the filmmaker, a source of painful indecision, of perpetual questions, that follows her, parallel to other, frequently antagonistic, concerns that flow through her life: to leave, to come back, to refuse to make a choice, to leave again. Akerman's hoarse, grating voice sends out, in *Down There*, autobiographical waves that echo the words of Georges Perec in the film *Ellis Island*:

> 'I don't know exactly what it means
> to be Jewish
> how I feel about being Jewish
> it is an obvious fact, sure, but a
> mediocre one as well, that doesn't connect me to anything;
> it is not a sign of belonging,
> it is not linked to a belief, a religion, a practice, a folklore, a language;
> it is more like a silence, an absence, a question,
> a questioning, a hesitation, a worry.'[6]

For Perec, the sense of belonging to Judaism is tempered by analytical distance, with which he constantly questions the notions of difference, remoteness, lack and absence. Chantal Akerman never manages either to solve the issues of Jewishness and of her relationship to Israel. Rather, they whirl about her – obsessions of identity that somehow torment the body, which at times give it strength, and at times worry it. The words of the filmmaker run through the static shots of *Down There*, expressing all at once conscious confusion, utopian desires and self-reflective criticisms ('I also know that this is a mirage').

In Chantal Akerman's films, the home is often a space of (self-imposed) imprisonment, of loss, of silences and wandering anxieties. In *Down There*, the flat is a place of self-reflective isolation. It is a manifestation of a cloistered nomadism that is the result of two types of seclusion: the voluntary reclusion of the filmmaker, sequestered in the dwelling that was provided for her in Tel Aviv, and the views out of the windows, obstructed by the buildings across the street. The eye of the viewer can only reach a fragmented, divided, outside world, where sameness begins anew every day: the same walls, the same terraces, the same anonymous figures that busy themselves with the same ordinary tasks. The framing of the shots varies (tight or wide shots, direct or high-angle shots); the texture of the images differs with the changing light. And yet, the real-life situations that are shown in these images are always the same and keep repeating themselves: an urban daily life that exists independently of the 'interior' life of the apartment, which is the true epicentre of the film.

The motif of the window gives the film its visual structure by providing a link between interior and exterior life, while limiting, blocking. Gérard Wacjman, in his delightful essay about windows, wrote that

> windows matter to everyone, in a personal manner, they matter to our innermost being, they state implicitly the way we stand in the world, gazed at by the world, away from the world. They enclose our privacy, they allow for the existence of a private space, that is our home, that is us.[7]

This cinematographic set-up in *Down There*, whereby the gaze is obsessively drawn to the window, the life outside, is like a recurring melody. Looking through the geometric grid that combines transparency and opacity, the filmmaker captures the mundane activities (resting, loitering, waiting) of an anonymous couple. The shots, fixed in place, sketch out a visible pantomime of everyday life, thus sending back an image of Akerman's own petrified life. Her words, her sentences, her questions, which she spells out with glaring simplicity in the voice-over, cannot get past the veiled windows. The venetian blinds radically alter the possibility of approaching the outside world, as there is no transparent, direct access. The gaze cannot wander freely, cannot enter easily *into* things; it has to deal with a network of lines, black cables, a 'process of construction or assembly',[8] that obstructs the view of the outside. Akerman uses them to block out access to the life outside. A geometry of vertical and horizontal lines creates stripes in space and blur the difference between within and without, fuses them together, makes them homogenous, belonging to the same material plasticity: the outside world is crossed out, taken out, almost denied. The viewer's gaze is held in place, and it is the fluctuating noise of exterior life that creates real, moving (acoustic) images. The exterior sounds and Akerman's inner voice produce dynamic mental pictures, while the viewer looks on, caught in the visual spider's web, constantly stumbling around in a circumscribed environment.

All those criss-crossing lines transform the cinematographic screen into a canvas that veils and covers the world. Because of the slats of the venetian blinds, the apartment becomes a sort of confessional:

> I feel so disconnected that I can't even manage to have a house with bread, butter, coffee, milk, toilet paper. Whenever I buy any of those things, it's like I've accomplished some heroic deed. […] There is something in me that's damaged, in my relationship to reality, to everyday life. How can you live a life where the air is not rarefied? It begins with bread, and a house, a modicum of order, a modicum of life …

Akerman uses humble things, *small, ordinary tasks*, to show the impossibility of building up the repetitiousness of daily life and thus of flowing within the continuity of life. *Blow Up My Town* may have displayed a rowdy and comical form of transgression, but *Down There* deals overtly with illness. The director speaks, but her words must face the muted whispers of the city and the subdued interior sounds. This near-silence creates a restful place, where Akerman can think and speak about pain. She never complains, never gives in to pathos, but prefers using plain, bitter language to describe her grievous relationship to life, her obsessions about exile, her mother, Israel, the home, the mundane …

However, *Down There* is not solely a film about seclusion; in contrast to the images of exterior immobility, cut through by the slats of the venetian blinds on the windows, there are a few shots of the sea and the sky, and their distant, shimmering light stands out radically. Akerman does not rush into the city. Rather, she uses low-angle shots to show the sky as a dome, an ever-fleeing horizon. The quiet sounds of this airy landscape are submerged, every once in a while, by the aggressive noises of passing military planes. Colonised by grey and black lights that move haltingly across the screen, the sky seems more about information than liberation, as the sound storm reminds one of the war-like atmosphere that hangs about Tel Aviv. These images of the empty blue sky echo the distant unrest of the Israeli–Palestinian conflict.

In much the same way, the images of the light-drenched sea and of the remote horizon contradict visually – as emphasised by the editing of *Down There* – the subdued light of the flat. It is an enclosed space, pathologically withdrawn from the world, paralysed by daily suffocations, while the sea is an open landscape from which one can travel to the ends of the world. As Jean-Marc Besse pointed out, an expanse, that is, a landscape stretching to the horizon,

> exists primevally. [...] A landscape, because it is an ordinary landscape, a landscape that blends together or sets up a primeval communication between men and the world, predates, therefore, any possibility of orientation, any landmark. A landscape is a radical disorientation, it rises out of the loss of landmarks, it is a way of letting oneself be invaded by the world.[9]

Chantal Akerman compresses together, on screen, immersive seclusion and the open perspective of the landscape. The various eerie shots of the sea give a material presence to the infinite, unreachable horizon, and the viewing subject, consequently, feels as if she had lost her bearings.

Down There makes the apartment into a den, where she can meditate at leisure. Because she juxtaposes blocked-out shots and expansive shots, she weaves together images of reclusion and fleeting vistas. But being blocked out does not necessarily mean a strict imprisonment: it represents a *fixed dynamic*. The way out is obstructed, the limit between the inside and the outside is clearly marked. It is a sort of *incarcerated anchoring*.

The editing of *Down There* does not attempt to connect sequentially the inside and the outside, the shuttered interior and the infinite horizon. On the contrary, it frequently goes abruptly from shots of the dwelling that offer solace and images of remote landscapes. Because what is outside is not directly determined by what is inside, the unique and powerful character of the exterior natural landscape is enhanced. The viewers are thus encouraged to 'dive into the landscapes',[10] as Alain Mons put it. All the more so since the editing, alternating constantly between open horizons and interior seclusions, tends to submerge them completely.

Akerman uses the same dialectics in her last film, *No Home Movie* (2015). The first image in it is a static shot of a wind-shorn tree in the Israeli desert. The director shows, with great patience, the scrawny shrub's resistance to this harsh climate. The tree as a visual metaphor for the human body has often been remarked upon: 'The details of its structure – roots, trunk, branches, leaves, etc. – represent an inexhaustible source of symbolic meanings that go from man to nature and from nature to man.'[11]

Considering the rest of *No Home Movie*, it is clear that the tree facing the wind at the beginning of the film stands as a metaphor for the filmmaker's mother, who, in her apartment in Brussels, is slowly losing vitality and wasting away. After the arid and empty desert, the viewers are abruptly transported to a park, most likely in Brussels, where the green grass shines. In a note that she wrote to go along with the film, Akerman says:

> After all the sand, it was necessary to show greenery, it was necessary to show the calm after the storm. [...] The story moves along at a slow pace, not unlike that apartment in Brussels where a woman walks about with the fragile grace of those for whom balance is difficult to maintain ...[12]

That woman is Natalia Akerman. In her book *Ma mère rit* (2013), Chantal Akerman wrote:

> I'm preparing for her death. How do you do that, someone asks. I try to imagine myself without her. And I think it'll be fine. Not for her, for me. Or the opposite. But I've heard that you can't really prepare yourself, so it's all a waste of time. She desperately wants to live. And you? Me? I don't know[13].

In this book, Akerman strings along freely little stories about life and daily thoughts. Written in a direct and uncluttered style, it does not give in to emotionality but truly treats everyday life with interest and gives it a great vitality by ridding it of all futility. *Ma mère rit* says everything plainly, without fuss, naturally, with conscious and disconcerting frankness. This text faces up to the little nothings, the tiny events that make up the banality of life; it records the faltering energy of life crushed by the pressures of time. Akerman describes 'ordinary obsessions' – the fact that her mother prepares her luggage a week before she is about to leave on a trip, for example – that are really silent anxieties, that can never be totally ignored when one belongs to a family that has been nearly destroyed by the Shoah.

Akerman, in *No Home Movie*, films her mother's daily life, even as she progressively runs out of energy. Static shots show Natalia, barricaded within this *place of her own*, hounded by old age, often exhausted, the realisation of her wild ideas stopped short. *No Home Movie* is not the 'movie sequel' of *Ma mère rit*; it is not her mother's filmed will and testament. Rather, it is Chantal Akerman's 'final film': it demonstrates the overall consistency of her œuvre, always dominated by the majestic figure of the mother. *No Home Movie* is imbued with a sort of cinematographic clumsiness,[14] which almost feels like artistic intuition. Akerman lets go of the filmmaking process she had been using so far in her career: she gives up on the long, formal, direct shots and offers instead an *aesthetics of doors left ajar*. She consistently captures the slow movements of the maternal body by looking through half-open doors. Places are not shown only from the front, but also obliquely, through narrow openings. Frequently, the camera is positioned in the doorframe, which emphasises not only the architectural geometry of the maternal home but also the limited nature of her mother's motions, as she slowly goes from the kitchen (to eat) to the living room (to rest) and the bedroom (to sleep). The camera stands back and divides space into small portions which frame the repetitious movements of the maternal body. The door, wrote Georges Perec, 'breaks up space, severs it, makes osmosis impossible and captivity mandatory: on one side, there is me and my home, intimacy, domesticity [...], on the other side, there are the others, the world, public, political'.[15]

Doors, in *No Home Movie*, are not boundaries; they do not separate. They are almost always left ajar, thus distancing the viewer from the intimacy of the ageing body. They are truly thresholds, but one cannot cross them because some secrets need to be preserved. The camera remains modestly out of the way, so that the Other may be discovered while not completely invading their private space. This distance is also created in another way, by frequently showing the two women from behind. The back is a protective barrier, it prevents the viewer from seeing what pours out of the private sphere. To *film from the back* means to create a kindly space, a territory around the intimacy of the body, preventing the movie from becoming obscene, as is too often the case.[16] *No Home Movie* shows, for instance, a difficult meal, but the viewer never sees directly the problems Chantal Akerman's mother has trouble swallowing her food. Filming from the back is a choice that allows for a certain amount of privacy while showing deterioration.

No Home Movies is structured by a number of tables, serving various purposes. The table in the kitchen, where mother and daughter eat their meals, brings about dialogues and sparks confidences. Sitting there, they talk about the father of the director, about religion and rites, about the various transformations of the mother's body. That particular table, in the kitchen of the Brussels apartment, evokes stability, functionality, the rhythms of daily life, in opposition to the hotel room tables in New York or in Oklahoma, from where Chantal Akerman skypes her mother. Those are tiny 'nomadic workshops'. In the editing, the sedentary kitchen table of the mother in Brussels is linked, in a fluid yet jarring back and forth, to the nomadic work tables of the daughter travelling in the United States.

As she is calling from New York, Chantal Akerman shows a close-up of her mother's 'ordinary face',[17] talking and gesturing affectionately, sitting at the table in her kitchen in Brussels. On the tiny computer screen, the home and the place of passage mix, as if the computer had become a *virtual room*, where the mother–daughter relationship can be maintained and the affectionate confessions can continue. For instance, they have, on Skype, the following conversation:

> *Chantal Akerman*: I want to show you how small the world is!
> *Natalia Akerman*: But why are you filming me?
> *C. A.*: I film everyone, mum. I just film you more than other people.

As the conversation goes on, the director reminds her mother that she has to work. The camera comes closer (or zooms in), her face becomes more and more blurry until it is only a colourful, striped, unidentifiable surface. The voice, though, remains clear:

> *N. A.*: I don't like it when I have my picture taken.
> *C. A.*: Don't worry, it's all blurry!

While Natalia's becomes less and less visible, her presence seems to grow; but the blurriness also demonstrates, in an ironic manner, the power of separation. The ephemeral power of the blurred frame softens the mischievous deformity of the old woman's face. Her sharp and lively voice is a reminder of her identity; it brings back the well-loved face that has disappeared from the screen, transforms its memory into an immediate presence. The blurriness seems less abstract than rational, less amnesic than mnemic.

Chantal Akeman records with slow solemnity the dynamic processes of the varying conditions of the body of Natalia, of her unrelenting weariness. The Brussels flat is more than a place to live in: it is a protective well, where the body can let go of weariness and try to get some energy back. In one of the last images of the film, Chantal Akerman and her sister talk to their mother to prevent her from falling asleep while she lies in an armchair.[18] This comfortable, recessive object is neither trite nor unsignificant. Often placed right at the centre of the screen, it represents the daily need for rest. In his lovely poetic essay about tables, Francis Ponge offers a noble portrait of an armchair:

> The armchair is, in a way, the bourgeois throne, and yet it is also the opposite of a throne, because it implies, from the one who sits in it, nothing of a hieratic nature. It is comfortable, maybe the most comfortable of chairs, not unlike the sofa or the daybed. One sinks into an armchair. It is where one can let go, what today is called to relax, it is where one can recuperate. It is the place that reminds one most of the mother's or the nanny's arms. The place to rest, to daydream, and even the place to sleep while seated in it.[19]

The armchair dedicated to Natalia Akerman's rest appears, in this scene, as a sign of early acceptance of death. As the old woman inevitably falls asleep, the camera moves haltingly towards the balcony. The film is overexposed, and a bright white light fills the screen – a ghostly white light, a portent of the director's mother impending disappearance.

A few moments later, a static, wide shot shows Chantal Akerman go in a bedroom, sit on the bed and tie her shoelaces. A heavy silence hangs in this

Figure 3.1 News from Home *(1976)*

Figure 3.2 News from Home *(1976)*

lonely room. The daughter is about to leave, undoubtedly, perhaps definitively. Then Akerman stands up and draws the curtains; the sombre light of day disappears and a great darkness blackens most of the screen. The film ends on a static shot of the small, light-filled hallway; there are two doors, one that leads to the kitchen, the other to the bedroom. On a side table, in this solemn and mellow atmosphere, we see a photograph of two young girls – most likely, Chantal Akerman and her sister. The director uses these

Figure 3.3 Down There *(2006)*

Figure 3.4 Down There *(2006)*

two images – one closed and dark, the other open and light – to evoke inexpressible, indestructible memories of childhood. In an interview from 2011, Nicole Brenez asked Chantal Akerman: 'Do you always use the word "girl" to talk about yourself?' 'Maybe, answered Akerman. Probably. I don't know. I never grew up. I've always been an old child.'[20]

Figure 3.5 No Home Movie *(2015)*

Figure 3.6 No Home Movie *(2015)*

Notes

1. Blanchot, *L'Entretien infini*, p. 452.
2. The mother of the writer Amos Oz committed suicide when he was twelve years old. Cf. Amos Oz, *A Tale of Love and Darkness*, trans. Nicholas de Lange: Boston: Houghton Mifflin Harcourt, 2004.
3. 'In modern times, aliyah has (...) been used to designate the "going up" to Israel of immigrants from other lands, just as in former times it meant going up to the Holy Land' (Britannica, The Editors of Encyclopaedia. 'aliyah'. *Encyclopedia Britannica*, 30 July 2019. Available at: <https://www.britannica.com/topic/aliyah> (last accessed 23 March 2022)).
4. On this topic, see Mathias Lavin, 'Ici comme ailleurs? Intériorisation de frontières dans *Là-Bas* de Chantal Akerman' [Here and There? Interiorised Borders in Chantal Akerman's *Down There*], in Corinne Maury and Philippe Ragel (eds), *Filmer les frontières* [Filming Borders]. Saint-Denis: PUV, 2016, pp. 171–80.
5. Alexis Nuselovici (Nouss). 'L'Exil comme expérience' [Exile as Experience]. FMSH-WP-2013-43, 2013. Available at: <https://halshs.archives-ouvertes.fr/halshs-00861245> (last accessed 7 June 2016).
6. Georges Perec, *Ellis Island*. Paris: POL, 1995, p. 58.
7. Gérard Wajcman, *Fenêtre: chroniques du regard et de l'intime* [Windows: A Chronicle of Gaze and Intimacy]. Lagrasse: Verdier, 2004, p. 18.
8. Ibid., p. 100.
9. Jean-Marc Besse, 'Entre géographie et paysage' [Between Geography and Landscape], in Michel Collot (ed.), *Les Enjeux du paysage* [The Stakes of Landscape]. Brussels: Ousia, 1997, p. 338.
10. Alain Mons, 'Le Bruit-silence ou la plongée paysagère' [Noise-silence or Diving into Landscapes], in Mottet (ed.), *Les Paysages du cinéma*, p. 236.
11. Robert Dumas, 'La Peinture de l'arbre à l'épreuve de la politique allemande' [Tree Painting and German Politics], in Jean Mottet (ed.), *L'Arbre dans le paysage* [Trees in Landscapes]. Seyssel: Champ Vallon, 2002, p. 29.
12. *Notes de Chantal Akerman*, movie press kit for *No Home Movie*, Zeugman Films Distribution, February 2016.
13. Chantal Akerman, *Ma mère rit* [My Mother Laughs]. Paris: Mercure de France, 2013, p. 61.
14. In the press kit, Akerman writes: 'This film is sometimes clumsy, but in this case, being clumsy is good. The film wanders about, and we don't really know where it is going. And yet, it can only really lead to one thing: death.' *Notes de Chantal Akerman*, p. 5.
15. Perec, *Espèces d'espaces*, p. 73.
16. See Éric de Kuyper, 'Aux origines du cinéma: le film de famille' [The Origins of Cinema: Family Movies], in Roger Odin, *Le Film de famille: usage privé, usage public* [Family Movies: Public Use, Private Use]. Paris: Méridiens Klincksieck, 1995, p. 17. De Kuyper points out that family movies, as soon as they are taken out of context, can only be described by the word 'obscene'.

17. See Jacques Aumont, *Du visage au cinéma* [Faces in Film]. Paris: Éditions de l'Étoile et Cahiers du cinéma, 1992, pp. 44–68.
18. In the press kit, Chantal Akerman describes the scene with great precision: 'So my sister and I tried to keep her awake, and it is a heart-breaking scene. We call out, mum, mum, mum. But she is deaf, even though she can still hear us. After that, once more, we leave her, we see deserts, we hear the wind. And then I'm back in the apartment' (*Notes de Chantal Akerman*).
19. Francis Ponge, *La Table* [The Table]. Paris, Gallimard, 1991, p. 113.
20. Nicole Brenez, *Chantal Akerman: The Pyjama Interview*. Useful Book #1, Vienna International Film Festival, 2011, quoted in Bax and Béghin (eds), *Chantal Akerman*, p. 60.

Part 2

The House as a Place of Declarations and Meditations

In Avi Mograbi's film-essays, which we will be examining here, the house functions as a focus for observations and confessions, where a web of statements and provocations occur and spend themselves out, connect with each other and isolate from one another. It is never a place that is totally, hermetically closed; it allows one to leave, to go away, to come back and, in this movement of passages, the being is relocated, stands up to meet the outside world, and opens up its upheavals. Thus, the house is a place where filmmaker Mograbi both speaks of himself and summons, within his familiar cell, the voices of the voiceless and the dramas of history. He establishes a topological link in which the 'outside' constantly shifts into the 'inside': the house is transformed and forms *windows for speaking*.

In contrast, Alexander Sokurov's house is a daily microcosm where mournful voices, isolated from the world, circulate. It is a place of silent meditation and echoes the Heideggerian thought of dwelling for which 'poetry builds the being of dwelling'.[1]

Through the analysis of what we will call the 'household films' of Avi Mograbi and Alexander Sokurov, through these places where both the self and a vision of the world are broadcast and projected, we will analyse the movement of speech and silence that engages the other's gaze. *To dwell* is to organise and to settle down, in the words of Benoît Goetz, 'spaces that are thought (spaces of thought)'.[2] In these film-essays, to speak, to look, to create and to reflect, with the house as starting point, does not mean to discover the *noumenon* of beings in order better to reveal the movement of communities (Mograbi), or to grasp the spirit of the Japanese house, where the image of the threshold establishes a point of mediation between the inside and the outside (Sokurov). Is it not in the familiar places that the outside world barges in, and, as the consequence of a disturbance, is the view of the outside not rearranged so that this strangeness becomes more familiar?

Notes

1. Martin Heidegger, *Essais et conférences* [1958], trans. André Préau. Paris: Gallimard, 1980, p. 243.
2. Goetz, *Théorie des maisons*, p. 35.

CHAPTER 4

Avi Mograbi: The Political Workshop

In the ritualised silence of an artist's studio (a painter, a photographer, a sculptor or a filmmaker), works are created. It is patient, generally solitary labour, and the creator, ideally, has no social duties or external pressures bearing down on them. Throughout the history of cinema, a plethora of films, fiction or non-fiction, have tried to show the creative process, and thus taken part in its mystification. Usually, the artist 'at work' is filmed in the original creative space, or else in a reconstructed set, or, sometimes, in a film studio.[1] These films, most of them destined for television broadcasting, document the artistic act, but do so by glossing over the original emergence and the maturing process of the work, which typically take place in a remote or religiously minded place. Other, rarer, films present the studio as a centrifugal spot, from which one art (cinema) looks at and reflects upon another art (painting, sculpture and so on).

> Being a total art form, [cinema] makes the separation and differences between the arts productive, given that these are, paradoxically, the main way in which they communicate and establish connections. In that sense, and this is what the films of Jean-Luc Godard demonstrate forcefully and intelligently, cinema serves as a point of *friction* between the arts. Whenever the art of cinema looks at the other arts, when it examines closely the many creative processes that they use, it demonstrates with great accuracy the differences between the arts, and the fact that their identity is constructed precisely through these differences.[2]

The studio, the workshop, the atelier stand, in a way, as silent megaphones for these differences, as mirrors that arts use to face one another, that illustrates their dissonances, the gaps that separate them and the similarities that bring them closer.

Objects in the studio spell out the artist's identity, and the space itself is a cartography of daily habits, precursive experiments of the creative act. The studio is both circumscribed and free, and because the artist's life takes place in it, the filmmaker can in turn film it and let the creative process unfold. The cutting room plays a similar role for the filmmaker: an enclosed laboratory, a cavern, where, through long and difficult operations, opinions and aesthetic choices are developed and affirmed. In *Where Does Your Hidden Smile Lie?*, Pedro Costa takes a modest, admiring and respectful peek inside the cutting room at the École du Fresnoy, where Jean-Marie Straub and Danièle Huillet have been working and quarrelling for many, many years. While students are watching them, they are hard at work preparing a third version of *Sicilia!* To use a phrase coined by Nicole Brenez, the two 'image labourers'[3] sit at the 35 mm editing table, talking and, sometimes, explosively and yet still with tenderness, loudly arguing. Editing, and re-editing, is difficult work, and, for the Straubs, it often leads to altruistic bouts of anger – which has a lot to do with the radically political nature of their films and their efforts to emancipate humiliated bodies.[4] Obstinate and fully engaged, the two artisan filmmakers shape, fashion, mould their cinematographic materials, in a long and patient labour of love. Danièle Huillet sits at the editing table, handles the film rushes, thinks about connecting all the different parts, polishes the film, while Jean-Marie Straub paces up and down the editing room, goes out to the corridor, gives the students a 'discourse on their method'. If the shooting itself was the first element, the cutting room is the second element, and the work that goes on there is a continuation of the first: one must listen still, with dignity and righteous anger, to the voices, so as to shape the cinematographic material, give it rhythm, grant it the political and poetic power of an explosion, with no discordant noises.

Unlike Jean-Marie Straub and Danièle Huillet, Avi Mograbi inserts his own body and his own voice directly in his films, inside the cinematographic screen. For the Israeli director, allowing his body to appear on screen is a political tool, a pacifist and interventionist weapon, a way to open a dialogue, and so, from the streets or from his home, to examine the Israeli–Palestinian conflict. Avi Mograbi's workshop is radically different from a painter's private, solitary, sometimes even remote atelier. It is both a home and an artist's studio, and as such, it is at once linked to the outside world and its unceasing violence, and to the family, since the director's wife and his child appear on screen every once in a while, minding their own business.

The apartment is a fallback, a retreat position and a command headquarters, but it is not used to influence the destinies of nations; rather, it serves as a place from which to question different communities' fractured, suspended histories. The films of Avi Mograbi are constructed around speech acts, both mischievous and sincere. Anger and doubt get swept up in an emotional maelstrom. The filmmaker's purpose is to find his place, both within this conflict and in the film he is making. The body is, in fact, a point of political philosophy: Avi Mograbi uses words, gestures and performative acts to participate in the daily struggle of the Israeli–Palestinian conflict. Player, actor, fabulist, he plays the fool yet remains self-aware; he is a multifaceted individual, petulant and generous. Avi Mograbi's character is disconcerting, to say the least. In his flat, his studio-home or out in the 'field of operations', he plays himself up as a 'collective agent',[5] who does not solve mysteries but questions them, increases them, multiplies them.

His private apartment is like a centre of political activism and, by the very fact that a camera is present, by the dialogue that is instigated between the director and the audience, it becomes a tool to think collectively and critically about conflicts. Avi Mograbi puts himself on stage, so to speak, he uses his own private life to paint a silly, ridiculous self-portrait, while hinting at the tragedy of the Israeli–Palestinian conflict.

THE LIVING-ROOM AS 'CONFESSION BOX'

In *How I Learned to Overcome My Fear and Love Arik Sharon* (1997) Avi Mograbi follows/hunts down Sharon, the notorious general turned politician for the Likud Party, during the 1996 election campaign. The beginning of the film shows the attempts made by the filmmaker to meet the politician, only to be thwarted every time by his staff. It seems impossible that the two should meet, especially taking into account the fact that they are at completely opposite ends of the political spectrum. However, day by day, Avi and 'Arik' slowly get acquainted. At first, Sharon seems rather friendly, and displays a jovial, paternal sort of benevolence; his 'opponent' is taken aback by this attitude and makes a show of tempering his intense loathing.

As the film progresses, the filmmaker played by Avi Mograbi pretends to be charmed by the previously detested Sharon. In an interview from 2015, Mograbi explains what led him to this comic stratagem:

> I looked closely at the magnetic ability that he seems to possess, and I understood that this could be the basis of the film that I was planning to make: how one person, seduced by the magnetism of a powerful personality, abandons his deepest ethical and political convictions. I then came up with the fictional idea. I looked for a real opportunity to show the character of the director freaking out over his intimate relationship with Sharon ...'[6]

Avi Mograbi fictionalises the appearance of Ariel Sharon in the life of the 'character of the director'. Sitting in his living room, he admits that his wife left him because she disagreed and disapproved of his growing political and personal sympathy for reputedly brutal and ruthless former general. At the beginning of the film, Avi Mograbi, in close-up, with the camera directly in front of him, looks at the audience with a sincere and worried expression and says: 'Tammi, my wife, just left me. It sounds stupid, but it's because of Ariel Sharon. Because I wanted to make a film about him.'

Alone on screen, sitting in his living room, Avi Mograbi reflects on this paradoxical idea: making a film about one's enemy. He is aware of the destabilising schizophrenia that is slowly taking hold of him, since he mentions his worry that he does not feel enough loathing for the man known by some as the 'Butcher of Beirut'. He says that the Likud has decided to begin its electoral campaign on the day of the Mimouna, and so he goes to Beit She'an without knowing if Sharon will be there. While pictures of the site of the rally are intermittently shown, he explains that there was an electrical problem and that the political rally might not take place.

> I have to admit that I asked myself if I was going to go help them. Tammi was against it. They are, after all, our political enemies. But when I realised what a failure, what a humiliation it'd be for the organisers, I grabbed my extension cords and my old quartz floodlight, I went and installed everything, and let there be light.

The pictures that are shown, taken from the images shot on location, provide a kind of narrative respite, whose purpose is to help understand and clarify the ever-moving position of the filmmaker/character in relation to his political adversary. Pondering the symbolic value of his attempt at solidarity, Mograbi fears it means he may be joining the enemy. These doubts raise more questions than is shown on screen: the ethics of the character and, by extension, those of the filmmaker himself, are at issue. By helping out the organisers of the Likud Party electoral rally, Mograbi puts an ironic twist on the notion that he is colluding with the (political, ideological) enemy. He stands simultaneously in and out of the images, and the narrative, as it gets more and more intense, only increases the ambiguity. In *Images documentaires*, François Niney wrote: 'How does one film the enemy without demonising them or exoticizing them, without resorting to the same kind of awful propaganda, but also without becoming their mouthpiece, without negotiating with them – since there can be no dialogue with the enemy?'[7]

Sharon invites Avi Mograbi to come and film his electoral visit to a group of rabbis. The director immediately spots a potential danger. From his living room, he says, after the fact: 'Suddenly, I have scruples. As long as I was the one chasing him, it was fine. I was at peace with my conscience. But these familiarities, these: 'Hey, I didn't see you yesterday, in Tiberias', these conversations about the birth of his heifer, all that was beginning to bother me.'

The character of the director becomes more and more fictional, and he moves further and further away from the real Mograbi; this detachment more or less removes all the complications involved in filming one's enemy, alluded to by François Niney. As the fictional aspects become more and more obvious, it progressively becomes possible for the two characters, the director and the general, the two enemies, to stand side by side on the cinematographic screen. The living room, the private and intimate space, turns out to be, in fact, a laboratory where political experiments take place. It is a sort of *confession box*.

> For many, many months, I did all sorts of experiments, alone, in my living room. I would write something, I would act it out in front of the camera, then I would watch the results … I kept going back and forth between the living room and the room where I do the editing, which is the one over there. I don't know where I got the idea to get so close to the objective. [...] It didn't come all at once, but it was a series of intuitions, using this method, because video cameras allow you to write while filming and to film while writing.[8]

In *How I Learned to Overcome My Fear and Love Arik Sharon*, the professional (the spare bedroom turned into a cutting room) and personal (the family living room) spaces are quite distinct. The living room scenes were filmed after the main shoot had finished. Mograbi sits directly in front of the camera, held by a friend of his, and he analyses, dissects his adventures after the fact, expressing his doubts and regrets.[9] This adds a fictional element to the narrative, and it also establishes a distant bond with the audience. Avi Mograbi does not quite resort to Michael Moore's 'approbatory' method, by which he constantly looks for the audience's support, and which uses comic expedients to set a Manichean trap for the audience. In the cutting room, Mograbi is often on the phone, trying with great energy to investigate Sharon's campaign and to make appointments to follow him around. Those scenes were filmed during the main shoot. Different voices are heard in each of these two spaces, but together, they form a home where professional and private are intermingled, where the flat is actually a workshop, where a dialogue with oneself takes places, where the images that were shot are analysed and critiqued.

The director sets a radiographic process in motion, as he talks to the camera, discusses the images that he shot previously and, with ever-present irony, reflects upon the summarily edited rushes. In a way, he seeks to distance himself from what he has seen, what he has experienced, what he has said. Among other things, he claims that Ariel Sharon's campaign rallies are 'boring, and the speeches are always the same, with no surprises', that Sharon 'only barely modifies them to fit the community he has to talk to', that he 'keeps repeating the same clichés'.[10] Speaking clearly, without using analytical language, Avi Mograbi tries to show the hegemony of visible politics,[11] to denounce the manipulative power of campaign images, and to decipher the 'ceremonial idiom'[12] that is the foundation of any political rally, and in particular those of the Likud. Georges Balandier writes:

> Political life depends heavily on the art of outward appearance, an art that is contingent on circumstances, that is ritualised by ceremonials, maintained by repeated commemorations. It is an art that is studied, nowadays, and taught by professionals. We know more and more about the ways the ceremonial idiom can be deciphered, about the different elements that contribute to efficient communication: spatial organisation, a program laid out as a narrative, etiquette and order of appearances, musical and verbal codes, rhetoric.[13]

The informal and mobile organisation of Mograbi's workplace, used for both familial and professional purposes, helps make it into a maieutic space, where daily rushes are submitted to critical enquiry. But the importance of these images of campaign rallies – which often seem quite disorganised – goes well beyond the predictable input of political propaganda: they show, from the inside, the working of the Likud ideology in favour of the colonisation programme in the occupied territories, of which Ariel Sharon was one of the most outspoken proponents. Avi Mograbi managed to film Sharon's visit to Beit Ariyeh, a settlement Sharon himself helped set up when he was Minister of Agriculture in the Begin government. Sharon receives a warm welcome and is declared an honorary citizen. In this scene, he sits at a table and starts talking with the settlement representatives: 'Some have followed my advice. Don't build a fence. A fence limits your expansion. Let the neighbours build a fence. They keep getting higher. If there was no camera here, I'd say … But they'd just take advantage of this to sell their movie.' But the filmmaker answers: 'You could do something nice for us too,' and everybody laughs. We should point out that words such as 'fence' or 'expansion' are very much part of *Eretz Israel*'s political and ideological lexicon and of their attempts to seal off the Palestinian territories – they will be central in Avi Mograbi's subsequent films.

The narrative keeps returning to the flat/workshop and alternating with exterior sequences. This creates a double movement: on the one hand, physical distance from the filmed content, as the director looks at his own material, comments on it, steps away from it, as it were. On the other hand, he also repeatedly returns to it, because his words always seek to analyse, examine, question the material, while sometimes digressing from it. In other words, Avi Mograbi's filmmaking process is that of an essayist, at least in the sense defined by Alain Ménil: 'Against the principle of continuous deduction or of an uninterrupted link between reason and discourse, a distinctive preference for digressions, interruptions, detours or rambles'.[14]

There are directors that use editing to analyse the images they produced, but Avi Mograbi does not do that. He does not dissect scenes in a scholarly fashion. He just sits in his living room, looking directly, amicably, at the audience, his body in close-up filling the cinematographic screen; the director/actor improvises, reflects, reacts, makes speeches. Mograbi's self-analysing cinema stands in great contrast to the methods of dialectical analysis, based on the principle of 'compare and contrast', used by the likes of Harun Farocki.[15] By squeezing everything he can out of archival material, Farocki composes, so to speak, a 'choreography of dialectical comparisons'.[16] In the words of Georges Didi-Huberman, Harun Farocki seems 'the man who turns contradiction into praxis, the man who has objections'.[17] Farocki's praxis is typical of dialectics as Walter Benjamin saw it:

> Dialectics, as Walter Benjamin wrote in his essay on *Ursprung*, is not just about intellectually organising things in history. Dialectics possesses its own rhythm, based on 'constantly spawning matter'. It is thus both *material* and *motion*, just like at the editing table, one must handle material, press buttons, find the right rhythm.[18]

It is therefore very important to distinguish Harun Farocki's dialectical editing from Avi Mograbi's self-analysis. As director and performer, Mograbi does not utilise a scholarly form of dialectics, masterfully handled, to question the world; he merely proposes a conversation, a dialogical confession based on humanistic sincerity. Harun Farocki uses an elaborate dialectical radiography, an archaeology of images that questions, with polished off-screen commentary, the impact of the past on the present; Avi Mograbi prefers an ever-changing voice, a constantly rewritten and modified discourse that mixes field anecdotes, family circumstances and political posturing. His body is placed at the centre of the entire system: while shooting, he moves and acts constantly, pressed on by immediate concerns, but once he gets back home, he *reacts*. The process of action/reaction has been written about at length by Jean Starobinski:

> for the journalists and orators of the French Revolution, the word 'reaction' is used quite seldom, and in a thoroughly neutral sense. It is a response, an action that goes in the opposite direction, perpetrated by a previously 'oppressed' party, or by a cause beset by enemies. 'It can be said figuratively of an oppressed party that seeks vengeance and acts in response', says the *Dictionnaire de l'Académie* of 1798. Can it be pure coincidence that the appearance of this lexical duo, revolution/reaction, is more or less contemporary with the polarisation of politics?[19]

For Avi Mograbi, reacting to the images he shot himself is reacting to reality, but it is also a form of political discourse, an opposition to a political adversary, either indirectly, from his home, or directly, by meeting the oppressor out in the world. Mograbi's revolt is comical, and it takes place outside and inside, frontally and diagonally.

At one point in *How I Learned to Overcome My Fear and Love Arik Sharon*, Avi Mograbi speaks in front of the camera, and talks about a recent, terrifying nightmare. Intermittently, on screen, we see images of mutilated bodies lying in the street – the victims of the Sabra and Shatila massacre of 1982. We also see the dark shadow of Sharon, shouting in a microphone: 'It's not the Lebanon War that made me leave the Ministry of Defence, but the fact that Christian Arabs massacred Muslim Arabs.' As an echo to these mutilated bodies, the editing inserts an extract from the Israeli military archives. Men are standing on a balcony and chanting: 'Come down, little plane, take us to Lebanon, we'll fight for Ariel Sharon, and come back in a coffin!' Abruptly, brutally, the victims of Sabra and Shatila make an appearance in this film, whose only subject, until then, had been a commented depiction of Ariel Sharon's electoral campaign for the Likud Party. This visual explosion of violence and tragedy – mutilated bodies left out on the street – brings back and revive the memory of Israel's bloody occupation of Lebanon as an 'invisible vision', as Jean Genet once put it.[20] Archival images of the massacre are introduced as if they were part of a nightmare, as narrated by the actor/director in his living room. Suddenly, cracks appear in the contemporary, factual images of the electoral campaign: behind them, an incriminating past, a bloody History arises. As François Niney points out,

> memory is not just an accumulation of facts, but is made up of assimilation and forgetfulness, of condensation and displacement (as in a dream, as in film editing). If this emotional function of integration does not take place, if the *collective* function of the objectification of history, with all that is repressed and all that is found again, with its blind spots and its discoveries, does not occur as well, then there is no actualisation, what is known is not reinvested in what is lived, and what is lived is not reinvested in what is known, there are, in short, no stories.[21]

How I Learned to Overcome My Fear and Love Arik Sharon is not a conformist film, completely focused on the Machiavellian and falsely generous character of Ariel Sharon. It is an actualisation, through a process of uncovering historical hints, of Sharon's complex figure, whereas a narrative about guilty support would have tried to keep it covered. The memory of History becomes active as it puts together different images and spatial temporalities, thus disrupting the linearity of the narrative and resetting it as a winding and tortuous path.

From the Wall to the Telephone

Avi Mograbi's films display a constant, tenacious willingness to look into the violence of the Israeli–Palestinian conflict. The Israeli West Bank Barrier, or, as it is known to its opponents, the Apartheid Wall, is a constant *topos* of Mograbi's work, and seems almost like an obsession. In *August: A Moment Before the Explosion* (2002), he films children throwing stones at Israeli patrol vehicles as they drive along the barrier construction site. Mograbi is violently assaulted by an Israeli soldier, who accuses him of creating a 'mob near the barrier'. A sharp dialogue, or rather two parallel monologues, ensue between the filmmaker, called a 'journalist', and the soldier, who eventually orders him to leave. Mograbi keeps filming, camera in hand, as he walks by the cement structures that will become the wall. A young child throws stones at him, shouting: 'Hezbollah! Hezbollah!', the name of the Shiite movement whose rising military strength is a great concern for the Israeli government.

Often, Avi Mograbi does more than just show the conflict; he gets physically involved in it. In *Avenge But One of My Two Eyes* (2005), many scenes were shot while he was with various associations, such as Ta'ayush, whose members regularly take soldiers to task at checkpoints and who try to bring humanitarian aid to the occupied territories. These encounters often become real border skirmishes, and verbal violence often turns into physical confrontation. As a militant, Avi Mograbi participated in and filmed these tense, violent situations at the uninhabitable border. At the Beit Furik checkpoint,[22] Israeli soldiers (not visible on camera) prevent a mother from meeting up with her daughter, who brought her some clothes. In a slight low-angle shot, the camera shows the exhaustion on the face of the woman, who has already been waiting for four hours. The mother shouts out wearily: 'I swear to Allah, death is better than this life. I'd rather die now than live like this.' Making her wait was, in this case, a violent political act, a punishment, a humiliation, a form of exterior imprisonment. Later in the film, a tank and a jeep stop a Palestinian family from crossing the border and taking their sick mother to the hospital. Mograbi's camera shows the jeep, armoured to protect it from thrown pebbles, in a sort of choreography, moving forward, backing up, trying to intimidate. An officer shouts orders in a loudspeaker: 'Go away!' The militants at the checkpoint call an ambulance, but when it gets there, it is also blocked by the jeep. A second ambulance, from the Red Crescent, arrives on the scene but ends up leaving empty.

By filming this systematic obstruction of free movement, these endless hours of forced waiting under the sun, Avi Mograbi indicates that an asymmetrical balance of power exists between those who make the decisions (the military) and those who suffer the consequences (the Palestinian people).

At the end of the film, Mograbi calls Israeli soldiers out at a checkpoint, and commands them to open a gate because, on the other side, Palestinian children on their way back from school are waiting in the sun. Upset by this flagrant injustice and abandoning his usual restraint, the filmmaker becomes upset and starts insulting the soldiers.

> 'Stop bothering me with your jeep and your forbidden areas! Open the gate and let these kids go home!'
> 'What is this, a sermon?' asks one of the soldiers.
> 'Yeah, you're all bloody idiots, that's what you are!'
> 'They're just looking for stuff to put on the news,' says another soldier.
> 'These kids are sitting there, waiting, and you don't tell them when you're gonna open the gate? Where are you from? What hole did you crawl out of? Under what stinking pile of rubbish did you grow up?'

The camera captures reality with raging strength, shows the stubborn faces of the soldiers who abuse their positions and wield a devious and contemptuous power. It is placed insolently close, in a way that transgresses the conventional distance that is supposed to stand between those who film and those who are filmed. The border becomes the stage of a war of words between the pacifist filmmaker and the soldiers. However, this moment of political anger should not be interpreted as a gratuitous explosion of raw emotion, and certainly not as a moment of release for entertainment's sake. As he bears witness to these lives that are entirely dependent on the whims of soldiers, Avi Mograbi gets to a point where he cannot put up with these circumstances any longer, and he bursts out. *Avenge But One of My Two Eyes* is built around a dual structure, violence and appeasement, screaming matches at the border and calm analysis on the telephone, out in the field and at home. As Jean-Luc Nancy wrote,

> Violence does not play power games. It does not play at all, it hates games, all games, the time intervals, the articulations, the moments of idleness, the rules that do not mean anything. Violence pushes the power games and the network of relationships aside, it crushes them, but it also spends itself out as it erupts. It stands below power, but above acts.[23]

From his home workshop, Mograbi is in constant contact, by telephone, with a Palestinian friend living in Hebron. This 'phone relationship'[24] is portrayed on a regular basis throughout the film, and it allows the director to joint together the real, physical experience and the dialogues that 'cover up', at least temporarily, the outbursts of violence. The phone becomes a method of discursive pacification, and it creates, by its intermittent appearance in the film, a sense of appeasement. The conversations help defuse the explosions that could be caused by the events shown previously, they temper the effects of the conflicts that were filmed, but without shutting them out, erasing or avoiding them. The anonymous Palestinian friend speaks quite frankly and expresses his outrage with almost stolid composure: 'I don't want to be a slave, here, in my own land, any more.' Avi Mograbi replies: 'We can't use force to change things.' Out in the field, the filmmaker enters the conflict, he takes part in it with great energy; at home, in his workshop, he talks, reflects, thinks. As the voice of the Palestinian Other enters the workshop, it creates a balance, an equilibrium. The intimate conversations are a response to the silence forced upon all by the violence of this conflict. The faceless Palestinian voice establishes, intermittently, indirectly, a kind of equality, by giving dignity back to the Palestinian people. The telephone becomes a political metaphor, a way to provoke a pacifist uprising, an image of the missing Palestinian people. Even the fact that Mograbi's family can be seen in the background reiterates this point: mundane domesticity, as opposed to the images of violence at the border.

THE WORKSHOP AS STAGE: FROM INDIGNANT IRONY TO BURLESQUE IDIOCY

Setting himself up in front of the camera, in his family home, represents for Avi Mograbi a kind of mischievous irony. While the narrative of *How I Learned to Overcome My Fear and Love Arik Sharon* focuses, as the title implies, on his fear that his increasingly close relationship with Ariel Sharon will turn into friendship, it also encourages the audience to detach itself and see, through it all, the political clairvoyance and pacifist mockery. Irony, write Pierre Schoentjes, 'pretends to take seriously the things it despises, it pretends to play by the other's rules, but only to show that these rules are idiotic or perverted'.[25] In his films, Avi Mograbi uses irony, and its 'cheerful indignation',[26] while sitting at home, but when he goes out in the world, he takes a political stand, physically and emotionally, and fights against all that is unjust, unacceptable, unbearable. It can thus be said that Mograbi's films are based on a dual structure: on the one hand, the filmmaker acts, reacts and takes part in the violent conflict between the Israeli and Palestinian communities; on the other hand, he turns his flat into a workshop, where he can speak freely and use a dramatised, analytical form of irony.

At the beginning of *August: A Moment Before the Explosion*, Avi Mograbi informs the audience that he thinks August is an intolerable month, because the weather is too hot and because nothing ever happens. So, in August, in the depressing heat, he films ordinary squabbles, the altercations that take place repeatedly, day in and day out, in Tel Aviv. He transforms his home into a domestic theatre workshop and plays many different roles: himself, his own wife, his producer ... He invents ludicrous situations that reconsider and reimagine the explosive reality. His living room becomes a laboratory where pacifist games are made up, where Mograbi creates what he calls a 'series of domestic episodes'[27] in which three quirky characters quarrel heatedly with one another. The director's wife (that is, Mograbi himself with a pink towel wrapped around his head) berates him for only making dark movies and asks him, for once, to make one 'that would make people smile', 'a movie that they will want to see again and again'.

Later, a producer named Roni (Mograbi still but now wearing a hat) walks angrily in the flat but the filmmaker is 'out'. His 'wife' (with the pink towel wrap) greets him. He has come to pick up the videotapes of the auditions for a film that Mograbi, the filmmaker, wants to make about the Cave of the Patriarchs Massacre.[28] The producer argues vehemently with Mograbi's wife, accusing her husband of deliberately sabotaging the production. He looks for the tapes everywhere, turning everything upside down in the apartment in the process, while the camera, placed in its usual spot in the living room, captures it all. These little domestic scenes are created using very basic special effects, such as split screens. Mograbi makes no attempt to hide the primitive nature of these visual tricks. He is even, to some extent, proud of them:

> I wanted the special effects to be as rudimentary as the props – a towel and a hat – that I use to become the wife or the producer. This roughness, this *low high tech* seemed appropriate to the comical, self-mocking aspects of these scenes.[29]

The goofy wackiness of events in the apartment stands in sharp contrast to the alienating fury that overtakes the Israeli streets. Avi Mograbi thinks up a stupid quarrel and thus draws the attention away from the images of urban violence. Writes Jean-Yves Jouannais,

> Idiocy, that intangible monument, can thus be said to be the result of a bet, an object that one would like to set down in some landscape, not to alter or distort it, but to give it an identity, to take away the contempt, the disgust or the absence that others considered appropriate.[30]

Avi Mograbi creates, inside his own home, a theatre workshop based on 'delusions of interpretation'[31] that bring up questions and doubts about the delusions of action of community violence. The chaotic and anarchic characters and the situational comedy enter into a sort of unbalanced struggle with reality. It is bickering as poetics, as a way to think about the political consequences of violence. The fictional quarrels are based on misunderstandings, disagreements and disputes, but they make sure always to maintain a connection, a comedic link to others. In contrast, the fighting that goes on in the streets of the country prevents, with its thoughtless violence, any possibility of a connection. As he goes back and forth between the outside world and his home/studio, the filmmaker does not use words and images to turn one ideology against another. The theatre workshop works rather as a window that looks, with great clearness and critical distance, upon the daily storm of violence in Israel.

Figure 4.1   August: A Moment Before the Eruption *(2002)*

Figure 4.2   August: A Moment Before the Eruption *(2002)*

Figure 4.3 How I Learned to Overcome My Fear and Love Arik Sharon *(1997)*

Figure 4.4 Avenge But One of My Two Eyes *(2005)*

Notes

1. See, for example, Henri-Georges Clouzot's *The Mystery of Picasso* (1956). It was shot in La Victorine studios, in Nice. The use of canvas, seen from behind and soaked through with paint, captures with great efficiency the creative process of the artist.
2. Pierre-Henri Frange, Gilles Mouëllic and Christophe Viart (eds), *Filmer l'acte de création*. Rennes: PUR, 2009, p. 20.
3. Nicole Brenez, 'Insurrections de l'amour en contexte matérialiste', in Jérôme Game (ed.), *Images des corps/Corps des images au cinéma*. Lyon: ENS Éditions, 2010, p. 185.
4. Nicole Brenez points out, quite rightly, that Pedro Costa's film 'focuses on creation as intervention, as act, as work, as praxis, just like, for the Straubs, art and cinema – and it is so with Cesare Pavese, Elio Vittorini, or even Charles Péguy, whom Jean-Marie Straub quotes – must help emancipate the workers, the peasants, the fighters, and help write the history of those who have no history' (Ibid., p. 187).
5. Christa Blümlinger, 'Le Peuple qui manque: à propos des installations d'Avi Mograbi', in *Avi Mograbi: The Details*. Rennes: Éditions Galerie Art et Essai, 2011, p. 87.
6. Avi Mograbi, *Mon occupation préférée*, interviews with Eugenio Renzi. Paris: Les Prairies Ordinaires, 2015, p. 71.
7. François Niney, 'Confondre l'ennemi sans se confondre avec lui', *Images documentaires*, 23 (1995), p. 24.
8. Mograbi, *Mon occupation préférée*, pp. 72–3.
9. Ibid., p. 72.
10. Ibid., p. 69.
11. Gérard Leblanc, *Scénarios du réel*, vol. 2. Paris: L'Harmattan, 1997, p. 13.
12. Georges Balandier, *Le Pouvoir sur scène*. Paris: Fayard, 2006, p. 171.
13. Ibid.
14. Alain Ménil, 'Entre utopie et hérésie: quelques remarques à propos de la notion d'essai', in Suzanne Liandrat-Guigues and Murielle Gagnebin (eds), *L'Essai et le cinéma*. Seyssel: Champ Vallon, 2004, p. 125.
15. Jacques Rancière, 'Les Incertitudes de la dialectique', *Trafic*, 93 (Spring 2015), p. 94.
16. Georges Didi-Huberman, *Remontages du temps subi: l'œil de l'histoire 2*. Paris: Les Éditions de Minuit, 2010, p. 80.
17. Ibid., p. 98.
18. Ibid., p. 145.
19. Jean Starobinski, *Action et réaction: vie et aventure d'un couple*. Paris: Seuil, 1999, p. 307.
20. Jean Genet, 'Quatre heures à Chatila', *Revue d'études palestiniennes*, 6 (Winter 1983). See also *L'Ennemi déclaré: textes et entretiens*. Paris: Gallimard, 1991, p. 247.
21. François Niney, *L'Épreuve du réel à l'écran: essai sur le principe de réalité documentaire*. Brussels: De Boeck, 2000, p. 248.

22. Mograbi, *Mon occupation préférée*, p. 155.
23. Jean-Luc Nancy, 'Image et violence', *Le Portique*, 6 (2000), online 24 March 2005. Available at <http://leportique.revues.org/451> (last accessed 8 June 2016).
24. See Emmanuelle André and Dork Zabunyan, *L'Attrait du téléphone*. Crisnée: Yellow Now, 2013, pp. 24–32.
25. Pierre Schoentjes, *Poétique de l'ironie*. Paris: Seuil, 2001, p. 200.
26. Ibid.
27. Mograbi, *Mon occupation préférée*, p. 139.
28. On 25 February 1994, an American–Israeli military physician and settler, Baruch Goldstein, entered the Ibrahimi mosque at the Cave of the Patriarchs in Hebron and fired on the Muslims who had gathered there to pray. He killed twenty-nine people before being killed himself. Avi Mograbi wrote an outline of a film that would be based on the trial of the unprecedented massacre. As he was not able to get access to the archives, Mograbi abandoned the project. He said he was particularly affected by the testimony of Baruch Goldstein's wife. In *August: A Moment Before the Explosion*, he uses rushes that are supposed to be from the auditions for the role of Goldstein's wife, for a film that does not exist, but that were in reality the auditions of three actresses for a chocolate advert. Cf. Mograbi, *Mon occupation préférée*, pp. 134–7.
29. Ibid., p. 133.
30. Jean-Yves Jouannais, *L'Idiotie*. Paris: Beaux-Arts Magazines/Livres, 2003, p. 26.
31. Kràl, *Le Burlesque*, p. 304.

CHAPTER 5

A Moving Inwardness: Alexander Sokurov's A Humble Life

In *A Humble Life* (1997), Alexander Sokurov shows the daily life of an old lady who lives by herself in a village in the mountains of Nara prefecture, in Japan. Her time is mostly spent sewing *mofuku*, or mourning kimonos. Her house is not presented as a domestic, functional space, but rather as an outer layer that strengthens and protects the lonely woman. Indeed, the traditional wooden house serves all at once as protection, as a place of meditation and as a workshop. Alexander Sokurov enters into this simple, unornamented architecture and introduces it as a form of poetic expression: for the filmmaker, it seems as if the dwelling was a way of thinking existentially about space. The Japanese house is an empty but active home, a site favourable to both delight and prolonged enchantment.

THE SPIRIT OF THE JAPANESE HOUSE

Late at night, clouds rush sideways in front of the camera, streaking before a mountain range. This image is followed by a static shot of a house, barely visible in the darkness. The director whispers calmly and solemnly: 'I arrived at dusk. The sound of the wind and fatigue prevented me from falling asleep.' Slowly, the camera inches closer to the house and comes inside. It lingers for a while on an oil lamp, then it examines from up close a hand stroking a tatami, while the sound of burning twigs and the chirp of crickets are heard. Later, Sokurov places his camera on the threshold of a sliding door, so as to bring together the inside and the outside as a continuous whole. Materials and fabrics are closely observed: packed-earth floors, the rush stems of the tatami. Slowly, the superimposed image of a Japanese-style room (*washitsu*), with its tatami flooring and rice paper (*shouji*) walls, appears. The audience can hear the sound of a wooden floor creaking, and one guesses that it is the house's lone occupant walking about. The filmmaker seems to be listening intently to the nervous chatter of the various materials, as if to reveal the quiet, spiritual sobriety of the walls and floors of this Japanese house.

A Humble Life does not represent the house as a constructed block, a shell made for protection or for privacy. European houses are essentially built on the notion that space is linear and functional, which encourages the use of perspective; Japanese architecture, on the other hand, relies on the notion of 'rhythmic space'[1] in order to create 'areolar spaces' where 'fields, context, juxtaposition, rather than articulation and hierarchic sequences',[2] are preferred. Exploring the house, for the filmmaker, means examining it beam by beam, looking at each angle of its frame, crossing each of its thresholds; it is a form of meditation, a way of losing oneself in this non-hierarchical space. In his book on Japanese architecture, Augustin Berque says that

> thresholds, in the technical organisation of space, serve a liminary function. Because it is areolar, even cellular in its structure, Japanese spatiality gives a great importance to thresholds: it is conducive to meditation because each cell exists in and of itself, and not as part of a whole.[3]

In *A Humble Life*, Alexander Sokurov warns the lady of the house of his presence; he waits, looks, stands in the doorway, careful not to offend her. Throughout the film, except at the very end when she reads a few haikus, the old lady never speaks. She goes about her day, in her slow and deliberate way, skilfully sewing light fabric to make it into mourning kimonos. The camera is constantly moving about, very slowly, as if to see all there was to see, as if it was fascinated by the beauty of the old house. Several times, the voice of the director pays tribute to it:

> This house is both delicate and solid. It is 130 years old. The walls everywhere are paper, from top to bottom, the doorways, the partitions and the doors. Everything bears the mark of perseverance, of tenacity, everything seems immutable, the century-old wooden beam, the sculpted wood. The temperature is barely above freezing, but the doors are open. It is very cold inside, there is not a single spot that is warm. The floor everywhere is packed earth.

The camera almost seems to touch and caress the materials and the textures that it encounters; every angle, every edge is brought into sharp relief. The house is made out to be a kind of philosophical armature, a sensitive spatiality open to the rhythms of the seasons and of nature.[4] The house appears almost as an empty shell, absolutely open to the outside, while inside, peacefully, ceremoniously, the daily rituals of life go on. Jacques Pezeu-Massabuau states that Japanese houses cultivate 'an open conception of material space', so that individual dwellings 'integrate the space occupied by the community as a whole'. Sokurov's camera moves around with no predetermined itinerary, going from room to room, from outside to inside, making no attempt at explaining the topography but seemingly integrating all the specific details of this traditional Japanese house. It moves along the lines of sight, points out the strength contained in this aesthetic emptiness, fixes it, salutes it. It is a thoughtful gaze, characterised by a sort of weightlessness, a straightforward grace, an unmasked beauty. The video camera[5] observes all the attributes of the house and presents its bareness as harmonious emptiness rather than apparent rusticity. Indeed, this emptiness is not nothingness: it is a pause, a respite, a whispered, serene peace.

Often, Western houses prefer fullness to emptiness, ornamentation to bareness. They fill up the architectural container, in particular by giving each room a technical function that takes over the feeling of space. Each room must therefore be furnished with all the necessary tools, so that it may fulfil its function. Roland Barthes writes,

> with us, furniture has an immobilizing vocation, whereas in Japan the house, often deconstructed, is scarcely more than a furnishing – mobile – element; in the Shikidai gallery, as in the ideal Japanese house, stripped of furniture (or scantily furnished), there is no site which designates the slightest propriety in the strict sense of the word – ownership: neither seat nor bed nor table out of which the body might constitute itself as the subject (or master) of a space: the center is rejected (painful frustration for Western man, everywhere 'furnished' with his armchair, his bed, proprietor of a domestic location).[6]

In *A Humble Life*, Sokurov's camera seeks to unveil the delicate forces of the house, to ennoble its harmonising energy. The static shots let in the wooded exterior's penetrating powers, they come in through the open doors, without intruding. The Japanese house is, in fact, a moving, ever-changing anchor, thus corresponding perfectly to Japanese spatial precepts, according to which 'inwardness must be intimately associated with motion'.[7]

Using long static shots and slow panoramic shots, Alexander Sokurov shows the Japanese house as completely open to the outside and not hermetically sealed. In the centre of an empty room, on a charcoal stove, a black cast-iron kettle is boiling. In the background, framed on each side by rice-paper walls with their wooden lattices, a garden appears through an opening. The entire wing of the house gives out on to the garden, lending an impression of depth to this green space. A dead tree trunk lies on the tatami floor, an echo, a muted alliance with the plants outside. The frail yet sculptural vegetal life is a powerful reminder of the fluid unity between the inside and the outside.

Later, the camera lingers on a tree near the doorstep of the house. It looks like an old engraving, with its twisted branches, with the shaded light that surrounds it. The filmmaker spends a long time looking at this corner of the garden, half-hidden by a wood partition, until slowly, almost ceremoniously, the camera turns away from the tree and shows the old lady doing her hair in the next room. A moment later, the camera, placed at a different spot in the garden, gazes upon the leaves of the same tree, but then it swivels down, along the pillar-like trunk, until the ground and a small stone basin forming a 'mineral tapestry'[8] can be seen. Interior and exterior spaces are united by the camera movements, and the common organicity becomes, day or night, a prelude to meditation. The garden is a condensed universe[9], which goes beyond its basic decorative function and creates a harmonious whole with the interior: the inside is nourished by the delineated vitality of the outside. From top to bottom, from the front or the side, the house of *A Humble Life* looks upon the world in a variety of ways, but the garden's beauty remains, like a series of ephemeral paintings.

Nevertheless, these perspectives on the garden should not be confused with the long shots of the mountains, with their heavy fogs that make them look almost like cottony landscapes. The solemnity of these images, of these vibrant pictures, is emphasised by the sounds Alexander Sokurov chose to add (the howling of the wind, some music). In their majesty, the great trees of the forest, their trunk neatly aligned, their branches filled with shreds of mist clinging to them, seem to represent the sovereign magnificence of nature, which thrives beyond humanity's control. As Baldine Saint-Girons suggested, a garden is a place where 'men give nature its just measure'[10]. This should be opposed to landscapes, which she defines in this manner:

> landscapes suppose that men meet a new measure through transhuman or transindividual nature. [...] Gardens are both 'art and memorial places', but it is a prearranged memory: men go there to meet others. Landscapes, on the other hand, transmit an unconscious memory that must be gleaned. In them, men can understand how they are anchored in a nature that is much greater than them.[11]

In *A Humble Life*, landscapes are paintings that show and demonstrate the beauty of nature; they are songs of life, a way of resisting death's call. In *Oriental Elegy* (1996), landscapes, men and houses are bound together in a sort of deathly immateriality. The residents of a Japanese village tell tales of death and mourning, to which Alexander Sokurov affixes an archipelago of nearly mystical landscapes of 'vanishing evaporation'.[12] He creates an apotheotic reality that is distended, that falls apart, that disappears only to be replaced by imaginary uncanniness.

The intense melancholy that seeps through Sokurov's 'Elegy' series creates a poetic lamentation, in which men and landscapes collaborate and unite to share overwhelming gloom. The various elegiac figures celebrated by Sokurov in these cinematographic essays[13] are, in his own words, 'a good and sad memory of what once was and will never come back. But it is not utterly lost, because its existence continues in me.'[14] *Oriental Elegy* focuses on an evanescent aesthetics, based on immateriality, vanishing images and melancholy.

While *Oriental Elegy* focuses on dizzying sublimity and the transience of time, *A Humble Life* shows a silent *awakening* caused by the harmonious beauty of the house and the calm motions of the old seamstress. Jean-Luc Nancy defined the difference between the beautiful and the sublime:

> In beauty, there is agreement, whereas the sublime is a syncopation tracing the outer edge of the agreement, it is the limits vanishing in a spasm and going off into the limitless, that is to say, into nothingness. [...] The instant is present in the instant and yet escapes it, it is the whole present and a cross-section of it (but it is as time, without a doubt, that one should interpret the sublime aesthetics: that may mean understanding time as a limit, time as a vanishing figure, which would be the very time of art?).[15]

However, Alexander Sokurov does not exoticise the Japanese house and rejects contemplation in any form.[16] The gaze is made to observe with more and more attention, as Sokurov probes the aesthetic characteristics of the house: he uncovers the house's identity, as the weight of the materials and the energy of the emptiness balance each other out. The static shots show both the penetrating link between the inside and the outside, and the persistence of shadows. The audience comes to understand that the house is not a single geometric space, but an existential topography. The precisely framed shots examine surfaces and volumes to give the whole its expressive unity and thus grant this humble place nobility. The director creates points of contact[17] between the audience and this oriental architectural skin: the house becomes a *vision* and loses its primary function as domestic dwelling.

There is double irresolution in *A Humble Life*: on the one hand, the Japanese house forms a miniature visual world, with no hierarchy, connected to earthly and celestial forces. On the other hand, the soft and fervent voice of the filmmaker expresses a kind of reverence – not one that is focused on the land, as is the case in Tarkovsky's films, but rather that looks to rise up towards beauty. Sokurov does not try to lead, to control, he does not try to colonise the cinematographic space; he only speaks intermittently, with great intensity, to express curiosity and reverence. His voice does not overwhelm the images; he speaks slowly, discreetly, barely above a whisper. The director describes his delight, but with practically no emphasis. It is almost as if words were mere suggestions, a means to create an opening in the cinematographic frame, to enter into it. The narration hints at a different mode of perception, one that would be based on purity and wonder, that would be inspired by this oriental beauty, that would acknowledge a debt with humility and faith.

Rather than hiding the unpredictable melody of creaking wooden beams, rather than overpowering the shrill bird calls that are a constant reminder of the open link between the inside and the outside, the narrator brings it all together. He gathers, he unites. He does not dismiss the ordinary background noises; he welcomes them, because their sudden, strange, dizzying vibrations are yet another expression of the beauty of the world.

> Noise is not an absurd remnant any more, fated to be erased as it always is in the basic soundscapes of ordinary films: Alexander Sokurov uses noises with parsimony, gives it a coherent, noble opacity, like a foreign language. Noises are hieroglyphs: one can feel the weight of their meanings, but the key is missing.[18]

This Japanese house, with its sculpted wood and endless silence, leads Alexander Sokurov to delve furtively into his memories of the Second World War in Russia. At the beginning of the film, a few old photographs are shown on screen: women and children posing in front of a dacha near a forest. These inserted images establish an enigmatic link between Russia and Japan, between the childhood dacha and the Japanese country house. But traditionally, Russian dachas are not permanent dwellings: they are summer residences, an escape from city life. Andrei Tarkovsky's *The Mirror* features a family dacha surrounded by an imaginal forest. But there are no daily chores being done in Tarkovsky's house; it is a fortress, a haven where memories and dreams can find solace. *The Mirror*'s dacha is rudimentary – practically a cabin, a sort of primitive space, an out-of-the-way place where dreams dominate reality, sublimate it, flee from it in order to find a new freedom. It may not be much more than a cabin, but it is still, to Tarkovsky, a refuge, a shelter, a place where dreams are weaved rather than a permanent dwelling weighed down by habits. The house of *A Humble Life*, by contrast, is a stable point, from which harmonies may be developed because of its 'spatial rhythms'.

FROM DOMESTIC GESTURES TO CRAFTING: A POETICS OF FORTIFICATION

Seated on a cushion, in a narrow corridor, only separated from the garden by a wooden lattice, the old Japanese lady is combing her hair in the half-light. Then the narrator's tentative voice is heard: 'It seemed she hadn't noticed me. I decided to come closer.' The camera moves forward and, staying at a respectful distance, shows her face reflected in a mirror. She gets up, leaves the room. For the audience, that moment in a dark corner represents the first time it sees the old lady. In *A Humble Life*, darkness is more important than light; it covers every room, as if to emphasise the solitary atmosphere in which the old seamstress lives. Junichirō Tanizaki wrote about the importance of shadows in Japanese culture in *In Praise of Shadows*:

> We delight in the mere sight of the delicate glow of fading rays clinging to the surface of a dusky wall, there to live out what little life remains to them. We never tire of the sight, for to us this pale glow and these dim shadows far surpass any ornament.[19]

A moment later, the old lady, with the camera standing slightly above her, is shown cutting twigs, which she then places calmly and meticulously in a small terracotta stove before starting a fire. Sokurov's voice is heard again: 'I remember that everything seemed interesting to me: the walls, the tools, the wind, the light, the sounds ... Her whole life.' The camera slowly creeps in, the fire crackles as Hiroko[20] blows through a bamboo tube to help kindle it. Later, we see her hands patiently, skilfully, determinedly drawing lines on white fabric to prepare it. The cloth and its voluptuous undulations fill the entire screen. 'I had never seen a mourning kimono being made,' says the narrator. We hear a piano melody, the song of birds, the muffled voice of a radio. The lady's hands, fingers crooked after years of manual labour, unfold the fabric and begin sewing. Alexander Sokurov uses close-ups to show her hands, her face, her skin, the texture of the fabric and the motions of her craft. The camera comes extremely close, as if actually to touch the waves of textile and the skin of the old lady's face. Gradually, it begins to feel as if her craft is really a kind of creative grace, rather than just professional techniques mastered by repetitions. It is a slow choreography, as the camera imperturbably glides on and the seamstress works unhurriedly. 'Being slow', wrote Pierre Sansot, 'is a passionate metamorphosis. It allows us to test out a person, a landscape, an event, to see what time will transform them into.'[21] As he films the old lady slowly preparing and crafting kimonos, Alexander Sokurov grants his images a temporal magnitude that transforms the narrative into a poetical fortification. The word fortification, however, should not be understood to mean a voluntary determination, but rather a concept of the rhythms of daily life, in which every gesture, every step is a powerless strength. Rhythmic harmonies allow the viewer's gaze to go beyond the place. The meticulous labour, the calm devotion of the old lady lead Sokurov to conclude that her body is a frail fortress.

The last shots of *A Humble Life* show a dark, empty room, with tatami flooring, in which stands a great folding screen. Sokurov narrates: 'I waited for her in the main room. Candles were lit. I looked at a statue of the Buddha.' The old lady walks in, sits on a cushion and greets the filmmaker.

She holds in her hand a notebook. She opens it and reads several haikus that she wrote herself.[22] After reading each one, she pauses, and Sokurov translates them in Russian.

> The Autumn comes,
> The water of the stream shivers,
> And sadness overtakes me.
>
> My husband died ten years ago,
> And today still suffering and sadness
> Grip my heart.
>
> The graceful white lily
> Towards the whispering brook
> Slowly bows.

This farewell ritual represents the first time the audience hears the old lady's voice. She is sitting directly in front of the camera, and she reads her poems serenely, in a melodious whisper. 'The haiku', wrote Roland Barthes, 'has the purity, the sphericality, and the very emptiness of a note of music,'[23] and that 'meaning is only a flash, a slash of light'.[24] These brief flares of emotion are a continuation, in a sense, of the aesthetics of *A Humble Life*: the old lady's very movements, every shot of the interior and exterior of the house appear to be illuminations, revelations, rather than meaningful, carefully constructed discourses. The haikus, as they are being read, convey simultaneously the presence of nature and the sorrow of losing a loved one. It

Figure 5.1 A Humble Life *(1997)*

is thus with a bereaved beauty that Alexander Sokurov's film ends: Hiroko's haikus are a reminder that life is impermanent, that the feeling of aesthetic completeness that is so dear to the filmmaker's heart can thrive only in the ephemeral. Beauty is a furtive bolt of lightning that instantly disappears in the dark mists of time.

Figure 5.2   A Humble Life *(1997)*

Figure 5.3   A Humble Life *(1997)*

Figure 5.4 A Humble Life *(1997)*

Notes

1. Augustin Berque, *Le Sens de l'espace au Japon: vivre, penser, bâtir*, with Maurice Sauzet. Paris: Éditions Arguments, 2004, p. 29.
2. Ibid., p. 74.
3. Ibid., p. 104.
4. Jacques Pezeu-Massabuau, 'La Maison japonaise: standardisation de l'espace habité et harmonie sociale', *Annales ESC*, 4 (1977), p. 696; quoted by Berque, *Le Sens de l'espace au Japon*, p. 86.
5. Alexei Fedorov was the cameraman.
6. Roland Barthes, *Empire of Signs*, trans. Richard Howard. New York: The Noonday Press, 1982, pp. 108–10.
7. Berque, *Le Sens de l'espace au Japon*, p. 102.
8. Barthes, *Empire of Signs*, p. 107.
9. Christian Godin and Laure Mühlethaler, *Édifier: l'architecture et le lieu*. Lagrasse: Verdier, 2005, p. 113.
10. Baldine Saint-Girons, 'Jardins et paysages: une opposition catégorielle', in Jackie Pigeaud and Jean-Paul Barbe (eds), *Histoires de jardins: lieux et imaginaire*. Paris: PUF, 2001, p. 54.
11. Ibid., p. 67.
12. Diane Arnaud, *Le Cinéma de Sokourov: figures d'enfermement*. Paris: L'Harmattan, 2005, p. 134.
13. *Oriental Elegy, Elegy from Russia, Elegy of a Voyage, Elegy of a Life*.
14. 'Interview d'Alexandre Sokourov donnée à Georges Nivat', in Murielle Gagnebin (ed.), *L'Ombre de l'image: de la falsification à l'infigurable*. Seyssel: Champ Vallon, 2002, p. 387.

15. Jean-Luc Nancy, 'L'Offrande sublime', in *Du sublime* [collective publication]. Paris: Belin, 1988, p. 76.
16. 'Interview d'Alexandre Sokourov donnée à Georges Nivat', in Gagnebin (ed.), *L'Ombre de l'image*, p. 388.
17. Godin and Mühlethaler, *Édifier*, p. 37.
18. Philippe Roger, 'La Poétique sonore d'Alexandre Sokourov', in François Albera and Michel Estève (eds), *Alexandre Sokourov*. Condé-sur-Noireau: Éditions Charles Corlet, CinémaAction, 2009, p. 78.
19. Junichirō Tanizaki, *In Praise of Shadows*, trans. Thomas J. Harper and Edward G. Seidensticker. Stony Creek: Leete's Island Books, 1977, p. 18.
20. Her name is given at the beginning of the film. The narrator says: 'Dear Hiroko, last night, I did not dream either. Did I even sleep, or was it just nothingness?'
21. Pierre Sansot, *Du bon usage de la lenteur*. Paris: Payot et Rivages, 2000, p. 124.
22. She reads eight haikus. Only three are transcribed here.
23. Barthes, *Empire of Signs*, p. 76.
24. Ibid., p. 83.

Part 3

The Forest: From Sensory Environment to Economic Site

Monumental grandeur, green density, heterogenous ecosystem, leafy maze: forests are a world beyond ours, a support for the imagination, full of enigmas and mysteries. In his study of the history of forests in the Western civilisation, Robert Harrison states that

> in the religions, mythologies, and literatures of the West, the forest appears as a place where the logic of distinction goes astray. Or where our subjective categories are confounded. Or where perceptions become promiscuous with one another, disclosing latent dimensions of time and consciousness.[1]

Movies often give forests limited roles; they are spectacular settings, full of symbolic protections, or inhabited by hostile or fantastic creatures. In the Hollywood blockbuster *Avatar*, James Cameron shows forests as a green, mystic, synthetic and obscure beauty, as an eerie environment where stories of futuristic myths are told. The movie borrows from countless other films, and so forests appear as nothing more than lush scenic ornamentations, a (super)natural, hyperbolic backdrop in which men and giant humanoids fight.

There are others, like Philippe Grandrieux, Naomi Kawase, Danièle Huillet and Jean-Marie Straub, or Lisandro Alonso, who look more humbly on the wooded world, in a more frontal and dualistic way; they remind us of the sensory power of the vegetal environment, they are aware of life's quivering reality. In their films, forests are an affirmation of a vigorous yet discreet strength; they are a *place for the living*, rather than a *space for the recluse*. Therefore, they appear in the pictures as something other than a simple decoration, a temporary and evasive participant. The camera occupies the undergrowth, feels its texture, hooks on to the plants' arteries, cuts into the bark of the trees: it proclaims that the forest's nature is to be lived in, to be explored. These filmmakers create narratives that connect the body to its organic environment, whose monumentality overwhelms and dominates us; they weave tactile poetry. Forests, in their films, are no longer a space to contemplate and become instead a place where one can put down roots, even if only for a time. They are no longer a landscape in which to get lost, and become an integral, macrocosmic foundation, where forces can be replenished. As Robert Harrison points out, 'we turn round to nature to found ourselves in the midst of something absolute which we do not possess and which in turn refuses to possess us. In this manner we appropriate nature as the place of dwelling.'[2] But how can one live in the woods without making them a home? How can one transform an exterior space, an unmanageable and often hostile space, into a place of germination where humans and nature can be reunited?

Notes

1. Robert Pogue Harrison, *Forests, the Shadow of Civilisation*. Chicago: University of Chicago Press, 1992, p. x.
2. Ibid., p. 227.

CHAPTER 6

Philippe Grandrieux's Forest-matter: A Multisensory Place

The violent thwacks of a young woodcutter's axe, his bold and rapid breathing, fill the first shot of Philippe Grandrieux's film *Un Lac* (2008). Two hands are seen in close-up; behind them, we can make out blurry, shining black filaments that ripple across the frame. After showing a few more frantic hacks, the camera looks up: dark trees sway against the pale dome of the sky. The trunk makes a brief, cracking sound, announcing its impending fall. These thundering noises jolt the images and seem to contract, compress them. It is as if the spasmodic sounds brutalised the lofty and serene verticality of the trees and shook them to their core. Sounds breach the two-dimensional perspective of the landscape, and the wounded depth of the plants stabs through the screen. One could think of these noises as punctures, that exist both physically (as the sound waves expand throughout the forested space) and aesthetically (they deface the beautiful landscape), or as a cinematographic manifesto, an artistic posture of sorts; because he favours the use of sound bursts to torment the elements, Philippe Grandrieux creates an auditory stratigraphy that takes over the appearance of the ecological structure. He unleashes a mobile and excruciating vison of matter that smashes through the illusion of the canvassed landscape.

POETICS OF THE UNSTABLE

For Philippe Grandrieux, every shot is an urge, a pressure, an energy that lays bare the nervous ripples of reality.[1] In that regard, images are not composed solely with the grammar of visual comprehension in mind, because they also aim to convey the physical and motive experience of perception, the body that makes the film and the body-camera meld into one, thus creating a centripetal force that changes reality and moves the senses polyphonically.

The activity of the maker of films pulls bubbling, swarming forces out of life, which resonates, in this sense, with the way phenomenology describes perception:

to move one's body is to aim at things through it; it is to allow oneself to respond to their call, which is made upon it independently of any representation. [...] We must therefore avoid saying that our body is *in* space, or *in* time. It *inhabits* space and time.[2]

After the tree has fallen violently to the ground, Philippe Grandrieux shows, from a close high-angle shot, the empty stare of Alexi, the woodcutter, as he listens to the slight rustling of leaves; the blows have ended, and the trees can finally go back to their usual, silent rumblings. We then see a Percheron horse pulling the timber through deep snow, with its master next to it; the rhythmic sound of axes can be heard in the distance. The camera follows the two partners, then moves closer and closer to Alexi's face. He seems out of breath. He stumbles, then falls in the snow. The boy is having an epileptic fit. A storm rages in his body and seemingly infects our perception of the forest: as nervous discharges course through him, the trees waver. The picture is no longer static, but moves, undulates, expands, as if torn apart. This blurriness, this quivering puts an end to the solid verticality of the forest, which becomes a place resonating with multiple sensory inputs, and yet also with a moon-like purity.

Grandrieux used blurry images in another film, but in a completely different way. *Sombre* tells the tale of Jean, a wandering puppeteer who feels strong urges to kill the women that he meets. *Un Lac* represented the forest as a sort of cathedral, a monumental dwelling place; *Sombre* shows thick, dense, overwhelming woods, which scratch and scrape those who try to enter them, to rush into them. Yet the woods let Jean in. This character, with his murderous sexuality, represents a kind of archetype, an evil wolf who preys on women but then hides in a den. The blurry images serve a very specific purpose, in this context – they help the forest assume the appearance of a lair. With its shadowy areas, with all its branches and leaves that prevent anyone from entering it, it becomes a living place, and only the animal (evil) part of humans can go in. The low, sepulchral light seems even more intense because of the deliberate blurriness of the images; the forest turns into a thick, aggressive mass. Life becomes corrupted, the forest that shelters Jean becomes opaque, and he, consequently, grows more and more monstrous and inhumane. The blurriness creates a hallucinatory absence of definition. It does not simply prevent clarity of vision; it transforms the image into a sort of gaping vacuum. The forest in *Sombre* is not a volume, a spatial expanse; it is a place permeated with ferocity, with a sickly torpor that rises out of Jean's body as he walks around.

Philippe Grandrieux thus instils a fluidity that favours the spreading out of forms, rather than their scaling. It is, in a way, a choreography of sensations.

However, the point is not to display a perfectly controlled stylistic process, to show artistic mastery; it is to engage the filmmaker's body in the creation of images, to capture the outpouring of life, to give rise, in the image itself, to an unstable tide. *To see* becomes the start of a journey, of an adventure of *touch*. Human figures and plant forms are interwoven, and the images show intense bursts of turbulence, of quivering that create a 'place of photographic epiphany',[3] as Gérard Leblanc put it. Philippe Grandrieux continues what Jean Epstein started, when he said he wanted 'all the volumes to move and ripen until they burst. Cyclical life of atoms, Brownian motion, as sensual as a woman's or a young man's waist. Hills harden, like muscles. The universe is nervous.'[4]

Yet, Philippe Grandrieux does not truly initiate a 'landscape dance',[5] as Jean Epstein wrote admiringly, in a text in which he railed against the overly 'picturesque' representation of 'Breton landscapes in documentary films'. For Grandrieux, the point was not to give autonomy to places and living elements, but to have them relate to one another as dependent entities: a place does not become actualised until living bodies dwell there and find a connection to it. The forest is not simply, for Jean, a place of passage, a hideout: it is also a lair for the predator. As Serge Margel put it:

> wherever the body happens to be at any given time, that place represents the present, the realisation or the reality of that constant, mobile tension in the body between creation and decay. The place *is* reality. It represents, in the body, the existential reality of the body, the reality of its ontological movement between constitution and unconstitution, between composition and decomposition, between life and death.[6]

TO TOUCH, TO BREATHE, TO GIVE RHYTHM

Alexi's body remains always silent and acts according to its instincts; its relationship to all living things is tactile, sensual. The young woodcutter returns with his sister to their ghostly house,[7] lost in a great, snowy expanse. Philippe Grandrieux shows a sort of incestuous embrace of the two bodies, prolonging it as the camera moves into the forest: Alexi's hand slowly strokes the branches of a tree that – the images being blurry – appear only as frail lines. The trees become great, colourful stained-glass windows, and the hand that caresses them seems to illuminate the forest: the woods are transformed into a world of innocent purity and grace. The sound of raindrops, the insistent close-up of the horse's mane make the living world a place of contiguous harmonies. In *Un Lac*, the forest unites everything, it forges a fraternal bond between humans, animals and plants, and it is those voluptuous, grainy, mobile images that bring them together. The camera barely grazes all those dissimilar singularities; a haptic power connects them all, resulting in *dermal alterity*. In this particularly magnetic scene, Alexi's face and the horse's head brush up against one another; they breathe together radiantly. But Philippe Grandrieux does not glorify a sort of anthropomorphic lyricism; he shows the power of symbiotic alliance.

After this moment of nearly shared respiration between Alexi and the horse, the man sighs brutally and goes back to the work of cutting trees down. Shots follow one another organically; Grandrieux sings the praises of this womb-like place where bodies touch, hold each other up, run out of breath. In other words, the forest never stands in the background: it is inhabitable, a place where human and animal bodies can settle in, linked together in a luminous and sensuous way. The arrival of Alexi's sister, Hege, prolongs this state of sensory emergency. She immediately gives him a water flask and he drinks greedily from it. The faces are seen from up close, so that the audience may see the radiant emotions on his face – a tear glides down his cheek, which his sister delicately wipes away. In a gesture of majestic freedom, he hugs Hege and brushes his cheek against hers. She then climbs up on the horse and, eyes closed, begins a kind of choreography, as she pets the animal and sings to it in a low voice. Meanwhile, her brother serenely holds the horse's bridle. All three of them, the horse and the siblings, set off at a trot in the forest. The camera follows them close, merrily showing one breathless face after another, jolted along by the horse's gait. Life is a joyous bustle.

Grandrieux shows the power of the forest as a liberating form of dance, as a stimulating, nurturing, expansive network that allows bodies and senses to interact. Trembling breaths, folded sounds, bursts of silence are produced by all bodies, human and animal as well as plants, and thus make the forest into a world alive with poetic rhythms. As a place, it is not represented by the space it occupies, but by its 'heartbeat'. In a slow and fast harmony, as the axe bites vigorously into the bark of the trees, the quickened breaths of the two woodcutters create the 'energetic sound waves'[8] of the film. Its rhythm comes from the skin, and not from words, from friction and not from speech. As Daniel Deshays eloquently puts it:

> Because it reveals the matter of objects, because it gives reality to the flesh of the bodies that produce speech, sound holds us, ravishes, overwhelms us. It is flesh of codes just as much as flesh of icons. And as sound pictures bring memories of flesh back to life, they rise and become a living presence, from the moment they are listened to – that is, in the sharp instant when the sensation arises.[9]

THE FOREST, A FLEETING SACREDNESS

If the power of flowing sounds, if their unstable pulses grant material reality, from the point of view of the audience, to the forest – a vibrating matter that realises the *Dasein* of a place – the chromatic intoxication[10] of the images turns the forest into a cosmogonic entity, which looks more like the moon than the earth. Quite often, the forest appears as a dark wall. The trees are no longer symbols of abundance; they become black threads, stern fibres. Rocks and snow, on the ground, bolster this uncanny feeling, as if the forest belonged to the night and not the day. Blacks and whites dominate, granting it a crystalline, terrifying purity. Philippe Grandrieux creates images made up of oxymoronic colours: white goes against black, softness is allied to fright, thus establishing a luminescence that generates terror.

Suddenly, Alexi and Jurgen, the stranger who came in to help out with the cutting of the trees, are walking by themselves in the forest, looking at the trees they are planning to cut. A series of medium-long shots show the bodies as mobile silhouettes. The forest seems more ghostly than real. The fog, the snow, the darkness of tree trunks irradiate throughout the images: it is a prodigious world, both drowsy and graceful. Consequently, the place seems less tangible, airier, and the forest only becomes more mysterious. In her analysis of *La Vie nouvelle*, Safia Benhaïm says that 'Philippe Grandrieux invents a place that represents a new type of mental and topographical layout, a hiatus, a territory that stands *in-between*, suspended between the two poles of pure mythos and a reality that is too dense.'[11] In *Un Lac*, the woods move constantly from imaginary construct to concrete manifestation. They cease to appear as a material structure and become a fantasy setting.

Light effects give the forest a triumphant appearance, a sometimes hazy, sometimes nocturnal, opaque and sooty texture. Yet, it would be simplistic to claim that the 'darkness' that forever permeates the forest is a deathly symbol, a living place turned into a petrified, grave-like backdrop. The forest is not overwhelmed by all-encompassing night; rather, it stands as a frozen shade, a place where all light is dimmed and the fog is thick. It exudes a fleeting sacredness, without being gloomy. True visual wizardry, since the image dazzles even more when light is at its dimmest, pervades the strictly physical space of the forest and transforms it into a dream-like painting.

In *Un Lac*, the air flows in draughts that pierce through the forest at night and grant it 'fragments of elusiveness', to use the phrase coined by Baldine Saint Girons. Night, she says,

> contradicts the geometric view of the world. [...] Night is a paradox, so sublime as to elude us just as it takes hold of us. [...] And just like the sublime,

night reveals a blind spot, from which knowledge erupts, but where knowledge is invalidated, opening itself up to an overflowing truth.[12]

Shadows come off snowy surfaces, revealing the forest's ancient primitivism; it is not that nature is suppressed, but rather that the supernatural overflows. Night denies its own status, even as it rejoices in becoming a moon shadow: the forest is indeed a paradoxical, hazy place, drawn to the land and the sky, caught between high and low, between the earth and the heavens.

Figure 6.1 Un Lac *(2008)*

Figure 6.2 Un Lac *(2008)*

Figure 6.3 Un Lac *(2008)*

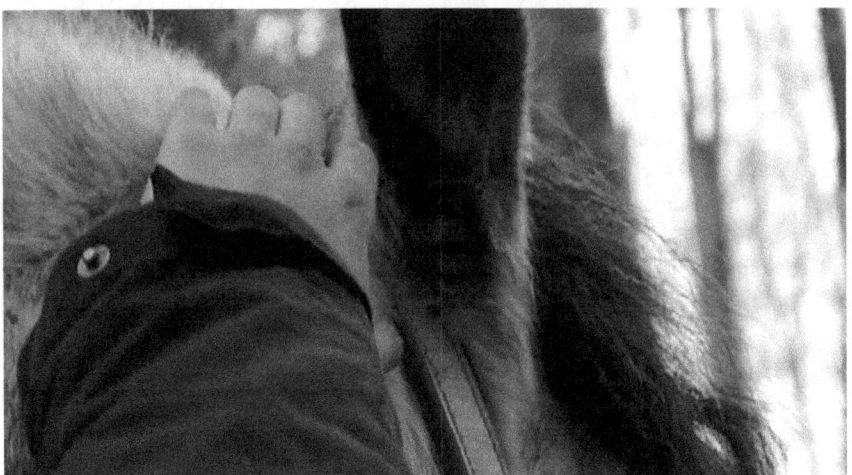

Figure 6.4 Un Lac *(2008)*

Notes

1. Philippe Grandrieux taught a master class during a retrospective organised by the magazine *Hors Champ* for the Festival du nouveau cinéma and presented by André Habib on 13 October 2012. He described in the following terms his relationship to the camera and the frame: 'The frame is an image that devours the eye. I personally prefer a fairly heavy camera, the physical strain of hoisting it on your shoulders. A 35 mm camera weighs about 27 kg, after all.

But [...] the demands on your body, the concrete energy necessary to counterbalance the weight of the camera, that is how you enter into a shot. These are very precise things, they are not ideas, they're never ideas, they're things that are directly involved. The body goes through them, they travel with the body, in the body. There is no active thought if the body does not activate the thought. Otherwise, it is disembodied, it goes nowhere.' *24 Images*, 160, from the extras of the DVD of *Un Lac*. Transcribed by *Hors Champ*, available at: <https://horschamp.qc.ca/article/grandrieux-de-a-g> (last accessed 22 March 2022).

2. Maurice Merleau-Ponty, *Phenomenology of Perception*, trans. Colin Smith. London: Routledge & Kegan Paul, 1962, p. 139.
3. Gérard Leblanc, 'La Poétique Epsteinienne', in Jacques Aumont (ed.), *Jean Epstein, cinéaste, poète, philosophe*. Paris: La Cinémathèque française, 1998, p. 33.
4. Jean Epstein, *Écrits sur le cinéma. Tome 1: 1921–1947*. Paris: Seghers, 1974, p. 11.
5. Ibid., p. 94.
6. Serge Margel, 'Au lieu de profondeur', in Catherine Malabou (ed.), *Plasticité*. Paris: Éditions Léo Scheer, 2000, p. 255.
7. In an interview with Claire Vassé, included in the press kit when the movie premiered in 2009, Philippe Grandrieux describes the house as an 'enclosed space, which we built entirely in the studio, a nocturnal network. It is a mental universe.'
8. Daniel Deshays, *Entendre le cinéma*. Paris: Klincksieck, 2010, p. 143.
9. Ibid., p. 27.
10. Marc Mercier, 'Pour en finir avec l'art orthochromatique', in Nicole Brenez (ed.), *La Vie nouvelle/Nouvelle Vision: à propos d'un film de Philippe Grandrieux*. Paris: Éditions Léo Scheer, 2005, p. 54.
11. Safia Benhaïm, 'L'Antre de Saturne', in Brenez (ed.), *La Vie nouvelle/Nouvelle Vision*, p. 111.
12. Baldine Saint Girons, *Les Marges de la nuit: pour une autre histoire de la peinture*. Paris: Les Éditions de l'Amateur, 2006, p. 159.

CHAPTER 7

Naomi Kawase's The Mourning Forest: *The March of Bodies, the Spiritual Journey*

In the Japanese countryside, not far from Nara, Machiko, a nurse with a sad and worried look on her face, begins a new job in a retirement home. There, she meets Shigeki, an older, somewhat eccentric man who cannot seem to get over the death of his wife, Mako, thirty-three years before. *The Mourning Forest* (2007) begins with a long shot of dense foliage, with the sound of bells in the background. In the next shot, a procession, at first hidden by tall grass, slowly makes its way through the fields. A group of men take down a tree, then carefully prepare and assemble chopsticks and wooden rings that will serve as offerings. The films cross-cuts back to the procession, which reaches its destination at the edge of a tea field. Then, the camera enters a dark and humid forest. A few minutes later, Machiko, back at work at the retirement home, lights an incense stick using the flame of a candle. Nearby, the photograph of a smiling young child can be seen. In ascetic silence, she prays before the altar for the child she has lost. Right from the start, *The Mourning Forest* presents the issue of loss. In respectful silence, it raises the question of getting over the death of the Other, of going on without them. As Jacques Derrida said:

> The death of the other, not only but all the more so when it concerns a loved one, does not suggest an absence, a disappearance, the end of *such and such* a life, that is to say, the possibility for a world (always unique) to appear to be alive for others. Death, every single time, is a declaration of the *total annihilation of the world*, the end of all possibilities, and *the end of the world as unique totality, every single time, therefore irreplaceable, therefore infinite*.[1]

The first part of *The Mourning Forest* shows bodies that are uncomfortable, but does not insist on the pain inflicted by sorrow. Naomi Kawase favours long shots of rice fields, with the forest, on the horizon, as a natural barrier. The retirement home is set in a remote area, surrounded by the generosity and harmony of nature. Landscapes are like deep green paintings, where the homogeneity of colour gives structure to space, as Machiko and Shigeki play hide and seek within the geometrical lines of the fields. They go for a drive, but Machiko loses control and runs the car off the road. They are stranded on a lonely road, surrounded by fields and woods. Machiko goes off to look for help; meanwhile, Shigeki walks out of the car with determination and enters the forest. The majestic height of the trees, the dense shade that almost feels like a prison, the lush vegetation all bring to mind the primeval forest. Augustin Berque says that

> in Japan, just like in Europe, there exists a myth of the primeval forest, site of great ancestral anxieties, but also reminder of our wistful yearning for an ever more remote nature. But contrary to Europe, [...] this primeval forest has been added to the mythological constellation of attributes that belong to Japan-ness. Indeed, in the mind of contemporary Japanese, it plays the role of original matrix.[2]

This view of nature as original matrix was already present in Naomi Kawase's first documentary films, where natural elements, such as flowers, trees or the sky, were used as a connection to the world, as a way to soothe one's anxieties and to dissolve the pain left by the father's absence.

A Healing Restraint

In *The Mourning Forest*, the way the characters walk, the way they stand, varies according to their physiology and psychology. Shigeki is impulsive and passionate, and so walks with a purpose; Machiko's gait is cautious, almost timid, as if travelling through a forest meant losing oneself in infinity, losing oneself in an emptiness full of plant life. As Nanine Charbonnel points out: 'The most feared of all spatial experiences is not knowing where one is, where one is going. To walk through a forest, through a desert, during the night: since Antiquity, these express the pain of isolation, the fear of stumbling.'[3]

There are two 'walkers' in Naomi Kawase's film but their purposes are at odds: Machiko wants to get out of the forest because she thinks of it as a dangerous dead-end, while Shigeki wants to run right into it and stay there. Machiko is Shigeki's care giver, but still, she follows him rather than guides him. As they walk together, in what appears more akin to disorientation and intuitive changes of direction than to a purposeful journey, she takes his hand and asks: 'Where are you going?' He answers serenely, as if stating an obvious fact: 'To see Mako!' Suddenly, Shigeki kneels in front of a high, dry trunk and declares that this rather anonymous spot is Mako's tomb. The camera, which had been leaning down towards the ground, looks up to the leafy roof and harvests its enigmatic shivers. The two bodies walk hesitatingly through the dense vegetation, as the camera looks on at once idly and analytically. The forest stands as a fortress of energy, a store of vitality that enfolds the two characters.

However, the fact that they are walking around under the canopy does not mean that they actually commune with the elements. Shigeki's eccentricities result from his oversensitivity, while Machiko, who sees the forest as a place where bodies exhaust themselves and disappear, acts on fear. When they come upon a stream that has swelled because of the rain, Shigeki simply crosses it in a few, quick steps; Machiko panics, screams, puts out her hand and begs him to come back. This moment of distress resonates with an earlier scene, where Machiko asks for the forgiveness of her partner, because the fact that she let go of her son's hand caused his accidental death. This is a moment of extreme pain for her, but the rain that falls on her seems to produce a sort of catharsis, as if her body was being cleansed of this deep anguish and revitalised.

Thus, an internal burden is lifted from Machiko. After this sequence, she and Shigeki warm themselves by the fire. Night has fallen. This is the second part of the story, during which the forest turns gradually into an initiatory place, a place where each may look for their own lost selves. The forest becomes more than a focal point: it is a land full of energy, where deeply buried emotional wounds, which the elements of nature manage to reveal, can be healed.[4]

The next morning, Shigeki wakes up and, in the low light, sees the back of his dead wife, Mako. He gets up and walks up to her; they dance together. Now the filmmaker demonstrates the forest's power to exorcise. The spirits of the dead awaken, and the grief that accompanies them is unearthed and thrown away, so that it may not continue eternally, buried under the skin of the living. The slow, immersive walk through the forest help the body to let go, because it is of the utmost importance they live in the present, to accept the sensations and the reinvigorating strength of this particular environment. When she enters the forest to find Shigeki, the nurse still believes in an illusion of rational control over the world. Her mobile phone, her last remaining link to the outside, her only way to resolve this inextricable situation, does not work. As it walks about the forest, as it overcomes obstacles, as it encounters the natural world, the female body tests its own mind, reflects cathartically on itself.

Indeed, all the senses are called upon during Shigeki and Machiko's walk: bodies bend down, stumble, touch each other.[5] Their disjointedness, their clumsiness reveal the stuttering character of their relationship to the forest. From then on, the point is not to keep sensations on the outside any more, but to internalise them, thus allowing the man and the woman to bind themselves to the vegetal world.

AN INITIATORY WALK

If the beginning of *The Mourning Forest* takes the audience into the faraway landscape, the second part of the film urges its characters to get away from what had been an essentially contemplative relationship to the forest and make it more active. The woods are dense, compact, almost like a wall: one must burst through to enter, which implies a physically different approach. Bodies lean on the natural elements, wrap themselves around them, in a sort of choreography; the forest is not just a landscape on to which tormented feelings of grief are projected. An initiation takes place there, and bodies temporarily set down roots and are transformed.[6]

In *The Mourning Forest*, Shigeki and Machiko walk around; they have no purpose, no destination. Walking is, in effect, an unsteady, stumbling motion, but as it gradually turns into a fragile progression, it shakes up the repressed regions of the mind. The camera's slow, tactile movements seem to brush up lightly against the world, and all living things' vital vibrations become perceptible. There is no hierarchy, whereby humans would submit to nature; instead, what gradually unfolds is the birth of a 'mesologic relationship'.[7]

As bodies and matter come closer, as the movement that binds everything in ecumenical kinship accelerates, the forest becomes a fortress both real and imagined, inside which the act of walking becomes a sacred, active form of immobility. According to Augustin Berque, places are different from 'choreutic processes', since they 'favour the concrete over the abstract, being rooted over moving about, the intrinsic over the relative, presence over representation, singularity over generality, experience over meaning'.[8] In *The Mourning Forest*, Naomi Kawase apprehends, with a walker's unsteady gait, the metamorphosis of bodies as well as their increasing sensory rooting. The forest is not just a natural ecosystem, it is a spiritual preserve where the spirit of the dead can be summoned. In this perspective, the dead tree scene is particularly noteworthy. Machiko and Shigeki have spent the night in the forest; they start walking again and, after stepping over a few fallen trunks, they stop and kneel before a huge, greyish dead tree, whose colour sets it apart from the surrounding greenery. The camera moves forward, gets closer to the bodies, seen from the back, meditating. Seemingly drawn by this enormous stem, Shigeki gets up and steps forward, just as a low-angle shot shows the awesome might of the tree. The camera moves down and we see Shigeki hugging the ageless bark. With its sacred dryness, its branches extended like celestial hands, it seems like a holy totem, in front of which one wishes to meditate and draw forth the invisible energies of the earth and the cosmos, rather than a sort of hallucinatory form.[9] Naomi Kawase makes an eternal sculpture of the dead tree, attributes a true ancestral power to it.

The forest is not just a static, unchanging witness any more. It is a power that supposes a return: the self goes out into the world to act. The forest is not just a projection of nature, or a poetic communion with the elements; it is a vital distancing from the present that makes it possible to dismiss 'the tragic character of death'[10] and grief. Because it is a moving union, which alternates between stasis and impulsion, the forest is more than an ecological reserve, than a natural ecosystem. In fact, it becomes a spiritual reserve, a place where the dead can be summoned, where a different relationship to mortality can be achieved and, therefore, where the living can find the strength to go on.

Figure 7.1 The Mourning Forest *(2007)*

Figure 7.2 The Mourning Forest *(2007)*

Figure 7.3 The Mourning Forest *(2007)*

Figure 7.4 The Mourning Forest *(2007)*

Notes

1. Jacques Derrida, 'Introduction', in *Chaque fois unique, la fin du monde*. Paris: Galilée, 2003, p. 9.
2. Augustin Berque, *Le Sauvage et l'artifice*. Paris: Gallimard, 1986, p. 113.
3. Nanine Charbonnel, 'Homo Viator ou Les Dix Métaphores de la marche', *Les Cahiers de médiologie*, 2 (Paris: Gallimard, 1996), p. 78.
4. Cf. Corinne Maury, *L'Attrait de la pluie*. Crisnée: Yellow Now, 2014, p. 77.
5. Jean Mottet analysed the importance of the sense of touch in *The Mourning Forest*: 'Du paysage à l'expérience sensible du monde: présence de la forêt dans

le cinéma japonais', in Claire Harpet, Philippe Billet and Jean-Philippe Pierron (eds), *À l'ombre des forêts: usages, images et imaginaires de la forêt*. Paris: L'Harmattan, 2014, p. 233.
6. On this topic, Jean Mottet points out that, in *The Mourning Forest*, 'the landscape is not situated any more, it is just a moment-in-the-world, where I can feel myself become a moment-in-the-world as well' ('Du paysage à l'expérience sensible du monde', p. 234). We should note, here, that in the second part of the film, the forest is not a landscape at all: it is an enclosed *world-place*. Perceptions also change: touch becomes more important than sight. The two walkers feel this 'primeval' forest with their skin just as much as they look at it.
7. The expression comes from Berque, *Le Sauvage et l'artifice*, pp. 286–7.
8. Ibid., p. 161.
9. We disagree with Jean Mottet's analysis, which claims that the dead tree of *The Mourning Forest* is a reminder of Apichatpong Weerasethakul's *Tropical Malady* (2004). We believe it should be seen as a form of dream-like decoration ('Du paysage à l'expérience sensible du monde', p. 235).
10. Vladimir Jankélévitch, *La Mort*. Paris: Flammarion, 1977, p. 393.

CHAPTER 8

Danièle Huillet and Jean-Marie Straub: The 'Sacred Sobriety' of the Undergrowth

The films of Danièle Huillet and Jean-Marie Straub make up a cinematographic constellation; they create radically dialectic, meteoric works that resist any typology. Their films storm and rage, criticise everything and everyone, refuse any compromise: they denounce fascism, capitalism, blind faith in progress, the society of the spectacle. Their cinema is unashamedly political and they use it to claim their unconditional belief in Marxist thought. In *Kommunisten* (2014), Jean-Marie Straub[1] quotes these sentences from Elio Vittorini: 'Communism does not want to build a collective soul. It wants to create a society where false differences are abolished. And once they are abolished, all the potentialities of true differences will become available.'[2]

Kommunisten was made after the death of Danièle Huillet in 2006; it presents, in condensed form, in one film, the entire trajectory of the Straub-Huillets, made up of resistance, protests, dialectic anger, refusals to submit. Jean-Marie Straub uses various fragments of their previous films (*Workers, Peasants* (2001), *Black Sin* (1988), *The Death of Empedocles* (1986), *Too Early/Too Late* (1981), *Fortini/Cani* (1976)) to create a homogeneous monument in which words and telluric forces endow the act of resistance with renewed vitality. In Straub's images, the earth and speech acts are indivisible, and their combined power turns the screen into a dialogic fortress. This is what Gilles Deleuze pointed out:

> [In the films of the Straub-Huillets,] history is inseparable from the earth [*terre*], struggle is underground [*sous terre*], and if we want to grasp an event, we must not show it, we must not pass along the event, but plunge into it, go through all the geological layers that are its internal history (and not simply a more or less distant past).[3]

For Jean-Marie Straub and Danièle Huillet, one of the bloody consequences of capitalism has been the destruction, the negation and the colonisation of nature. Their works never use nature as a backdrop, or pretend to; they never subjugate nature by placing actors in it as if they were pieces on a chessboard. The Straubs,[4] in their later films, strongly advocated for a 'return to nature'. Nevertheless, even if the two filmmakers sought an open-ended confrontation with the rustling richness of eternal forces, one should not conclude from it that they give in to lyrical nostalgia. Indeed, they aim to make the old world blossom in today's reality because it must face the new world, rebel against it and fight to prevent its foretold disappearance.

WALKING THE LAND: BETWEEN GEOGRAPHY AND GEOLOGY

The Straubs' political, ethical and technical positions, defended by dialogues and protests, assert themselves before the movie shoot begins, just in the way they survey the land, hoping to find the place with the right lines of sight, where the points of view will be predetermined, restricted, perhaps even narrowed. Before the filming can even begin, geographical research is required. As Jean-Marie Straub himself said:

> To make a film on this planet, you have to be something of a geographer. Geography means to describe the land – 'geo' means land, and 'graphy' means to write. And you have to be more than that, you have to know something about geology. You can't film a tree or a mountain if you don't know what's underneath.[5]

As opposed to Luc Moullet, who roams territories with the help of maps,[6] the Straubs choose a piece of land and settle there, and then proceed to say, to cry out poetic and literary texts from Hölderlin, Cesare Pavese, Franz Kafka, Elio Vittorini or Charles Péguy. As early as *The Death of Empedocles* (1987), they instigated an unheard-of harmony and solidarity between mythology and ecology.[7] The making of films, in other words, begins with a walk. The point is to tame space, without colonising or domesticating it, and certainly without dominating it. This gradual process is all about 'becoming a place',[8] and the Straubs begin their encounter with telluric elements by listening carefully to the silent and stormy forces of nature, to their subtle shifts, to their vocal unpredictability. Each take includes something unexpected, something that moves according to the temperamental, impetuous forces of nature. It may be light variations or the vibration of the sounds of seasons. The shots' composition lets the natural environment breathe and bloom, lets it move in its own, free, sovereign way. Renato Berta, who was director of photography on many of the Straubs' films, said:

> We let the shot live, nature is exactly as we film it, and so I'm never 100 per cent sure of the final result ... There are all kinds of surprises in Danièle and Jean-Marie's films. A leaf that happens to fall just at the right moment, that's unusual for them! A lizard sort of strolls by ... And when we were editing, that shot would become the lizard shot.[9]

In their films, elements of the landscape grant reality to words, they give life to literary texts. Therefore, filmmaking for them demands that they listen, that they let in, within the rigidity of the screen frame, all of nature's sobriety, its fragility and its generosity, that they welcome its presence. Constructed, decorated movie sets are often heavy and crippling, and so the Straubs prefer the power of living things. The very act of filming is, first and foremost for the two filmmakers, the presentation of an unfiltered dialogue, and absolutely not a forced imitation of reality. The point is to find out what reality has to offer and incorporate it within the lucid rigour of cinematographic pictures.

Their first features focused on archaeological sites[10]: ruins stand in them as noble traces of the past, and from worn-out stones arise the murmurs of History. In a different way, *The Death of Empedocles* separates clearly, through Hölderlin's voice, humans and nature. As is often the case in the Straubs' films, trees are reminders of the solemn columns of antique theatres, yet do not imitate or replace them. Trees are like beams, and bodies can lean against them to 'declaim' the literary text. In *From the Clouds to the Resistance* (1979), Nephele sits on a branch and, with a voice made lovely from worry, she warns Issione of the risks he is taking by resisting the gods. In the first part of the film, taken from Cesare Pavese's *Dialogues with Leuco*, the filmmakers maintain a conversation between the human voices and the murmurs of nature. But the point is not simply to illustrate the text; nor is it to take away nature's powers of harmony, which would reduce it to a backdrop, hidden within the picture. The film leaves room for the unexpected, for moments of pure, elemental vitality, personified by the enchanted presence of the birds and of the breaths of wind. This effervescence of nature is not just an echo or a lyrical reminder: it reinforces and extends the tension that already existed in Pavese's text, in its rhythm that simultaneously lifted it towards the heavenly dome and threw it down into the very bowels of the earth.

THE BUTI RAVINE, A PRIMEVAL PLACE

For these unabashedly political filmmakers, the renaissance of the literary text in cinema implies that a historic as well as geological site is unearthed, and that its ancestral, ancient power is used to proclaim its defiance to the world. The Straubs first came to Buti, in Tuscany, for the stage production of *Sicilia!*, just before they started shooting the film version in 1999. It was on this occasion that they first saw the nearby Apuan Alps.[11] The discovery of the woods and the ravine near Buti changed their relationship to that place: the ancient stones and the heroic ruins are now forever linked to the debut of the two filmmakers, while the surrounding areas, covered with forests and steep slopes, are the perfect setting for bringing literary texts to life.

The relationship to Buti began with *Workers, Peasants*, continued faithfully with *Humiliated* (2003), *Quei Loro Incontri* (2006), *Le Genou d'Artémide* (2008), *Le Streghe* (2009) and *L'Inconsolable* (2011).

During a retrospective of their works in Metz in 2011, Jean-Marie Straub shared as always, after a showing of *Le Genou d'Artémide* and *Le Streghe*, questions, comments and opinions with the audience. One spectator asked: 'How did you choose the forest, the places, where the films were shot?' Jean-Marie Straub answered:

> It was random. I just sort of found myself there, twelve years ago. It was random, because somebody had left us there, in the middle of the night. He said: you can just stay there, in this house. We had to live somewhere. We had gone there to shoot *Sicilia!* Or, in any case, for the theatre rehearsals. They put us up there, in a house that was right up near the road. It took me many years to get up the nerve to go down in that ravine. I admired it from above, but I was timid. It always takes me a long time to get used to things. Then, one day, I went down, and it was love at first sight. This particular ravine extends to more than two kilometres. It goes down, then it turns. We shot a lot of scenes down in that ravine. But first, we had to get used to it. If things exist in the movies, it's because the filmmaker is not a parachutist.[12]

In B movies, in crime dramas, ravines are most often used as a backdrop for death and disappearance: the place where the accident occurs after a vertiginous fall, where shady and troublesome characters meet their end. The Straubs turn the cliché around: for them, the ravine is more than a wooded valley, a suitable place to shoot scenes. It is a limited place, both wild and modest. It is a notch, a gash, a dazzling setting for the literary text.

The Straubs' respect and admiration for John Ford is well known, though they did not idolise him. As the years went by, Jean-Marie Straub began to consider the Buti ravine as their equivalent of Ford's Monument Valley. It is true that the buttes and mesas of the plateau in the Western United States seem more uncontrollable than tameable, whereas the overgrown, narrow ravine resembles a farmable patch of land. Its welcoming simplicity, the serenity of its clearings lead one to poetic as well as political contemplation. Nature there is modest, it stands apart from the rest of the world. The Buti ravine possesses for the Straubs a sort of primitive discretion. Because of the immediacy of time there, it becomes possible to *situate* the voice of the people, to put the harshness and violence of History (for example, in *Workers, Peasants*) into words.

The film begins with the camera panning slowly, patiently, stubbornly, through the undergrowth, showing the living community of moss, grass, earth, leaves, trees, ferns, stones and birdsong. Often, in what we shall from now on call the 'Buti films', the Straubs use static shots and slow pans that give a sense of sanctity to the lonely, at times sunny, at times shady woods. But these takes never present nature as a moving postcard. Instead, they allow the audience to breathe in the smells of the undergrowth, to hear the persistent murmur of this telluric place. The Straubs see nature as a heterogeneity in motion, simultaneously grand and tiny, impossible to describe with a global and unanimous definition. Each Buti film separately, and all of them together, fix indelibly, record this essential and inexhaustible place, the undergrowth, and allow the viewer to return to it at will. Because it is a place we can come back to, where we can settle, it becomes a topographical floor, the space where the Straubs' working methods can unfold, and these methods, in turn, produce new visions, re-visions.

Images in *Workers, Peasants* are polished, as if the Straubs were artisans patiently transforming matter. They show the upheavals caused by light and wind, they show, by way of uncompromising cinematographic repetitions, the *temperament* of a place; the audience's point of view is renewed because it gets rid of its certainties. The two filmmakers described in the following terms their cinematographic use of rigorous, stationary pictures:

> Disquiet is more real, more painful when it's a subversion of matter. We know that the best – and fastest – way to be amazed is to look fixedly at a single object. One day, that object, and it will seem like a miracle, will look to us as if we were seeing it for the first time.[13]

In *Quei loro incontri*, the static shots and pans draw up a map of the terrain, focus on sounds and sights so as to create an ever-rising tension. They stifle any desire for digression, any willingness to daydream. The images give the audience the opportunity to be 'un-blinded' from tedious and predictable views of the world. Thus, the many shots of the undergrowth give the Buti ravine the look of a subterranean place, where the secrets of life are held. Yet, it cannot be assimilated to the dense, vegetable monumentality of the forest, nor indeed its labyrinthine expanse. The undergrowth is smaller, more modest, its harmony is frailer; it is an opening, a narrow one, through which humans can come without intruding.

The harmonious simplicity of the Buti ravine allows the Straubs to initiate a dialogue between the community of men (*Workers, Peasants*) and the community of the gods (*Quei loro incontri*). The woods impose a great silence on the images, protect the power of the literary texts of Elio Vittorini and Cesare Pavese, and revitalise their incantatory purity. It is not by chance, therefore, that the Straubs chose to set Pavese's last five *Dialogues with Leuco* there, in that out-of-the way, out-of-the world, woody ravine. It is a fraction, a minority, standing apart from the majority, from the whole, and that is precisely what makes it an exceptional place to hear Pavese's poetic and mythical text. For him,

> The main particularity, if not of poetry, at least of mythical fables, is their consecration of *unique places*, linked to a fact, to a gesture, to an event. Meaning is attributed to a place that was specifically chosen, set aside from the rest of the world. Thus are sanctuaries born.[14]

The Buti ravine is a natural bastion, one of Pavese's *unique places*, where through the agency of time, literature is honoured and saved from disappearance.

Workers, Peasants was adapted from Elio Vittorini's novel, *Women of Messina*,[15] about men and women who get back together at the end of the Second World War, in the ruins of a village situated between Bologna and Modena. Despite their age difference, despite their differences in social class and political affiliations, these refugees, who come from all over Italy, try to deal with the harshness of their daily lives, with cold temperatures and poverty. Little by little, the community becomes organised and life gets back on track. But conflicts, irreconcilable difference of opinions emerge, and the utopianism, the solidarity of the project falter. After opening with a 360-degree pan that patiently explores the slopes of the ravine in waning light, an authoritative long shot looks fixedly at three bodies on the wet ground. At the centre of the image, widow Biliotti is sitting next to the basin of a washhouse. To her right stands Pompeo Manera, sturdy, immobile, and to her left is Cattarin, who is leaning with her right hand on the side of the basin. The widow is holding a notebook as she firmly describes the cruelty of their daily lives:

> In the first days of November a bit of snow fell,
> then it melted, then came the rest,
> and it stayed until early March, and the spinach and the cabbage,
> we had to dig through the snow to harvest them.

Even in their early work, the Straubs disliked and rejected flashy action scenes because 'spectacular' movies, from their point of view, are akin to an artificial ruckus, an ostentatious agitation of bodies. For this militant couple,[16] cinema is about affirming a position of revolt, and not about unbridled action. They mean to film words, which means, for them, that bodies must be *grounded* before they can even begin expressing themselves. A vertical, polarised posture is necessary because the actor's body needs to represent an indignant immobility.

The image of the tribunal, of a court open to the vagaries of time, has often been used to describe the Olympian diction of Straubian voices.

However, architecturally, courts of law are designed to be hierarchical, to structure speech, to have it restrained by rules rather than overwhelm unexpectedly. Instead, the Straubs establish a form of equality shared by all speech acts; they favour rhythmic bodies and voices over faces saturated with *pathos*, the tension of texts over the gimmicks of representation. In *Workers, Peasants*, widow Biliotti makes words 'rise'; she 'uplifts' the literary text without interpreting it, without overacting. Speaking is a duty, which means that words must be declaimed; the Straubs made this a permanent feature, by following a *principle of allegation*, in the legal sense of the word: 'A text, a passage must be cited as if it was evidence of what we're saying.' Legal speech, therefore, becomes poeticised by the Straubs because its expression is no longer stuck within the confines of the tribunal, but lives instead in the sacred chants of the Buti ravine's nature.

Often during the film, the peasants and the workers must face their reality; they have to deal with each other's values and differences in daily life, which inevitably leads to either amicable disagreements or fiery conflicts. Elio Vittorini's text is never read to favour either the peasants or the workers, the female or the male bodies. Words are spoken clearly, at a sharp and unequivocal rate, and that only makes the relationship between workers and peasants, the irreconcilable differences between their struggles and their daily lives, darker, harsher and more heart-wrenching. The voice speaks at a cadence that is never plaintive; it never denounces, it is never complicit. For the Straubs, speech gives depth and life to acts.

The voices of the workers and peasants are deep, their words are rough, their fates are cruel, but through it all, the ravine's undergrowth gives evidence of the serenity and unity of all living things. The soothing, continuous music of the mountain stream, the birdsong, the rustle of leaves in the trees, the architectural anarchy of the branches do not seek to appease the quarrelsome power of the text, but to make it even more concrete, denser. On screen, the natural site becomes a pure, material presence, a pure substance that hands can grab on to, where bodies can stand and carry on with their allegations. For the Straubs, a body that stands still possesses a vigour that is grounded, rooted in the earth. This irritated some critics, and they likened the Straubs' films to a motionless theatre; inactive bodies, to them, could mean only static passivity. It is important to contradict these hasty judgements because these films are not simply a series of aesthetic poses. Many of them depict unmoving bodies, but this should be not understood to mean that they lack vitality: it is an aesthetics that is transmitted by exulting, corporeal, graceful, imposing voices.

In *Quei loro incontri*, the dialogues between Dionysus and Demeter reveal a fundamental imbalance between mortals and gods. In the Buti ravine, the

Straubs show Dionysus, hands extended, leaning against the small trunk of a tree, while Demeter sits nearby on a boulder, one hand touching the stone, the other on her knee. Their voices are a constant reminder of the fateful difference between them: men die, gods do not. Demeter says:

> Everything they touch becomes time, action, expectation and hope. For them, dying is also something. [...] And what about the stories they tell about us? Sometimes, I wonder if I really am Gaia, Rhea, Cybele, the Mother Goddess, as they say. They know how to give us names that are a revelation to us, Iacchus, and they tear us away from the oppressive eternity of fate, bring us back to the time and the countries where we are.

Grazia Orsi speaks Demeter's words with no emotional intonation, her body like a statue, solid, cohesive and humble, in a form of solidarity with telluric elements. By using Cesare Pavese's mythological texts, in which the gods in turn show understanding and scorn towards mortals, by returning to Elio Vittorini's utopian eloquence that tends to scatter the community rather than unite it, the Straubs bring together ancient and modern times. Men's lives are cruel because they have to suffer constant indignities and do not know harmony.

Likewise, in *Workers, Peasants*, the Straubs do not shift Elio Vittorini's text to a set that looks like, or even imitates, the ruins of the village of Messina. Quite the contrary: they fuse words and bodies together in a material, real place – the calm and varied setting of the Buti undergrowth – in order to reveal and sharpen the cruelty of life, which separates mortals and gods, and differentiates each and every man as well. Invariably, they choose to come back to this place, the Buti ravine, this *locus* to which its delicate beauty grants sanctity.

As for *The Death of Empedocles* (1986) and *Black Sin* (1988), they both trace a link to the poetic works of Friedrich Hölderlin, while celebrating nature – not in any grand or rhetorical way, but by showing, from film to film, a continued attachment to a specific place. According to Jacques Rancière, there was a change in the way the Straubs worked after *Workers, Peasants*. In a conversation with audience after a showing of that film, he said that 'it changes from one type of theatre to another. From Brecht, let's say, to Hölderlin. Or, if you prefer, from dialectics to lyricism.'[17] Marxist ideology says that nature is something that must be tamed, transformed, moulded, in order to emancipate the workers and the peasants of the community. But in *Workers, Peasants*, the nature is down in the ravine, and it is rough, wild; its noises often cancel out the sound of voices. 'One could say', adds Jacques Rancière, 'that the Straubs' politics and their film direction take a stand for the inhumanity of nature. Nature is a power, a continuous grumbling that limits humans.'[18]

We believe this point of view could be more nuanced, however, because nature in this film is more than a restrictive inhumanity. The Buti ravine, in its wildness (there are no agricultural, industrial or mining activities there), may seem inhuman, but one should not infer from this that the Straubs took a stand for a nature that limits humans. The undergrowth is an atemporal, mellifluous presence, an organic harmony, and as such, it can give life to a literary text, ennoble its poetic materiality, elevate its political might. Nature is an active setting rather than a dialectical landscape.

In the woods of the Buti ravine, the two filmmakers compose visual hymns that salute the great unity of nature as an *awakening*. Françoise Dastur wrote about the link between sanctity and nature in Hölderlin's poems:

> nature is said to be *heilig*, holy. But a more exact translation of the word would really be *whole*, or *unscathed*, because *heilig* comes from the verb *heilen*, which means to care for, to restore a being to wholeness. If nature is said to be *heilig*, it should not be taken to mean that it is divine and as such opposed to all that is human, but rather that one should see in nature the whole of beings, and not just part of them. Modern thought tends to do just that, when it contrasts nature with spirit, culture and freedom.[19]

In the 'Buti films', the lichen, the trees, the leaves are quivering evidence of the 'sobriety of the sacred',[20] so essential to Hölderlin's view of nature. As the Straubs set up a confrontation between the words of Cesare Pavese and Elio Vittorini, and this *integral whole* that is the woods of the Buti ravine, they own up, in a way, to this claim in *Grund zum Empedokles*: 'In pure life, nature and art are only opposed harmonically. Art is a flowering, the perfection of nature. Nature only becomes divine when it fuses with art, a different, but harmonious species.'[21]

Le Genou d'Artémide stages the second conversation of the *Dialogues with Leuco*, titled 'The Wild Beast'. It is yet another link between the Straubs and Pavese's mythological text. Seen from the back, Endymion is sitting next to the basin of a washhouse. He is talking to a stranger who is just passing through, and is telling the story of Artemis's apparition:

> Have you ever met someone who was many things at once, who carried them all inside them, and their every gesture, their every thought seem to you to contain infinite things from your earth and your sky, and words, memories, days past that you will never know anything about, and future days, certainties, and another earth, another sky that you will never be able to possess?

Filming from behind, seeing characters from behind is a recurring theme in the Straubs' filmography[22]; it is often interpreted as political insolence because it prevents us from seeing properly. It goes defiantly against the power of the *pathos* that is produced by the actors' exaggerated faces. The audience can only listen closely to the entire text and look at the humble scenery. Endymion's back is like a screen, on which are projected the shadows of the woods, as if the opaque body took on itself the ethereal power of nature, covered itself in its telluric radiance.

In *Le Genou d'Artémide*, Jean-Marie Straub interweaves Hölderlin's poetic songs and Pavese's mythological text; neither dominates, neither stifles the other. In fact, both texts seem to call to each other, to answer one another, each strengthening the other. Straub uses the living force of this particular locale, the Buti ravine, and gives these woods the power of primordial speech. The mundane, yet pure and indomitable soundtrack affirms a great political attachment to nature – it must not be colonised, it must not be destroyed – as well as an unbreakable poetic connection to the earth, where the 'incarnation of the text'[23] can take root and from which it radiates. The conclusion of *Le Genou d'Artémide* is quite politically minded, as it attempts to deal with the living ghosts of the past. A series of pan shots anxiously picture the silent burden of History: several tombstones commemorate the resistance of Italian Partigiani who died in these woods towards the end of the Second World War. The weary yet unsubdued bodies lay beneath the maquis sullied by barbaric struggles. Jean-Marie Straub films with 'necrophiliac piety'[24] this land that has known both terror and grace, this place that is both historic and marginal, this ravine that is also a monument. Mighty indignation finds an anchor in this telluric environment.

Figure 8.1 Workers, Peasants *(2001)*

Figure 8.2   Workers, Peasants *(2001)*

Figure 8.3   Le Genou d'Artémide *(2008)*

Figure 8.4 Le Genou d'Artémide *(2008)*

Notes

1. Danièle Huillet passed away in 2006. She does appear, nevertheless, in the very last shot of *Kommunisten*.
2. Interview with Elio Vittorini by Dionys Mascolo and Edgar Morin, published in *Lettres françaises*, 160 (June 1947), reproduced in the movie press kit handed out at the premiere.
3. Deleuze, *Cinema 2. The Time-Image*, p. 254.
4. It has become common usage to use this name for the 'inseparable couple'.
5. 'Rencontres avec Jean-Marie Straub et Danièle Huillet, École supérieure des beaux-arts du Mans, mars 1994', in Jean-Louis Raymond (ed.), *Rencontres avec Jean-Marie Straub et Danièle Huillet*. Paris and Le Mans: Les Éditions Beaux-arts de Paris/École supérieure des beaux-arts du Mans, 2008, p. 19.
6. See 'La carte et le territoire', in *Luc Moullet, notre alpin quotidien: entretien avec Emmanuel Burdeau et Jean Narboni*. Nantes: Capricci, 2009, pp. 15–54.
7. See Dominique Païni, 'Le Front d'Empédocle', in *Jean-Marie Straub, Danièle Huillet/Hölderlin, Cézanne*. Lédignan: Antigone, 1990, p. 19.
8. Ibid., p. 22.
9. Interview with Renato Berta, 'Jean-Marie, vous avez déclaré que vous étiez plus intéressé par le son que par l'image, mais ce n'est pas vrai! Dites-moi la vérité: vous êtes plus intéressé par l'image que par le son!' 'The lizard shot', in *L'Internationale straubienne: à propos des films de Danièle Huillet et Jean-Marie Straub*. Paris: Éditions de l'œil/Centre Pompidou, 2016, p. 39.
10. José Moure has pointed this out: 'Sophocles' tragedy, *Antigones*, was staged in the Segesta theatre, in Sicily. Schoenberg's opera, *Moses and Aaron*, was produced in the Alba Fucens amphitheatre, in Abruzzo. Corneille's tragedy, *Othon*, was literally staged on the Palatine Hill' (*Vers une esthétique du vide au cinéma*, p. 187).

11. The rehearsals took place in the Teatro Francesco di Bartolo, in Buti, in 1997. The performances took place in April 1998; the representation of 6 April 1998, was filmed. It was released with the title *Sicilia! The Theatre Version*. The film version came out in 1999. The script was based on a text by Elio Vittorini: a man, who has been in exile in the United States for many years, revisits the places where he grew up in Sicily. Travelling from Messina to Syracuse, he meets all kinds of people. He then goes to his mother's house. The film was shot in Buti and in Sicily. See Jean-Charles Fitoussi, 'Le Temps d'un retour, notes de tournage de *Sicilia!*', *La Lettre du cinéma*, 8 (Winter 1999).
12. Jean-Marie Straub, 'Après *Le Genou d'Artémide* et *Le Streghe*', *Le Portique*, 33 (2014), document 7, online 5 February 2016. Available at: <http://leportique.revues.org/2764> (last accessed 11 January 2017).
13. *Quei loro incontri* press kit (2006), distributed by Pierre Grise Distribution, 2008. Available at: <http://www.gncr.fr/flms-soutenus/ces-rencontres-avec-eux> (last accessed 2 February 2017).
14. Cesare Pavese, *August Holiday*. French edition: *Vacance d'août, La Vigne* [1945], trans. from Italian by Pierre Laroche and Gilles de Van, in *Œuvres*. Paris: Gallimard, 2008, p. 471.
15. The Straubs used Chapters 44, 45, 46 and 47 of Vittorini's novel, published in 1949. The title refers to these women who rebuilt their village after an earthquake.
16. Marie-Anne Guérin, 'Oh! Cette coulante liquidité de l'air', in *L'Internationale straubienne*, p. 381.
17. Philippe Lafosse, *L'Étrange Cas de Madame Huillet et Monsieur Straub: comédie policière avec Danièle Huillet, Jean-Marie Straub et le public*. Toulouse and Ivry-sur-Seine: Ombres/À propos, 2007, p. 142 (transcription of a conversation with Philippe Lafosse, Jacques Rancière and the audience, after a showing of *Workers, Peasants*, Jean-Vigo Theatre, Nice, 16 Februry 2004).
18. Ibid., p. 146.
19. Françoise Dastur, *Hölderlin, le retournement natal*. Paris: Encre Marine, 1997, p. 108.
20. Ibid., p. 138.
21. Friedrich Hölderlin, *Grund zum Empedokles*, quoted by Dastur, *Hölderlin, le retournement natal*, p. 113.
22. Cf. Davide Vasse, 'Le Dos et le sol: de quelques dos dans le cinéma de Danièle Huillet et Jean-Marie Straub', in Benjamin Thomas, *Tourner le dos au cinéma: sur l'envers du personnage au cinéma*. Saint-Denis: PUV, 2012, pp. 111–22.
23. Raymond (ed.), *Rencontres avec Jean-Marie Straub et Danièle Huillet*, p. 86.
24. As Serge Daney points out: 'in *Fortini/Cani*, the camera travels up and down the Italian countryside where, during the Second World War, entire civilian populations were massacred. [...] One could reach the conclusion that this is a sort of necrophiliac piety' (*La Rampe*. Paris: Petite Bibliothèque des Cahiers du cinéma, 1996, p. 14).

CHAPTER 9

Lisandro Alonso's La Libertad *and* Los Muertos: *The Dual Forest*

Lisandro Alonso's *La Libertad* (2001) takes place in central Argentina's pampa,[1] an immense, wide open territory, a 'wooded steppe'.[2] However, the director does not take his audience along for a never-ending stroll; instead, with several long takes, he establishes the exact boundaries of his work. A young woodcutter, Misael, after building a temporary shelter in the pampa, surveys a wooded area, identifies the trees that can be cut down and marks where they will be axed based on their size. With graceful dexterity, he uses his axe to remove the bark. He then makes a bundle of this modest treasure, which he intends to sell later, and places it at the edge of the forest lot. Lisandro Alonso shows all this hard work while remaining at a respectful distance. The camera follows every wonderfully skilful gesture. This is reality, powerful yet untouched by any sermon about deforestation, unsullied by allegorical interpretations, unspoiled by any meditation on the generosity of nature. Trees are felled and pruned; the filmmaker is only a mindful observer, and it is the young man's activity that gives the pictures their energy. These woods are only a work site, the means to produce a modest income. The long duration of the shots underscores the woodcutter's progress, but also shows the austerity of his life: all he does is cut, transport and sell wood. Lisandro Alonso shows that basic survival activities (hunting armadillos for food, starting a fire) are really acts of autonomous resistance. The forest, in *La Libertad*, is not just a lush environment or a wild ecosystem; it is a set of habits, a place of endlessly repeated, exhausting work.

THE WOODED PAMPA, A MODEST PRODUCTION SITE

With his axe, Misael carefully removes all the branches that are in the way and starts digging around the base. The camera is placed directly in front of him and looks steadily at his precise motions, emphasising the calm, ordinary courage of this young man. The picture then moves closer to the trunk and the audience can see the axe rhythmically biting into the wood, until the whole tree falls to the ground. The woodcutter then starts cutting into the tree with a chainsaw, slowly, methodically transforming this living being into wood pieces. Because he refuses to edit any of this work out, Alonso demonstrates that this wooded area really is a *production site*, a place of everyday hard work, a place of labour.

Anne Cauquelin defines a site as a 'third space, the result of the dialectics of space and place'.[3] She adds:

> Space is the position, the situation, the setting that can be readily identified on a map. [...] A site is built, and people settle there. [...] Place, however, is a site that has received the characteristics of memorisation, of enfolding, of environment, whether from the physical environment, or from the context, from behaviours – transmitted through customs – or from the archives.[4]

According to Yves Belmont, a site

> possesses a status that makes it an anthropological item, and this item in turn refers to an entire *economy*, i.e., an organisation of both life and territory. In other words, this economy is symbolic, political, just as much as it is prosaic.[5]

Cinema has often featured industrial sites, places that witnessed the world's economic transformations, where the burden of past economic glory and the promise of better days intersect. In *West of the Tracks* (2004), Wang Bing portrays the slow decay of Tie Xi, a gigantic industrial complex, after the rapid political and economic changes that occurred in China. Sergei Loznitsa's *Fabrika* (2004) patiently shows the disappearance of an entire industrial world in post-Soviet Russia and presents in long, formal, exacting static shots the archaic motions of workers in a smelter and in a brick factory – movements both profoundly human and mechanical, stuck in brutal and unending temporality.

In *La Libertad*, the 'natural' production site used by Misael seems more small-scale and traditional. Geographically isolated, the site demands that the woodcutter organise his day around his work, and live in a temporary and rudimentary camp. Conditions are hard, temporarily yet also durably[6]; therefore, the wooded lot in the pampa needs to be appropriated in order to convert the site and make it into a place, maybe even Misael's own place. In the words of Gilles Tiberghien, to 'settle' somewhere means the 'capacity to make room as a first condition to build, that is to give a place an existence entirely related to oneself. The place can then make space possible, within its own limits.'[7] Misael's camp is only a temporary, provisional shelter; just like a shed, it is a 'vulnerable body'[8] whose very vulnerability creates a constant synergy with the outside. For the woodcutter, this temporary refuge is a place of transit, not a place of dwelling. *La Libertad* presents the moods both as a place of work, where the activity of woodcutting is carried out, and as a place of residence and self-sufficiency. The film is edited so as to slow down events, to celebrate the daily circumstances of Misael's life; Lisandro Alonso criss-crosses the forest to show its value as a resource and to propose his own singular vision of the perimeter.

After a short pursuit and an efficient strike, Misael, the logger turned hunter, catches an armadillo with his bare hands, looking for his evening meal. During this scene, Alonso leaves the wooded lot and goes into a much denser forest. Static long takes show Misael walking with great energy, surrounded by the varied sounds of nature. The loud songs of the birds seem like a music concert, lively and variegated.

FROM EXPLOITATION SITE TO PREDATORY LANDSCAPE

In *La Libertad*, the forest is a resource; in *Los Muertos*, however, it is a predatory and ungenerous place. This Alonso film from 2004 tells the story, in a silent, troubled and opaque way, of a man who is freed from prison and goes to see his daughter in the remote regions of Corrientes and Misiones. Lisandro Alonso shows the journey of his main character, Argentino Vargas, a strange and silent man, as he crosses the wetlands along the Paraná River. In *Los Muertos*, the forest looks like an impenetrable jungle, and it hangs over the narrative as a mysterious, lush, colourful presence. The film begins with a lively, yet deliberately blurry low-angle shot: the camera moves along the ground and, suddenly, finds the bodies of two children, lying down, covered in blood, while we see the legs of a man pacing around them, a machete in his hand (we will learn, later, that Vargas was sent to prison for the murder of his two brothers). In this very first shot of *Los Muertos*, the forest is soiled by the man's barbaric act, yet it helps to hide the horror. Its representation is, in fact, shaped by contradictory forces: on the one hand, the forest is an exuberant living entity; on the other, it is a constant reminder of the two murders that took place within it.

The opening long take stigmatises the forest because it is a corrupted place, haunted by the sacrilegious death of the two children. Indeed, every subsequent shot that involves the forest in some way is linked to the torpidity of a horrendous past. Alonso makes no attempt, in *Los Muertos*, to solve the mystery of the double murders, or even to judge Vargas's act. He merely follows, in stubborn and heavy silence, this strange, instinctive man who was deprived of his freedom for many years and now comes home to his family.

He makes the long journey on a small boat on the Paraná River: the forest is always present, at the edge of the frame, as an oppressive outline that skirts the river. Michel Collot writes,

> As it opens up the view, perspective also closes it by hiding parts of the landscape, in particular that part that goes on over the horizon. This is where the invisible infiltrates the visible, requiring the imagination to fill in the gaps left by the lack of perception.[9]

In *Los Muertos*, the forest is like a *moving margin*; it is something to punch through, never a place to explore. Only twice does Vargas enter the forest: once to fumigate a wild beehive located in a tree stump because he wants to gather the honey, and the second time when he finally arrives at his daughter's camp. This last scene, the conclusion of the film, features a dynamic boy who seems perfectly in sync with the natural environment; he climbs a tree, grabs a fruit and eats it. As it turns out, this boy is the ex-prisoner's grandson, and their meeting puts an end to the heavy pressure Vargas was under during his trip on the river.

In *Los Muertos*, the forest is a barrier. Vargas runs along next to it but never enters it. It is a wall but it does not keep in the wilderness; it keeps out the savagery of the outside world. One is reminded here of Martin Heidegger's definition: 'the limit is not the place where something ends, but rather, as the Greeks had already observed, a place where something begins to exist (*sein Wesen beginnt*)'.[10] In other words, the Lisandro Alonso films represent forests in radically different ways. It is a hinterland, in *Los Muertos*, an alcove in the landscape, the site of a double homicide; in *La Libertad*, the forest is exploited for its natural resources, a place of work and life. *Los Muertos* presents the forest in a fragmented perspective, as a place that can be *visited*, but not a site that can be *occupied*. However, it would be simplistic to see the forest of *Los Muertos* only as a horizon; every take, every image hides a reminiscence of the two murders.

In *La Libertad*, Lisandro Alonso's camera is often quite mobile, its motions relentless and daring. Again and again, it is projected forward, at a brisk pace; it dives in between the trees and touches all living things. The nimble movements of the camera lightly brush against the trunks, the grass and the sky and bring them all together in similar, multisensory perceptions. Because he focuses on the senses of hearing and touch, the director establishes a contact, a closeness with all parts of the forest. This refusal to rely on sight as the dominant sense brings to mind the utopian wishes of Paul Arnould: 'it would be possible to dream of a forest that would not be measured by sight, by glances and by landscapes'.[11] The choreographed motions of the camera, the rich soundtrack aim to capture the variety of the environment: the high grass of the pampa, the sharp cries of the animals, the dry yet sturdy trees. We see a spirited ecosystem that goes in and out of balance and oscillates between hyperbolic life and allegorical death.

The forest, in *La Libertad*, thus possesses two distinct dimensions: as a site for economic exploration and as an ecology. When the camera shows labour, it is generally stable, static and directly in front of its subject; the aim is to demonstrate the technical aspects of cutting and pruning trees. But sometimes, the camera moves, as if to gather and fuse together in great cinematographic motions the vast disparity of all living entities throughout the vegetal world. It seems that Alonso is not looking to get back to elementals,[12] but to initiate a geophysical journey through a territory that is both economic site and biological reserve. Indeed, *La Libertad* does not idealise nature, as if it was a Garden of Eden to be preserved, nor does it seek to trivialise its presence; instead, Lisandro Alonso characterises the forest as a field of enquiry, both technical and sensory. Within this circumscribed area, humans live their lives and establish ephemeral relationships with the forest.

Figure 9.1   La Libertad *(2001)*

Figure 9.2   La Libertad *(2001)*

Figure 9.3 La Libertad *(2001)*

Figure 9.4 La Libertad *(2001)*

Notes

1. *La Libertad* (2001) was Alonso's film school graduation piece.
2. Jean Demangeot, *Les Milieux naturels du globe*. Paris: Armand Colin, 1996, p. 263.
3. Cauquelin, *Le Site et le paysage*, p. 85.
4. Ibid.
5. Yves Belmont, 'Sites et lieux', in Younès and Mangematin (eds), *Lieux contemporains*, p. 72.
6. While talking on the phone to a friend, Misael reminds him that he will be staying on site for a month and a half and asks him to go and see his mother.
7. Gilles A. Tiberghien, 'Demeurer, habiter, transiter: une poétique de la cabane', in Augustin Berque, Alessia de Biase and Philippe Bonnin (eds), *L'Habiter dans sa poétique première: actes du colloque de Cerisy-la-Salle*. Paris: Éditions donner lieu, p. 93.

8. Ibid., p. 98.
9. Collot, *La Pensée-paysage*, p. 111.
10. Martin Heidegger, *Essais et Conférences*, trans. André Préau. Paris: Gallimard, 1980, p. 183.
11. Paul Arnould, 'La forêt: le sens et les sens', in Andrée Corvol, Paul Arnould and Micheline Hotyat (eds), *La Forêt: perceptions et représentations*. Paris: L'Harmattan, 1997, p. 392.
12. Jean Mottet, 'Prologue', in Jean Mottet (ed.), *L'Herbe dans tous ses états*. Seyssel: Champ Vallon, 2011, p. 7.

Part 4

The Banlieue: *Off-centred, Isolated*

As early as the 1970s, many works of fiction surveyed the French *banlieues* and filmed them as if they were a world unto their own: territories standing away from the big cities, where the same scenarios of social exclusion and pain are endlessly repeated. The neighbourhoods, the council housing form the basis of these narratives, and space is structured around them in a purely contextual way. The camera stays close to the characters, hangs around the group, focuses on their individual destinies. These '*banlieusards*' are, most often, teenagers trying to tame their rebellious energy, to realise their desire to achieve success or to get out and away from there. In almost every film, they end up confronting law enforcement. And the architectural space, meanwhile, the buildings, the staircases, the high-rises, appear mainly as stigmatised containers.

In movies such as *Tea in the Harem* (Mehdi Charef, 1985), *La Haine* (Mathieu Kassovitz, 1995), *Inner City* (Jean-François Richet, 1995), *Douce France* (Malik Chibane, 1995), *Ma 6-T va crack-er* (Jean-François Richet, 1997) or *Bye-Bye* (Karim Dridi, 1995), the *banlieue* is represented as a dreadful landscape, or as a territory that is to be occupied, or as an unusual setting for a love story and all related conflicts. In short, in most films *about* the *banlieue*, the fictional narrative uses sociology and geography to depict in an exceedingly emotional manner the fate of the '*banlieusard*', a lost cause who may be redeemable or even rehabilitated. As Thierry Paquot said: 'to shoot a film in the banlieue does not mean filming the banlieue'.[1]

Eric Rohmer's *Boyfriends and Girlfriends* (1987)[2] is one notable exception: the Parisian *banlieue* is new, architecturally interesting, and it is home to young men and women whose only worry in life is experiencing it fully and experimenting with blossoming desires. In this modern and luminous setting, Rohmer's young bodies exchange various 'kinds of courtesies'[3] and discuss in affected whispers the delightful contradictions of their feelings. In an interview in the newspaper *Libération*, Rohmer said:

> Almost everything in *Boyfriends and Girlfriends* takes place in the new town of Cergy: it is the laboratory for the experiment, the utopian space that allows the narrative and the characters to develop unhindered. Back then, the Saint-Christophe neighbourhood, the train station, the prefecture looked as if they had come out of nowhere. My intention was to present this new life in a pleasant light, as opposed to other films (Godard, Mocky) that focused on the oppressive, totalitarian aspect of this urban future. [...] Cergy was a protected space, it was isolated, pacific, and love and friendship could unfold freely there, like in one of those plays where innocent young people meet in some sort of primeval nature so that the playwright can describe the birth and evolution of their feelings.[4]

In contrast, Dominique Cabrera's *Chroniques d'une banlieue ordinaire* (1992) asks previous residents of the Val Fourré district in Mantes-la-Jolie to come back to their housing estate, to see their old 'towers' once again. Having been declared insalubrious, they were to be demolished by controlled implosion on 26 September 1992.[5] The camera follows with mindful modesty the ex-residents as they go through the flats where they used to live. Some of them had left more than twenty years before. The audience sees shot after shot of deteriorated walls, empty rooms, abandoned spaces, run-down stairwells, looted electrical equipment. The ex-residents, some of them quite emotional, tell the stories of their lives in these now deserted places, and of shared times that were often happy. There is power in these words that bring back remembrances of past homes, power that can overcome and supplant the images of empty and anonymous spaces. Yet, Dominique Cabrera does not propose a eulogy of the 'towers'. She organises the diverse and sometimes contradictory accounts to create a polyphonic architecture – she weaves together the positive and the negative words and thus transmits something of the complexity of this utopian project of the 1960s that aimed to provide affordable housing for all. Place, in this case, becomes an architectural palimpsest, on which are written, said, repeated and rewritten publicly the intimate confidences of the residents. Cabrera filmed the *words* of those who lived in a *place*, and thus brought together home and territory; in other words, she filmed the *words of a place*.

How can a film represent the *banlieue* without letting the story, the narration and the characters overwhelm the audience's attention? How can a film represent these eccentric, isolated territories without giving in to the negative stereotypes, without resorting to the images of a condemned world, just beyond the borders of the great city, irremediably collapsing? Pedro Costa, Tariq Teguia and Pier Paolo Pasolini use the *banlieue* as a place of contact, of complicated connections where one comes and one goes, a place where humble relationships are perennially established (*Colossal Youth*,

Pedro Costa), where new and wild freedoms are invented (*Mamma Roma*, Pier Paolo Pasolini), where the urge to leave is strongest (*Rome Rather than You*, Tariq Teguia). In their films, buildings seem damaged rather than preserved, degraded rather than repaired. How, then, do they try to rehabilitate them?

Notes

1. Thierry Paquot, 'Les banlieues au cinéma: filmothèque', in Thierry Paquot (ed.), *Banlieues/Une anthologie*. Lausanne: PPUR, 2008, p. 149.
2. In 1975, Rohmer directed four documentaries for television about the creation of new housing estates: *Enfance d'une ville*, *La Diversité du paysage urbain*, *La Forme d'une ville* and *Le Logement à la demande*.
3. Dominique Païni, *Le Cinéma, un art moderne*. Paris: Cahiers du cinéma, 1997, p. 70.
4. Éric Rohmer, interview with Antoine de Baecque, 'Architecture-fiction. La vie en villes. Cergy-Pontoise', *Libération* (29 March 2002).
5. Called 'Tours des Écrivains' (Writers' Towers), these four high-rises had been built in 1965.

CHAPTER 10

Pasolini's Wastelands

On 2 November 1975, Pier Paolo Pasolini's mutilated body was found near a beach in Ostia, on a piece of wasteland. His death in this isolated place, on the outskirts of the city where Jean-André shot his film, *Pasolini l'enragé*, in 1966,[1] resonates with his life as a civil poet,[2] a lively agitator and exceptional filmmaker. Throughout his meteor-like life, he passionately defended those who did not have a voice, those who were on the fringe. In his first novels (*The Ragazzi* and *A Violent Life*) and in his Roman film trilogy (*Accattone, Mamma Roma, La Ricotta*), Pasolini gave the outskirts of Rome and their various *borgate*[3] (areas where the residents built their houses themselves because they could find no other place to live) great importance. In these suburban zones live the poorest of the poor, the underclass that were banished from the noble centre of the city. As Pasolini explained in an interview:

> I arrived in Rome from Friuli. I came from the countryside, from a community of peasants, where everything was clean, exact, moral, honest, and I found myself in the gigantic cauldron of the Roman suburbs. I experienced extraordinary emotional trauma, it was a shock to the nerves, truly. I discovered the Roman underclass, their pains, their filth, their cynicism, their unknown Catholicism, their stoic paganism, etc. Really, it was emotional trauma, a traumatic discovery that overwhelmed me.[4]

In his book, Hervé Joubert-Laurencin wrote: 'the other quality that immediately makes Pasolini a great director, in his first trilogy, is his choice of always shooting in real and astonishing settings, in half-deserted places, on the outskirts of cities'.[5] And he adds right away, referring in part to the masterful integration of the site of Mount Testaccio in *Accattone*: 'truly, he possesses a genius of places'.[6]

FROM UTOPIA TO ANACHRONISM

The *banlieue*, for Pier Paolo Pasolini, is a nervous universe, where words, gestures and shouts signify the extreme poverty of a community washed up on the outskirts of the city. The *banlieue* is an edge, yet it is separate from the centre, from the historic heart out of which radiate the power and domination of the bourgeoisie, where the most fortunate bask in their privileges. Pasolini's first films immerge themselves in the raw reality of these suburban spaces, with all their wastelands, such as the neighbourhood of Pigneto in *Accattone*, or the housing complex of INA Casa, Cecafumo, in *Mamma Roma* (1962). By its very nature, the wasteland is an undecided space, it is 'in a temporary, undetermined, unfinished state'.[7] In these films, Pasolini aims to establish a link between the life of places and the life of bodies, in essence creating a sort of perpetual motion that makes space into something both poetic and political, while simultaneously moving it away from any kind of representative exposition.

Pasolini shoots the arrival of Mamma Roma (Anna Magnani) and her son in the Roman suburbs with a tracking shot. They are moving back to her old flat, in the ancient neighbourhood of Casal Bertone. The camera shows grey, run-down buildings, while we hear the voice of the mother saying cheerfully to Ettore, her son:

> 'That's our house, there ... Do you see it? That window, up there, the sunny one. You can see trousers hung out to dry. Last floor. It'll only be for a few days. After that, you'll get to see the house ... A beautiful house! You'll only meet nice people, in a nice neighbourhood.'

As they climb up the stairs of this building where they intend to stay 'only for a few days', the camera pans serenely around and looks at all the little rascals, as Mamma Roma likes to call them, crammed together on the steps. We see alternatively the curious, astonished face of Ettore and the mischievous faces of the urchins. As she opens the door, the mother says spitefully: 'You won't find such scoundrels at the other house!' Pasolini uses the accusatory words to mock Mamma Roma, her desire to enter the middle class, her wish for an orderly and honourable life for her son. Later, she buys a flat in a new housing project in Cecafumo. In front of the building, Ettore will meet the neighbourhood boys, who will become his future companions in the nearby wasteland.

Systematically, the filmmaker shows Mamma Roma at close range, so as to heighten the emotional impact of her face, the vigour in her voice, the generous brutality of her gestures. When she first arrives on the outskirts of Rome, Mamma Roma, just freed from the supervision of her pimp, is generally filmed in interiors, in her flat or in the church where she goes to pray. As the prostitute becomes a mother again, she goes from the outside to the inside. This life represents a radical change, since trying to conform to norms while living in the margins implies a ritualisation of interior gestures and the creation of institutionalised, quotidian, domestic and moral relationships.

When, later in the film, Mamma Roma returns to prostitution, the director shows her at night, walking on dark pavements, in essence both veiling and unveiling her. On the other hand, Ettore, the son who was lost and then found again, appears on screen only as distant, blurry figure. Pasolini frequently resorts to panoramic shots, either to reveal the entire extent of the wasteland or to follow along with the teenager as he loiters in that nameless place. The camera does not actually come any closer to him until the very end, when a close-up shows a sick, feverish boy: lying down, dying, he resembles Mantegna's *Lamentation of Christ*, as if he was history's sacrificed body.

When his mother comes to pick him up and take him to the outskirts of Rome, Ettore has just spent the previous sixteen years in a boarding school. Once there, he seems to while away most of his time in an abandoned piece of wasteland, that serves as a sort of open base and secondary home. There, the local boys make existential discoveries and experience sexuality for the first time with Bruna, 'the She-Wolf'.

According to an architecture specialist, 'a lot that can be considered to be vacant is suspended between past and present, between the disappearance of an object and the beginning of a new project. The lot is vacant ever since an object disappeared, and what is vacant is the memory of that disappearance; a vacant lot presupposes that an object has been forgotten.'[8] By its very nature, the wasteland is an undecided space, it is 'in a temporary, undetermined, unfinished state'[9]. In *Mamma Roma*, Pier Paolo Pasolini constantly gives new relevance to the presence of the wasteland in his narrative, through his use of pans and long takes that allow the audience to revisit that space and make a precise topographical image of it. Wild grass, mounds of earth, architectural ruins, traces of a vanished past: a wasteland is an undefined, abandoned, disorderly space. In it are juxtaposed ruins and wastelands, traces of times past and clues of what will come. For this reason, it would not be sufficient to claim that Pasolini associates wastelands exclusively with notions of disappearance and abandonment. Many, many different things confront one another along the distended lines of time. In *Mamma Roma*, columns of black stone and partially collapsed arches are scattered across the wasteland: it is not an arid space, with no history. The vestiges of the past are everywhere and quite obvious. As Richard Bégin points out:

> Ruins do imply a revival of the past; however, they also, and mainly, represent the appearance of absence, the *presence of absence*. They are the direct consequence of some forgotten event, without which they would not exist, and they remain. Ruins are an event unto themselves, in the present, and they arouse in the mind of the traveller something like a spiritual awakening. Traces, remains, ruins or debris, they endure *here and now*, in the form of

fragments, of fallen remains resulting from the fragmentation of the origins, of the absolute.[10]

In *Mamma Roma*, the wasteland consists of vegetation and ancient ruins; it brings together the forces of nature and fragments of culture.[11] Antiquity is made manifest through the presence of scattered traces, and the audience is faced with what Georges Didi-Huberman called 'the return of repressed history'.[12] Next to crumbling stelae, vegetation grows: the past next to the present, wilderness next to the sacred. *Mamma Roma*'s wasteland is a contemporary place, but also a place where the temporality of the here and now meets an archaic, anachronistic temporality.[13] The wasteland is a contemporary reflection, in a way that reminds one of Giorgio Agamben:

> The ones who can call themselves contemporary are only those who do not allow themselves to be blinded by the lights of the century, and so manage to get a glimpse of the shadows in those lights, of their intimate obscurity. [...] The contemporary is the one whose eyes are struck by the beam of darkness that comes from his own time.[14]

A LANDMARK OF REBELLIOUS ALTERITIES

In most movies, wastelands are essentially an empty and confused space, without identity or unity. Marcel Carné's *Wasteland* (1960) is a good example. It tells the story of a group of young boys and girls that survive by pickpocketing and fight amongst themselves in the Parisian *banlieue*. The wasteland, in this narrative, is a backdrop whose main functions are to stimulate the conflicts and to emphasise the marginality of these young people. The camera closes in on their rebellious energy, and the wasteland appears only in the background, as some odd sort of postcard. The characters are shown on screen standing in front of the waste ground, and often standing *against* it. Marcel Carné focuses on the faces, on the dialogues; the wasteland is behind them, empty and lifeless. Pasolini, by contrast, does not allow this space to fade into the background. He makes it into a landmark, a place of sociability, of sharing. The wasteland is the collective possession of Ettore and the other kids; they fight each other there, but they also play football.

In *Mamma Roma*, therefore, the wasteland does not amount to a non-place. According to Marc Augé, 'the space of non-places creates neither singular identity, nor relations. Only solitude, and similitude.'[15] It is an informal meeting place, a space where reality is experienced, where habits take root; it is an out-of-the-way place, yet it is there that relationships can be established, that a sort of insolent brotherhood can be formed. It is an enclosure that stands at the centre of all attachments, where ways of speaking, ways of acting are shaped; it is an *extended hole* where the free bodies of feral youths hang out, where they can reject all social norms and avoid career expectations. In one particular scene, Mamma Roma rebukes her son precisely for not working and spending entire days loitering in the streets.

A frequently repeated scene shows Ettore walking back and forth in the wasteland: in effect, this creates a continuing link between body and space. Land is not a just geographical surface that one can cross, or a political symbol; it is an area where the body feels and exists. Because Ettore and his friends keep coming back to the wasteland, it becomes a central point, a hub, a place where daily dreariness can turn into an uncertain future. Bruce Bégout writes: 'Always, daily life wavers between controlling the present and discovering something new, between safety and adventure, between the exotic and the endotic. [...] What is ambivalent about the mundane is that it can never be reduced to a single attitude; it constantly oscillates between the familiar order and the willingness to leap into the unknown.'[16]

In *Accattone*, there are only two scenes that involve a piece of waste ground. The first time, Accattone and Stella take a brief rest there; the second time, Maddalena is raped by the friends of her ex-pimp, who was denounced to the authorities.[17] The second occurrence takes place at night, thus obscuring and partially hiding the violent act. The wasteland is defiled; it is not at all the ontological place that gives structure to the life of the boys of *Mamma Roma*. In *Accattone*, suburban spaces are anarchic, set up along vanishing points, and the characters walk across them quite tentatively. Often, white lights link together small pockets of space, offset contrasts, abolish differences; a single, general perception brings together these degraded and miserable spaces. Architectural space, in this unified perspective, could be qualified as *set design as witness*. The Roman suburbs represent a well-organised, unbroken reality. Jean Collet said as much:

> This is why, maybe, sets are really just ideas of sets; they are light rather than matter. For Rossellini, stones are not grey or black, they are smooth or rough. They're stones. In this particular case, the earth and the sky exhibit the same, blinding whiteness. *Accattone* is a white world rather than a shantytown under the Roman sun.[18]

In *Mamma Roma*, by contrast, Ettore belongs to the wasteland. Pasolini wraps him up in it: he keeps showing the boy in it, using wide shots, as if to emphasise the fact that he is physically rooted in that marginal place. But even though the narrative is centred on the teenager's wanderings around the wasteland, that does not mean that Ettore simply meanders about with no destination in mind; nor does it mean that he is some incarnation of Benjamin's *flâneur*, who slowly makes observations about life. And he certainly is not some pensive, lonely Baudelairian stroller. Pasolini creates the character of a familiar wanderer, a regular loiterer: a person who intends to domesticate the outside world. Thus, the wasteland can be considered as a house without a roof, a habitual haven. The filmmaker, in other words, establishes a cinematographically balanced situation, wherein humans and places stand in perceptual equality – and the wasteland is the fulcrum: its function is to be a *daily landmark*, rather than an occasional crossing point.

After the sudden onset of Ettore's illness, filmed as if it was a painting about the death of Christ, Pasolini concludes the narrative with two wide shots of this new city: the architecture that, for Mamma Roma, represented

Figure 10.1   Mamma Roma *(1962)*

Figure 10.2   Mamma Roma *(1962)*

and personified a social and moral transformation, has now turned into the thick walls of a prison that blocks out all possible futures. Mamma Roma's terrified eyes watch these soulless masses, and she sees a horizon that is closing instead of opening. There is no freedom. In *Mamma Roma*, extreme poverty pervades the wasteland – a place without recognition, without legitimacy, but familiar, permeable and permanently open. In uncertain times, it is also a place suffused with the experiences of incandescent youth.

Figure 10.3 Mamma Roma *(1962)*

Figure 10.4 Mamma Roma *(1962)*

Notes

1. The film was part of a series, 'Cinéastes de notre temps'.
2. I am referring here to a lecture given by Alberto Moravia at Yale University in 1980, titled 'Pasolini, Civil Poet'.
3. '... the *borgate basse* are the most ancient clusters, mostly self-built, while the *borgate alte* came about when the Fascist regime decided to move certain populations away from the city. As for the *borgate* of the developers, they are the most recent. For a long time, the residents felt like they were living in a world apart, with different sociological characteristics from the great housing projects' (Colette Vallat, 'Centre et habitat précaire, périphérie et habitat illégal. Quelle place pour les grands ensemble en Italie?', in Frédéric Dufaux and Annie Fourcault (eds), *Le Monde des grands ensembles*. Paris: Créaphis, 2004, p. 228).
4. Pier Paolo Pasolini, *L'Inédit de New York*, interview with Giuseppe Cardillo, presented by Luigi Fontanella, trans. Anne Bourguignon. Paris: Arléa, 2008, p. 60.
5. Hervé Joubert-Laurencin, *Pasolini, portrait du poète en cinéaste*. Paris: Cahiers du cinéma, 1995, p. 56.
6. Ibid.
7. Paola Berenstein-Jacques, Alain Guez and Antonella Tufano, 'Trialogue: lieu/mi-lieu/non-lieu', in Younès and Mangematin (eds), *Lieux contemporains*, p. 131.
8. Ibid., p. 127.
9. Ibid., p. 131.
10. Richard Bégin, 'L'Époque de la survivance: de la mémoire des ruines dans *À l'ouest des rails* de Wang Bing', *Cinémas: revue d'études cinématographiques/Cinémas: Journal of Film Studies*, 15: 2–3 (2005), p. 88.
11. Anne-Violaine Houcke said that 'so-called *modern* cinema carries along, in its formal exploration, pieces of Antiquity, in a way that takes it forcefully away from traditional, spectacular restitutions, while refusing to make a *tabula rasa* of the past' ('Le Retour de l'antique dans le cinéma italien moderne: de Warburg à Fellini et Pasolini', *Mise au point*, 3 (2011), online 30 August 2012. Available at: <http.//map.revues.org/992> (last accessed 22 December 2015)).
12. Georges Didi-Huberman, *Survivance des lucioles*. Paris: Les Éditions de Minuit, 2009, p. 92.
13. The presence of Antiquity in Pasolini's films could also be analysed in *Oedipus Rex* (1967), *Medea* (1969) and *Notes Towards an African Orestes* (1970).
14. Giorgio Agamben, 'What is the Contemporary?', in *What is an Apparatus and Other Essays*, trans. David Kishik and Stefan Pedatella. Stanford: Stanford University Press, 2009, p. 45.
15. Augé, *Non-places*, p. 103.
16. Bégout, *La Découverte du quotidien*, pp. 42–3.
17. Accattone (which means 'beggar' in Italian) is a small-time pimp in the Roman suburbs. He barely makes a living, but manages to get by thanks to the 'help' of Maddelena, who gives him some of her earnings, and Nannina, the wife of

Cicio, the pimp who was denounced and who is in prison. When Maddelena is no longer able to help him out, Accattone turns instead to Stella.
18. Jean Collet, 'Le Blanc et le noir', in *Pier Paolo Pasolini, Accattone*, vol. II, *Dossier*. Paris: Éditions Macula, 2015, p. 124. This article was originally published in *Les Cahiers du cinéma*, 132 (June 1962), pp. 44–7.

CHAPTER 11

Pedro Costa's Colossal Youth: *From the Slums to the Sanitised Apartment*

The Cape Verdean slums of Fontainhas, north-west of Lisbon, are the setting of Pedro Costa's trilogy, *Ossos* (1997), *In Vanda's Room* (2000) and *Colossal Youth* (2006). Most of the residents of the neighbourhood are outcasts, dropouts and labourers, who were forced to build a dwelling in this uninhabitable place. They moved into these vacant, abandoned areas and transformed a place of exile into an inclusive home. These 'places for the displaced'[1] are indeed interstices, narrow openings, in whose gaps are told the stories of brutalised humans and upended temporalities.

In 1999, when Pedro Costa was about to shoot *In Vanda's Room*, the destruction of Fontainhas had already begun. He set his film up around two mutually exclusive, yet contiguous spaces: the *inside*, which mostly means Vanda's room, where she and her sister use heroin, and the *outside*, about to be demolished, where dark, narrow streets are lined with tiny shacks that disappear, day by day, torn down by excavators.

THE DILAPIDATED FRAGILITY OF FONTAINHAS

By the time shooting began for *Colossal Youth* in 2006, Fontainhas had been completely demolished and rebuilt. Pedro Costa had decided to return and revisit the ghostly traces of the old neighbourhood, scattered across the new constructions, when he met a Cape Verdean immigrant, Ventura.[2]

> I had seen Ventura many times while shooting the other films. He was a true outcast, a solitary outlaw, an outsider. He always fascinated me. I talked to him and learned he had been one of the first to build a house in the neighbourhood. He had arrived in Lisbon by himself, with no family. Slowly, from to 1975 to 1980, Ventura's life and the history of the neighbourhood became completely intertwined. He told me about his problems, about his romantic life. From that came the idea that Ventura was a sort of archetypal figure of this past.[3]

Colossal Youth is constructed around a 'fictional framework' based on Ventura's life, but it was constantly modified while the film was being shot, partly because of the working method that was used, based on repetition and improvisation. Costa summed it up in these terms:

> The idea was to do a scene, then forget it, and then do it again three months, six months later. It wasn't the same any more, the actors remembered it, but something else had developed. It's as if the scene needed to be forgotten to be done again.[4]

At the beginning of the film, Clotilde has decided to leave her husband, Ventura, a Cape Verdean labourer who lives in one of the shacks common in Fontainhas. When he complains about this situation to his daughter, Bete, she says that her mother has been dead for a long time. He leaves her miserable little room next to a construction site and meets up with his adoptive daughter, Vanda, who lives in the basement of a new building. She explains that she is enrolled in an addiction treatment programme. Later, we see Ventura repeatedly reading out loud, with his friend and roommate, Lento, a letter written to convince the woman he loves to come back to him from Cape Verde, where she lives. He wanders endlessly between the old neighbourhood and the new, where he must go and see a new apartment for himself and his family.

Right from the start of the film, Pedro Costa places the audience in a narrow alleyway that could have been in the recently demolished Fontainhas, but is in fact in another, adjacent, neighbourhood. Ventura is standing in it, lost in his thoughts, head down. Another man, wearing overalls and smoking a cigarette, is next to him, leaning against a brick wall. The image is constructed is such a way that the walls almost seem like massive, gigantic columns. Costa, however, does not just show an architectural space; he tries to capture the 'emotion-matter'[5] of the bumps, holes, notches and grooves, which together form 'matter that is in itself expressive'.[6] These masses of concrete, shapeless, worn-out, run-down, dirty, give this space a kind of hieratic verticality. Pedro Costa harnesses the geometrical forces of the place. In a sense, this 'topological aesthetics' is somewhat similar to Yasujirō Ozu's. Because he systematically uses a camera with a 50mm focal lens, which he places exactly 1 metre above the ground, 'the height of someone who is sitting down', Ozu favours static shots that are structured by pure and harmonious horizontal and vertical lines, such as that created by the partitions inside a traditional Japanese house.[7] Ozu's camera is not 'anthropocentric'[8]: it composes images that are geometrically perfect, and the characters move around within them. Similarly, Pedro Costa chooses stylistically bare images because he wants to take advantage of the architectural elements present in Fontainhas: through rigorously constructed and edited shots, he unveils the dilapidated and maze-like frailty of the area. Alleyways, walls, tiny houses are all shown from the front, directly, with long, static shots that aptly describe the gaudy soul and dislocated spirit of the neighbourhood.

In this particular, grey-tinted shot, the bodies of Ventura and his companion are not in the background, but they are not in the foreground either; they are proportionate, in a relationship of equality with the structures of the construction materials – while those materials are the traces of time's corrosion, the architectural memory of the area. The resistant flesh of the bodies, the worn-out cement are at a tonal equilibrium; they form a perceptive block, with no hierarchy. Both the lengthy static shots, which mark the passage of time, and the relation between bodies and construction materials convey a sense of space, not as a simple volumetric construct, but as a shapeless architectural form that possesses bonding properties. Nevertheless, formalistic cinema and the plastic capabilities of images do not create *beauty* because, being too well made, too cultivated, it would have obscured and hidden the raw materials of reality and silenced the voices trying desperately to express their hardships. There were those who accused Costa of using others' misery to his own aesthetic ends. Jacques Rancière, the philosopher, answered their criticisms:

> Pedro Costa filmed places exactly as they were: the houses of the poor are usually gaudier than those of the rich, and their raw colours seem more suited to please lovers of modern art, in contrast to the standardised adornments of the petit bourgeois. By Rilke's time, gutted houses already seemed to show poets both fantastic sceneries and a stratigraphy of ways of living.[9]

Bodies Attached to Places

In *In Vanda's Room* as well as in *Colossal Youth*, the disorderly appearance of the slums is actually organised in a way that draws the viewer in. The slum/place displays no harmony, but it is capable of affecting the audience with 'its intrinsic flaws', as Alain Mons put it.[10] The stories of these underdogs, of these victims of exploitation, are caught up in the rigidity of the static shots. Thus, the bodies never weaken, and those who expect them to fall, those who look forward to the spectacle of their debasement and decay, see instead Pedro Costa's aesthetics of dignity and magnification. The filmmaker sets out the bodies of his characters as if they were statues of flesh, and their specific gestures, their calm, strong voices, their uneventful tensions declare solemnly, publicly their right to exist. Costa does not use postures or any kind of 'theatrical dandyism', but rather jumbles together blocks of heterogeneous presence. Generally, the figurative organisation of shots is such that bodies, gestures, tables and walls are linked together by their very differences, attached by their direct, rustic humility. Costa brings things and bodies together in the orderly abyss of the shot frame, and destitution becomes an unvarnished strength.

Quite often, the filmmaker favours static shots to show Lento and Ventura, in their shack, playing cards, waiting, listening to music or once more reading out loud the love letter … In one of them, in a sombre light that does not hide bodies but contains them, Lento is seated, at the right edge of the frame. At the centre stands an old, worn-out, simple table. Lento is drawing something right on the surface of the furniture, and the scraping sound of the pen gives the impression that he is in fact trying to sand it. Ventura enters the shot and stands still, then he sets down on the table a record player and a bottle he had been holding. He sits in front of Lento, with his back to the audience. The empty, grey space fills with lively music. Lento is still doodling on the table, and because of that, every once in a while, the record player moves and the melody skips a beat. Ventura's hand dashes across the screen and grabs Lento's, to calm down his nervousness. It is most likely that this scene was improvised, yet every gesture, every look suggests great tension without ever resorting to psychological triggers. Lento's quick and neurotic doodles on the table are as eloquent and insistent as words, silent though they may be, and Ventura's lithe, forceful, almost brutal grab reveals an authority that is more paternal than brotherly in nature. 'What is characteristic of a gesture', writes Giorgio Agamben, 'is that the point is not to produce or to do anything, but to support and to take responsibility. In other words, gestures belong to the realm of *ethos*, and that realm is most specifically human.'[11] Ventura's body is not just plonked down in space, in a sitting or standing position; silently, or with words, it holds a gestural or postural position, which goes along with and even intensifies the appearance of the place's architecture. Exactly as Danièle Huillet and Jean-Marie Straub did in their own films, Pedro Costa uses the power of immobility; bodies do not move or gesticulate, and yet they vibrate and thus send tremors through space. They fill it, give it nobility, but do not erase it. The use of low-angle, static shots and of short focal length accentuate both the strong energy emanating from Ventura's body and the dull appearance of the walls and ceiling. The stability, the insistence of the camera, the geometric arrangements of the frame, where bodies and walls seem to weigh on each other, transform the room into a signifier of the brutal poverty of the room. Throughout the film, Pedro Costa constantly emphasises both the character of the place and the importance of movement in this familiar space. He depicts the temperament of interiors, through the binding yet discordant mood of gestures and the active role played by objects and walls.

In an attempt to define the importance of earth and land in the films of Danièle Huillet and Jean-Marie Straub, Daniel Dobbels wrote: 'The land "carries the abyss", part epigraph, part film; it is stapled to every shot, to these Straubian shots that are, in the words of Serge Daney, "like a tomb".[12] The verb *staple* is quite appropriate in this case because it implies both stability and vigour. The land is hooked on to the image, but it is not an unmoving backdrop or even decorative scenery; indeed, it grants strength to the political and ethical values promoted by the Straubs. In *Colossal Youth*, Costa brings together, in each shot, bodies and shanty/homes, and establishes a historical relationship between men and architecture. The rigidity, the possessiveness of the images 'staple' together, to use Daniel Dobbels's word, Fontainhas and the men who live there. As Pedro Costa said:

> In *Vanda*, I found the right focal length, a length nearer to my own sensibilities. It's very, very wide, it requires a lot of space. Lines are a little bit wobbly, especially vertical lines, so this requires quite a lot of attention. People were going mad during the *Colossal Youth* shoot, even the actors, because I kept getting somewhat lost. And even when I wasn't lost, it would take a very long time to get the position of the camera just right. Width, depth, height, there is only a single point where all three dimensions are together, only one possible point, so that vertical lines are straight, and that's very hard to find. One millimetre off, and the lines get curvy or start leaning to the left.[13]

This might be precisely where the mystery of Pedro Costa's cinema lies, in the way bodies are tied to space, in the fact that their grace is anchored to the places where they dwell, in the way that these fragile bodies avoid becoming icons of decay.

From Fabricated Place to Planned Space

The area around the shack represents a collective territory. The neighbourhood is, metaphorically, a great communal house or a small land of exile. Its community is brought together by its language (creole), its history (immigrants from Cape Verde), its ways of living. As Benoît Goetz put it: 'The body creates an architecture. We use our bodies to modify the space around us. Dwelling should be thought of as a generalised choreography.'[14] Ventura's body (apparently, he fell down some scaffolding while doing masonry work[15]) both *talks*, chanting words as if they were shards of political and poetic thought, and *builds*, since he built, among other things, his own house in Fontainhas. As Pedro Costa said:

> The whole area of Fontainhas, every little wall that you can see in the film, was built at night, on the weekends, in secret, by people like Ventura, masons who had day jobs and came here at night or on Sundays to build their own little houses. Or Vanda's father. These houses, they're part of their bodies.

> And now they've been amputated. The new white houses were designed in a laboratory. They still lived in Fontainhas when people they'd never seen before, who perhaps came from Cape Verde as well, came and built this monstrous, cold desert.[16]

Because the mixed and inclusive shell of Fontainhas was reduced to rubble by bulldozers, Ventura and Bete need to relocate to a new neighbourhood called 'Casal Boba'. There, high blocks of flats show off their geometrical architecture, their harrowing whiteness. From grey to white, from place to space, from emptiness to fullness, from noise to silence, Costa films a difficult, rough, nearly impossible transition. Without saying it expressly, he examines the murkiness, the worries involved in any change: how does one go from a noisy, hectic community to a sanitised space where loneliness looms? Costa's take on this issue is similar to Ivan Illich's:

> the art of living somewhere is an activity that goes well beyond the architect. Not only because it is a popular form of art, not only because it moves in waves that no architect can control. [...] Architects can only build. The vernacular residents create axioms of space, within which they dwell.[17]

When he films Ventura's broken-down shack and then the new flat, the filmmaker demonstrates the balance of power, the aesthetic gap. He does not simply oppose and contrast the two. He does not establish a sort of fake competition between the two dwellings because, in that case, the difference would have been too simplistic and the architectural peculiarities of both spaces would have been neutralised. As Ventura sits, waiting to see the new flat, his image is surrounded, trapped between two white facades: the overbearing presence of these walls completely cuts the inside off from the outside, as if interiors were something intimate that needs to be hidden, veiled. Space seems to be reduced to only two dimensions, as if to insist on the fact that social housing is a system that duplicates itself, creates sameness and negates the human value of difference. These are flat, colourless shots, with no perspective: Ventura is about to enter a place that is not a place, but an empty space, a space that tells no stories, that has no history. Pedro Costa's radical choice to use low-angle shots with a wide lens and short focal length, in effect, turns the screen upside-down. As Jean-Louis Comolli wrote: 'the low-angle shots, the short focal length emphasise the stiffness of the perspectives, the coldness of the right angles, they present a human desert'.[18]

While Ventura sits and waits to visit a flat in the new 'city', a man in a suit steps in front of the camera and calls him out. They greet each other; Ventura presents himself as a retired assistant mason, the other says he is André Semedo, that he used to be a locksmith and has now become an administrator. Each then states which city and which specific Cape Verdean island they are from. A close-up of the shiny doorknob being turned by a hand indicates that they are about to enter the apartment – a probable reference, or homage, even, to Robert Bresson's use of thresholds. Ventura says: 'I ache all over. My head hurts. I can't open the door.' Once inside, the two men walk slowly in circles through the empty spaces. All of a sudden, André Semedo states, his voice strong and firm: 'It's so nice to be protected by the household gods!' With deliberate slowness, Ventura replies: 'This apartment is too small.' This is not a conversation, but two simultaneous monologues; Pedro Costa shows that it is impossible to relate to a space that is white and empty, just as it is impossible to relate to the person that represents it. Ventura asks for more bedrooms because of all his 'adopted' children, and the agent replies sternly: 'Bring me documents!' The second time, the agent points out that Ventura is alone once again, and says insistently that, usually, people come with their wife and children. This sounds like a critique; it is as if Ventura's loneliness, at that moment, in that sterile and empty flat, becomes official. The agent praises the size of this new, second-floor apartment, and lists all the different pieces of furniture that could fit in the living room, ending with: 'Such a change, that's the future!' He then carries on with an enumeration of all the shops and services available in the neighbourhood. Ventura upsets this neat commercial demonstration by pointing out a spider crawling on the living room ceiling. He then separates himself by going into another room, where he waits, behind the closed door, for the agent to finish his speech: 'You also have rights and responsibilities, of course, and if you miss a payment …'

This is in no way a lazy denunciation of social housing. Pedro Costa's film, in fact, aims to go much further, and questions the difference between a fabricated place, built by the very people who live there, and a planned space, created by politics of urbanisation. Costa shows the violence of separation, the wide gap between two ways of living, two vastly different worlds. Writes Jean-Marc Besse,

> The politics of the household (as opposed to the politics of housing) depend on the possibility, for the people, to become more than just residents, to dwell in their homes. To use an analogy, one could say that the issue is to go from the language of housing to the speech of the household.[19]

Pedro Costa's film criticises political power's insistence on a transition that is purely functional and not existential. *Colossal Youth* points out that no one listens or pays any attention to these destitute people, that they exist, from an institutional point of view, only in official administrative documents. Even so, the point is not to present the slums as luminous territories, nor is it to sublimate its generous and creative poverty; there are no winners, no losers. The back-and-forth between the slums that must be abandoned and the new flat implies that the bridge linking the marginalised and the socialised worlds was never really built. The space of the future is overmanaged, the old neighbourhoods are destroyed too quickly, projects are built without considering the history and memory of places. Those who used to live in these poor areas have been forgotten, yet the walls, the run-down streets tell their stories: stories of belonging, of lively habits, and no one should be allowed to sweep away that past in the name of the ideological cult of Novelty.

Figure 11.1   Colossal Youth *(2006)*

Figure 11.2   Colossal Youth *(2006)*

Figure 11.3 Colossal Youth *(2006)*

Figure 11.4 Colossal Youth *(2006)*

Notes

1. See Michel Agier, *Le Couloir des exiles: être étranger dans un monde commun.* Bellecombe-en-Bauges: Éditions du Croquant, 2011, pp. 78–9.
2. 'Because the neighbourhood had been destroyed, I wanted to make a new film, to add something, something fictional. I thought about the birth of Fontainhas, about the first men who settled there in 1970 and 1972, about those who built those shacks. They left their country, Cape Verde, Guinea, Angola, Mozambique where there was war, where they couldn't find any work. They settled there, and

they waited until their wives came' (Interview with Pedro Costa by Emmanuel Burdeau and Thierry Lounas, *Cahiers du cinéma*, 619 (January 2007), pp. 74–8).
3. Interview with Pedro Costa by Jean-Sébastien Chauvin, *Colossal Youth* press kit, 2006.
4. *Dans la chambre de Vanda: conversation avec Pedro Costa*. Nantes, Capricci, 2008, p. 66.
5. This expression is taken from Michel Collot's book, *La Matière-émotion*. Paris: PUF, 1997, p. 2: 'emotions are not purely subjective. It is an affective response from a subject upon encountering an entity or a thing from the outside world, which he or she may then try to interiorise by creating another object, source of a similar yet new emotion: a poem or a work of art.'
6. Ibid., p. 61.
7. See David Bordwell, *Ozu and the Poetics of Cinema*. London and Princeton: British Film Institute and Princeton University Press, 1988, pp. 75–9.
8. 'This is why I have insisted on the non-anthropocentric qualities of the camera placement.' Ibid., p. 79.
9. Jacques Rancière, *Les Écarts du cinéma*. Paris: La Fabrique Éditions, 2011, pp. 139–40.
10. Alain Mons, 'L'Intervalle des lieux', *Le Portique*, 12 (2003), online 15 June 2006. Available at: <http://leportique.revues.org/578> (last accessed 8 September 2015).
11. Giorgio Agamben, 'Notes sur le geste', *Trafic*, 1 (Winter 1991), p. 35.
12. Daniel Dobbels, 'L'Exergue', in Païni and Tesson (eds), *Jean-Marie Straub, Danièle Huillet, Hölderlin/Cézanne*, p. 14.
13. *Dans la chambre de Vanda: conversation avec Pedro Costa*, p. 98.
14. Goetz, *Théorie des maisons*, p. 14.
15. This particular episode of Ventura's life was shot at the Gulbenkian Foundation.
16. *Dans la chambre de Vanda: conversation avec Pedro Costa*, p. 165.
17. Ivan Illich, *Dans le miroir du passé: conférences et discours, 1978–1990*. Paris: Éditions Descartes et Cie, 1994, pp. 65–6.
18. Jean-Louis Comolli and Vincent Sorrel, *Cinéma, mode d'emploi: de l'argentique au numérique*. Paris: Éditions Verdier, 2015, p. 97.
19. Besse, *Habiter un monde à mon image*, p. 161.

CHAPTER 12

Tariq Teguia and the Algerian Banlieue: *A Field of Ruins*

In his first video essay, *Ferrailles d'attente* (1998), Tariq Teguia filmed in slow motion various landscapes around Algiers. The city appeared uninhabited, petrified, caught in some sort of monochromatic torpor. For his first feature film, *Rome Rather Than You* (2006), Teguia chose to focus on a specific *banlieue* that was being built at the time, La Madrague. In this gigantic, deserted, paralysed construction site, the director chronicles the lives of young men and women imprisoned in this dark and broken-down place. To set a film in a new Algerian *banlieue* in the 1990s is a political rather than sentimental choice: its characters are trapped in an area undermined by a hidden war, a war with no front lines. Even so, Teguia does not make his characters into caricatures or archetypes. He prefers to emphasise the persistent presence of the surroundings, to show the way walls interact with bodies, overwhelm them, block out their future ...

From Scrapped Landscape to Utopian Map

In *Ferrailles d'attente*, a slow lateral dolly shot surveys an old ochre wall, while the soundtrack produces a 'crumply' sound created by sampling, as if to accentuate the fitful, confined feeling. Then great white capital letters appear on screen: 'MACHINE À SURVIVRE' (SURVIVAL MACHINE). An urban landscape, perpetually deconstructed, is revealed. Walls, sheets of metal, piles of wooden pallets seem to fence everything in. In his first short, Tariq Teguia exposes an architectural fault line, an architectonic chaos: steel cables lying beside the roads, houses with no roofs and no windows, rough walls striated by iron beams going up towards the sky. The loud clatter of scrap iron fills the screen, disrupts this already quite harsh urban setting. There are no words in this narrative, but the jerky movements of the camera tell their own story, just like the series of black and white photographic portraits that break up its structure, every once in a while. These silent images reveal the helplessness of the young Algerian people. Regularly, words and fragments of sentences ('to dwell', 'vacant property') appear on screen, enigmatic and alarming.[1] The use of these metaphors ('survival machine', 'what's nicest about this place is the silence') gives deeper meaning to these alienated, unmoving urban visions.

In *Ferrailles d'attente*, Teguia uses low-angle shots to create anxiety; buildings do not look like stable structures, but seem unbalanced. The frame does not delineate a solid geometry, but induces aggressive undulations: the ground itself seems to crack, and the urban construction site, abandoned because of the economic crisis and the ongoing civil war, turns into vertically aligned ruins. Chromatically, the faded ochres, the dark blues, the sparkling whites (created by overexposing the film) transform the urban landscape into a moving, phantasmic space.

In this video essay, Tariq Teguia portrays a landscape of negations, uninhabited rather than inhabited, where the architecture seems to be about to collapse even as it is being built. He enters these interrupted construction sites, these countless abandoned projects, as if Algeria was a country with a suspended present.

In *La Clôture* (2003), he criss-crosses the streets of Algiers and looks particularly at male bodies, men who wait with restless resignation for time to pass and for life to peter out. *Ferrailles d'attente* focused mainly on the urban landscapes, on building sites that did not hint in any way at a better future, while *La Clôture* lets Algerians speak. As the camera looks straight at them, they express their indignation and their blistering anger. As the film goes from man to man, from face to face, the audience listens to these muffled, stuttering yet imposing voices. Here are a few samples:

> Fehti, 28 years old, Algerian, sadly. I've been a student for twenty-five years, and in the end, I have fame but no recognition. Twenty-eight years of grief, twenty-eight years of 'disgustingness'. I've been complaining for twenty-eight years. What, should I commit suicide? I could never do it, I'm a coward!
>
> Kader, 32 years old. There aren't enough words in the dictionary, it's too deep. We can't take it any more. What should we do? Work? For what purpose? Things never get any better. Run away, go abroad, that's not possible. You go out with your girlfriend, and then the cops come and stop you, because it's immoral, it's against religion, or it's because our society is not ready to accept it. It makes no sense, what we're going through. If you want Algerians to live, then don't show them that things are better elsewhere. Show 'em a world in ruins. Take away the parables! Take away all images from the outside.

Placed at regular intervals in *La Clôture*, these outbursts are shot very simply; what gives them their strength is the incredible power of their rebelliousness and outrage. They erupt publicly, these liberating shouts, and their exuberant, raw energy subsequently becomes a sort of inner experience: the *outraged I* becomes a *kinship*, a *we*. *La Clôture* offers no explanations: these voices express vital impulses, they dish out disturbing truths, they convey pure and immediate consciousness. In his phenomenological analysis of voices, Jacques Derrida says:

> It is this purity that makes it fit for universality. [...] It is this universality which dictates that, *de jure* and by virtue of its structure, no consciousness is possible without the voice. The voice is the being which is present to itself in the form of universality, as con-sciousness.[2]

In *La Clôture*, these angry yet lucid male voices[3] express the impossibility of staying in the country, of living in the city or in the street; they are saying that the Algerian civil society of the 1990s is stuck in this state of confinement and inaction.

In the fictional feature-length film *Rome Rather Than You*, Tariq Teguia continues his political exploration of the Algerian *banlieues*, this time in the Algiers suburb of La Madrague. As the decade-long civil war rages on, Kamel and Zina wander around the city. Kamel wants to leave the country and reach the European Eldorado, while Zina, claiming that she is happy to let events decide her fate, dismisses all his arguments with clairvoyant frankness. One scene in particular seems quite representative of the narrative's take on geopolitics. Kamel and Zina sit next to each other on a bridge, with their backs to the audience. They watch the incessant flow of cars and the ceaseless activity of the port of Algiers. Naively hopeful and impatient, Kamel lists all the European cities where he would like to go and live (Marseille, Barcelona, Naples); he even mentions America, because 'the king there is just, and no one is persecuted', and then Australia. Zina answers him with lucid firmness: 'What would you do in Australia? There's only sheep and kangaroos, over there. Why would leave your beloved neighbourhood?' Kamel replies: 'Long live globalation!' Then, on a black background, the following words appear, in French and Arabic: 'Making your border overlap someone else's, that's waging war.' We then return to Kamel and Zina sitting on the bridge. 'Money and things travel,' she says, 'but not men.' He replies: 'Arab means *those who move*.' He has tried to go to Europe and was turned away, yet he talks about these cities as if they were islands of hope. His list draws up the map of a world where there are no borders, an archipelago of possible escapes, a subjective topography, as he merely enumerates the places he dreams of going to. As Kamel denies the existence of international borders and their use as tools of surveillance, Zina replies drily: 'Arab, what it really means is *those who are turned away*.' In effect, she redefines borders as political and legal markers.[4] When the two friends finally get inside Bosco's house (he is a sailor who sells fake identity papers), they walk back and forth in that abandoned place, then approach two big maps pinned on a wall. Zina points to a spot on one of them and says: 'We are here.' Kamel immediately points to another spot and replies: 'Yeah, and we'd like to be there.' Just like in the previous scene, Kamel is looking for an escape, while Zina wants to know where she is, where she is anchored. The map turns out to be a subjective view of the world, which needs to be appropriated by choosing a fixed point or by moving around. More than just an iconographic illustration, the map is 'a place that represents territories as worlds of reference'.[5] For Zina, a map situates one geographically; for Kamel, it is 'emotional, an interiorised utopia',[6] as Jean-Marc Besse wrote.

In *Rome Rather Than You*, Tariq Teguia reduces everything to only one neighbourhood, one phantom location, La Madrague, the new project where the new concrete architecture is meant to entice the affluent to come and live. During the first thirty minutes of the film, the bright light of day shines on the streets and docks of Algiers, as Kamel and Zina wander about freely and easily; but the second half of the film takes place in an obscurity that stresses the sense of paralysis induced by the curfew, in this *banlieue* where a secret, subterranean war is being waged. Teguia shifts abruptly from walking to wandering, from opening to shutting down, from light to darkness. 'We tried to map out Algiers and its *banlieues*, we criss-crossed it, we looked at the city, but from the back, a city under curfew, with its own particular rhythm, its own singular weightiness.'[7]

The long car ride across La Madrague, while Kamel and Zina are looking for Bosco, could have made the film into a sort of road movie (Kamel borrowed the vehicle from his uncle, claiming 'an urgent situation'). Yet, that is hardly the case, because both of them are, in fact, prisoners of this *banlieue*, and every road disorients them and culminates in a dead end. Most road movies 'see modernity as an era of increased mobility, of moving away from fixed space-times, and thus as a form of return to nomadism, even if temporary, briefly running away from the "iron cage"'.[8] It is a trip with no point of return, with no fixed destination or predetermined duration, with no itinerary. To leave, in this case, is to give up any possibility of return; the road goes on and on, infinite, 'forever lost'.[9] To quote François Dagognet, the road is 'beginning without end', it is 'capable of ending the domination of circularity; it will save us from confinement and its forced immobility. We will not be prisoners any more.'[10] Kamel and Zina's ride across La Madrague is undeniably circular, arduous, constantly interrupted by numerous dead ends. Just as in Tariq Teguia's first shorts, *Rome Rather Than You* depicts a dark and narrowly confined urban geography. The characters' pressing desire to leave the country, to escape from the war and from themselves, leads them to a paradoxical *halted flight*: in La Madrague, all their hopes are buried forever.

LA MADRAGUE, CONTEMPORARY RUINS

La Madrague is located on the Mediterranean coast, about 20 kilometres from central Algiers. Tariq Teguia, in *Rome Rather Than You*, gives a sense of how far that really is by using a forward tracking shot twice, following Kamel and Zina along the side of a road, as if they were in a procession. Yet, they end up in that concrete no-man's-land, surrounded by construction site waste. A long, static shot of a simple, grey, unplastered wall marks the transition from the codified space of the anonymous streets of Algiers to this desert of unfinished houses, as if the filmmaker wanted to convey metaphorically the sense of impending imprisonment. The car driven by Kamel then follows at low speed a convoluted path in a maze of alleys and small streets, between unfinished buildings, around piles of construction materials, accompanied by the slightly jerky forward motion of the camera. Unhurriedly, this progression reveals to the audience a series of concrete stakes, meant to uphold the floors of the future buildings. Zina then asks: 'Where are we going?' Kamel answers: 'To see a guy who sells hope. He has a house with a garage, two floors, and visible beams.' Zina replies: 'You're messing with me. Everything looks the same, every house has two floors, two garages and visible beams.' In this chaotic yet uniform environment, Kamel and Zina desperately look for Bosco's house. As Kamel points out: 'They only put the address when everything is finished.' This is truly a phantomatic *banlieue*; Teguia locks his characters up in an unfinished *banlieue*, where things in the process of being built look like ruins, like fragments, like failure. The architecture of the *banlieue* can thus be described as *constructed degradation*. Teguia films La Madrague as if it was contemporary, vertical ruins. Houses are jumbled together, in this new, off-centred area, like so many concrete islands, where it is impossible to live or dwell.

In films, ruins are quite often associated with feelings of melancholy; they bring the past back to life, but as a 'grieving memory'.[11] In the not-yet-built Algerian *banlieue*, however, ruins are a living reality, an ungainly, poorly constructed truth. These contemporary, moribund ruins are quite different from ancient ruins, made sacred by the passage of time. As Richard Bégin writes,

> To observe ruins, remnants or debris means, in a way, that you're making an *event* of this debris; *what once was* is made to reappear, or, at the very least, you are made conscious of a time *before*. Thus, the traces of an era can be seen as the origins of that other era, of that phenomenological *epokhè*, which we will call the *era of survival*.[12]

Therefore, it is neither before nor after that the 'constructed ruins' of *Rome Rather Than You* can be observed. They are an absence of memory, a raw reality that cancels all imaginary beliefs, that mirrors the overall paralysis of a country. These vertical ruins are soulless fortifications, a crippled architectural pattern that represents only a collapse that left no rubble behind. Tariq Teguia films a disaster-*banlieue*, fragmented, ripped apart, but with no visible wreckage, more akin to a cave-in than to a construction.

In this 'critically ill' *banlieue*, in this disused, crime-ridden place, there is no urban existence, even as some underground, secret lives persist. In that sense, it seems less like a tamed functionality or a sanctified monument than a desecrated power. I agree with Benoît Goetz when he writes: 'To reduce architecture to its monumentality is to overlook its function as event.'[13] The basis of Tariq Teguia's elliptical narrative is the destructive force of political events, which breaks down any possibility of building one's life, day by day; even the faces of the residents of the community seem wrecked. Usually, something links together architecture and urban life; the Algerian filmmaker shows what happens when that link snaps.

In *Rome Rather Than You*, the dreadful reality of the unfinished walls bears witness to these countless censored and devastated lives; all these building materials strewn about are more than architectural components. They represent the broken-down relationships, the scattering of a community, they are the image of an Algerian civil society that has been blown away to pieces. The disgraceful aesthetics of La Madrague weigh upon every shot, every scene, like an invisible political presence, a nomadic, elusive obsession. Teguia uses the surrounding architecture, the scattered signs of construction and destruction, and the rhythm of the night, to make these silent voices heard, to denounce and criticise the state, and the state of the country.

THE PLASTIC EURHYTHMICS OF PLACE

La Madrague, in Tariq Teguia's film, is not a continuous territory; the plasticity of its appearance makes it feel, intrinsically, like a prison. The sombre colours, the reds, the blacks, the greys, create on the cinematographic screen a sort of *plastic eurhythmics* that transforms every place into an unliveable, unbearable nowhere ... When Kamel goes into a restaurant to ask where he can find Bosco, the entire space is covered in, and closed off by bright red curtains – the very same hue that reappears later, in the middle of the night, when a policeman bullies some of Kamel's associates. Visible outside and inside of dwellings, this red colour always appears in the shadows and transfigures these dark environments, nullifies their topography, delocalises them and makes 'transitory burrows' of them. 'Cinema', wrote Elie Faure, 'is first and foremost plastic: it represents a sort of moving architecture which is in constant accord, in a state of equilibrium dynamically pursued – with the surroundings and landscapes where it is erected and falls to the earth again.'[14]

In *Rome Rather Than You*, coloured surfaces, plastic matters absorb architectural spaces. The night setting of many shots also contributes to a feeling of disorientation and spatial confusion, thus enhancing and strengthening the enigmatic and strange expressiveness of the locations.

In *Les Marges de la nuit*, Baldine Saint Girons wrote:

> And so we come to this paradoxical conclusion, that colours shine brightest during the night. [...] The great painters of night scenes go even further than engravers in their efforts to explain the *fiat* of the night, its true processes. Not only do they reveal the inseparable nature of the visible and the invisible, not only do they demonstrate that all vision must come up against an impossible aesthetics, they reveal how 'coloured sensations' that assail from within and without are organised and disorganised.[15]

The colour red, being amalgamated in *Rome Rather Than You* with the night, reaffirms the dangers of the underground war whose tragic spectacle cannot be seen on the bodies themselves, but inside the various locations. The nocturnal chromatic force erases the facades and buildings, only to make them later blast out on screen as charged explosives, as distillations of the invisible war against the Armed Islamic Group of Algeria. These night scenes, full of colours, could be connected to certain American photographic aesthetics, most prominently Robert Frank's, whom Tariq Teguia often refers to.[16] Frank did shoot – in black and white, though, in his case – sprawling nights that stretch out the drifting spatiality of places. In *Rome Rather Than You*, places are filmed as if they were wounded flesh, as if they were substitutes for bodies. Teguia depicts a mobile, diffused, unstable terror, and the dehumanised, uninhabitable architectural spaces, with their dreadful chromatics, contribute to the creation of this terror.

Whenever a place is not plastically altered, in *Rome Rather Than You*, then the poetry and metaphors of language take over. As Kamel and Zina get to La Madrague, they look stubbornly for Bosco, and when they do not find him, they stop on a deserted beach. Zina blames Kamel for landing them in this soulless place: 'You talked about the sea, and we end up in this mangy neighbourhood!' Teguia films the beach from above but leaves no room, in the frame, for the sea itself. The majestic horizon having been forcibly removed by the director, the seaside area looks almost like a narrow, sandy piece of waste ground. The word 'mangy' compares the beach to diseased skin; the powerful imagery of language, which Teguia uses to complement and enrich the sense of sight, transforms the place to make it worthy of rejection. Reality is reconfigured, disfigured; words are fragments of images, unbound by the restrictive borders of the screen frame. By bringing together the plasticity of the walls and buildings and the evocative power of language,

Teguia playfully drops, throughout the narrative, phrases that operate as topographical and cartographical enigmas. 'You will join a republic of runaway slaves, I'm not the one to say, it's D. H. Lawrence.' So says, in the red night, the police officer.

Figure 12.1   La Clôture *(2003)*

Figure 12.2   Rome Rather Than You *(2006)*

Figure 12.3   Rome Rather Than You *(2006)*

Figure 12.4 Rome Rather Than You *(2006)*

Notes

1. These inserts could also be construed as a homage to Robert Frank, who was the subject of Tariq Teguia's doctoral dissertation, and who often engraved words directly on his photographic negatives or wrote directly on the image.
2. Jacques Derrida, *Speech and Phenomena, and Other Essays on Husserl's Theory of Signs*, trans. David B. Allison. Evanston, IL: Northwestern University Press, 1973, pp. 79–80.
3. In 2009, at a retrospective of Tariq Teguia's films at the Festival des Films d'Afrique du Pays d'Apt, someone in the audience asked: 'Your movies are great. But where are the women?' This was the director's answer: 'In *Ferrailles d'attente*, the person the camera gets closest to is a woman, with the word "risqué" written on screen. In *La Clôture*, I filmed young women. But the point was to cause a stir, and the way women talked and presented themselves was much more modest, more restrained. They didn't show the same violence as the men did when they talked about their profound feelings of failure. Because I wanted this film to be a violent declaration, I decided to edit the women out. I didn't want to pretend that I was responding to some need for equality, and, in a way, what I did also reflects the situation of women in Algeria. There are women in the streets, but never after a certain time of day, and not at all in some neighbourhoods. One could say that women are absent from public life in Algeria. I knew that some people would notice their absence in the film. But it does bring up the issue of our public and political space. Women are locked away. Both men and women have their own barriers, even if, sometimes, they actually overlap' ('La Leçon de cinéma de Tariq Teguia', Festival des Films d'Afrique du Pays d'Apt, 2009, interview with Olivier Bardet. Available at: <http://www.africultures.com/php/?nav=articleetno=9014> (last accessed 23 September 2016).
4. Michel Foucher, *L'Obsession des frontières*. Paris: Perrin, 2007, p. 21.

5. Jean-Marc Besse, 'Cartographie et pensée visuelle: réflexions sur la schématisation graphique', in Isabelle Laboulais (ed.), *Les Usages des cartes (xviie–xixe siècles): pour une approche pragmatique des productions cartographiques*. Strasbourg: PUS, 2008, pp. 19–32.
6. Jean-Marc Besse, 'Cartographier les lieux de nulle part', *Notre histoire*, 233 (2005), p. 20.
7. See *Cinéaste au centre, discussion entre Tariq Teguia et Jacques Rancière*. Paris: Centre Georges-Pompidou, 8 March 2015. Available at <https://www.centrepompidou.fr/cpv/resource/cdy6bG9/r5XgG78> (last accessed 16 March 2022).
8. Walter Moser, 'Présentation. Le Road movie: un genre issu d'une constellation moderne de locomotion et de médiamotion', *Cinémas: revue d'études cinématographiques/Cinemas: Journal of Film Studies*, 18: 2–3 (Spring 2008), p. 14.
9. This is a reference to the beautiful title of a piece by Mathieu Darras, 'Routes à jamais perdues', *Positif*, 545–6 (July/August 2006), pp. 21–3.
10. François Dagognet, 'Route, anti-route et méta-route', *Les Cahiers de médiologie*, 2 (2nd semester, 1996), p. 20.
11. André Habib, *L'Attrait de la ruine*. Crisnée: Yellow Now, 2011, p. 11.
12. Bégin, 'L'Époque de la survivance', p. 91.
13. Ibid., p. 36.
14. Elie Faure, *The Art of Cineplastics*, trans. Walter Pach. Boston: The Four Seas Company, 1923, p. 24.
15. Saint Girons, *Les Marges de la nuit*, p. 137.
16. Tariq Teguia's doctoral dissertation was titled *Robert Frank, fictions cartographiques*.

Part 5

The Strangeness of Places and the Solitude of Men

To live in a remote place is often considered as a form of punishment. Those who live 'far away from everything' are all but forgotten, prevented from benefiting from possible future developments, forced aside, kept away from the crowd. Films have long been interested in wild natural spaces, in part because they were still 'unexplored'; but they seldom show any interest in inhabited but debased areas, in lost and muted lands, deemed unworthy of attention or celebration.

Yet, life goes on in these 'lands of nowhere', in these neglected geographical spaces. Generally, whenever 'nowhere' is mentioned or brought up, it is in a derogatory context, as an unsignificant, negligible or even contemptible space. The word itself, 'nowhere', is unequivocal: it is an absence, a deficiency, a shapeless, soulless waste. It is an expanse that cannot be named, that cannot be described, an emptiness, a sterile nothingness. Nevertheless, some contemporary filmmakers, following the examples of Béla Tarr and Bruno Dumont, have turned these assertions around and produced fertile works of art. They go to the ends of the world, to places that are often disparaged for being too rural, too unrefined, and they capture their blunt light, they map out these territories where forms of existential dereliction thrive.

However, these 'nowheres' that appear in the films of Béla Tarr and Bruno Dumont are strangely languid; there are no explicit agonies, as if they were petrified by the banality and cruelty of human stories that occur within them. By praising the dull traces of these non-places, by giving a definite form, on screen, to defective lives, by fixing the image of a moving paralysis, they give meaning to them, even if that meaning is only a sense of despondency and exhaustion. Yet, Béla Tarr, Sharunas Bartas and Bruno Dumont succeed in giving a form to the shapelessness of nowhere, by giving their ugly paleness the quality of expressive bewilderment. How do they do it? How do they turn 'nowhere' into laconic *loci*, how do they reveal the underlying poetry? How do they represent, cinematographically, the immured, cut-off, entrenched isolation of these places? How can a film develop and give life to the 'spirit of nowhere' and bring forth the dystopian forces of these places?

CHAPTER 13

Bruno Dumont's Hamlets: Cursed and Isolated Places

In France, the very notion of *hameau*, or hamlet, supposes a tension between two antagonistic ideas: remoteness and community. On the one hand, a hamlet is usually linked, at least administratively speaking, to a village; the hamlet is dependent on it, but it stands apart, it keeps at a distance. On the other hand, any hamlet will contain a number of houses and farmhouses, often quite close to one another, while around the hamlet, a few isolated farms will create a sort of archipelago, a loose network, traditionally separated by fields – family properties, often quite small. These farms are scattered about, close enough that they can see one another, but at some distance nevertheless. It is in such hamlets on the Opal Coast of northern France that Bruno Dumont shot *Hors Satan* in 2011 and *P'tit Quinquin* in 2014.

Hors Satan begins under a rainy light, in front of a closed door. A hand knocks vigorously, the door opens slightly, and another hand gives a sandwich to the person who is standing outside. A long shot follows, which shows the various houses and outbuildings of the farm where the young girl lives who will become the vagrant's friend and accomplice. As the film begins, the director thus sets up two different spaces: one is inhabited by men, made up of several farms huddled together, and the other is a landscape, the dunes of the Opal Coast. Between the constructed world and the natural world, the two main characters (the young girl and the vagrant) go constantly back and forth. In *Hors Satan*, bodies have a significant presence, while both the hamlet and the landscape as a whole are seized by feelings of strangeness and beauty, by an oscillation between inertia and energy, and, in fact, this fluctuation punctuates the entire narrative and the unfolding of its enigma. In truth, the notion of narrative – a transparent and rational story, told in a straight line – is incidental. As Bruno Dumont himself said about stories: 'You need one, of course, but it's of secondary importance. I write about places, not about stories.'[1]

Defective, Luminous

After praying silently for a long time while facing the wild landscape of the sea dunes, the vagrant walks on the road that leads to the hamlet and finds the young girl crying near her family's farm. They do not say a word; she only nods, and they start walking together. The silence is heavy, and they walk at a brisk pace, which seems to hint at the fact that the girl has just been through a horrible experience. They head towards the dunes, making sure that nobody can see them, and they stop when they get to a campfire. The wind howls endlessly, emphasising the feeling of being out in the wilderness. They finally start talking, a short, quick dialogue. 'I can't take it any more, you understand?,' she says. The vagrant, letting his feet hover dangerously over the flames, answers: 'Only one thing to do.' *A posteriori*, the scene could be interpreted as a purification ritual, a confrontation with fire. In any case, the man gets up and walks towards a water tower, at the foot of which he has hidden a hunting rifle. Then, they both hurry back to the farm.

In just a few seconds, the images go from beauty to defect, from wilderness to civilisation, from natural spaces to rusty metal sheets. In a medium shot, the camera watches the man and the young girl hide behind a dilapidated wall. The vagrant then aims with his rifle, but just when he is about to shoot, the scene changes. Bruno Dumont opts for a wide shot, showing a cowshed covered in rusty metal sheets with, in the foreground, a pile of tarp and worn-out agricultural machines. A man comes out, pushing a wheelbarrow full of manure, and he is immediately shot down by the vagrant.

The man and the young girl stay awhile inside a storage structure near the cowshed, then they go back out into the fields. They kneel in the grass, and the camera being behind and slightly below them, their bodies are seen up against the sky. The vagrant's hands open up a bit, as if he wanted to absorb the raw energy of nature.

Several times during the course of the film, Bruno Dumont resorts to wide shots of the dilapidated farm, interspersed with high-angle or low-angle shots of the natural areas that surround the buildings. These are not the idealised images of immaculate and flowery farms; these buildings are ugly and in terrible shape. It is as if time had stopped and everything was petrified, blocked, as if there was no way out. Old material, broken machines, rusty odds and ends, piles of rubbish litter the area, a dire statement of the devastating effects of time. There are no plans to embellish or maintain this rural *domus*. Dumont's camera focuses on the disharmony, the neglect and the deterioration of the farm. In the words of the anthropologist and architect Philippe Bonnin, *Hors Satan* looks at 'an unremarkable heritage', worn out, disused.

> For farmers [he adds], there is no point in wasting energy maintaining what has outlived its purpose [...], even if it was inherited. However, according to the principle that one should never throw anything away, everything is kept despite its poor conditions. If anything is worth moving, it's things that are in

the way, that directly prevent the actual agricultural work from taking place. If a disused building still stands, it is because it is assumed that it will eventually find a new use.[2]

In the first ten minutes of the film, the source of the evil that plagues the hamlet is thus clearly identified: in that neglected place, laws do not apply, and the mother and the daughter must submit to the authority of the stepfather. Nothing but a 'hard-working shadow', that man, who most likely sexually abused the young girl, barely appears on screen before being gunned down; the mother, meanwhile, with her masculine face, her short, closely cropped hair, displays an aggressive and slavish brutishness. The gendarmes come to investigate the murder of the stepfather. After they leave, a close-up shows the hands of the girl, picking up breadcrumbs from the table; the mother's hands appear in the frame, grabbing and holding her daughter's. 'Forgive me, she says humbly, for the harm he's caused you.' In *Hors Satan*, mothers live in a sequestered world and the roughness of rural life forces them into silence. After hearing the apology from her mother, the young girl gets up, hugs her and leaves. As she walks in front of the run-down outbuildings, she takes a deep breath, as if she was relieved, and then goes and meets up with the vagrant.

Between the enclosed space of the farm and the wide-open landscape of the dunes,[3] the light changes radically and completely: the dark and sombre atmosphere of the farm becomes generous and bright sunlight out in the dunes. As the characters go from one environment to the other, the light changes with them, to demonstrate the antagonistic nature of the two worlds, to contrast, in a true dichotomy, depravity and grace. The farm and the hamlet are tormented by oppressive perversions but an innocent beauty shines on the dunes. They represent a wild, indomitable, uncontrollable, primordial freedom. Even under heavy, misty skies, the fleeting light that radiates over the dunes is so intense as to be almost incandescent. Bruno Dumont and Yves Cape, his director of photography, film the Opal Coast using mainly static shots, in CinemaScope, so as to transform this natural landscape into a pure, sovereign, dazzling, almost brutal form. The horizon is often placed in the top quarter of the frame,[4] giving the impression that the ground and the sky are coming together. It becomes, to quote Michel Collot, 'a structure that truly determines the emergence of a "meaning of meanings"'.[5]

The horizon is not anonymously infinite in this film, nor is it a static background; it is a line determined by the vagrant's presence and aura, by his religious gaze constantly fixed on that distant space.

The many scenes in which the vagrant's body is shown in nearly magnetic contact with the dunes could be seen as a respectful reference to

Andrei Tarkovsky, who filmed nature in the Zone in a way that highlighted its tumultuous beauty, who showed the stalker lying on the ground for a long time, as if the earth was a womb. In *Hors Satan*, the vagrant lies down on the dune grass – receptive to feelings and impressions, he becomes one with nature, like the lunatic or the child in Tarkovsky's works. Shut off from the rational world, Dumont's two marginal characters embrace the mysteries of the world, as they tune in, each in their lonely and spiritual way, and listen to the song of the elements. In Tarkovsky's films, the lunatic 'locks himself in to find himself'.[6] In contrast, the hermit of *Hors Satan* lives in the wild, open spaces of the dunes and marshes of the Opal Coast. But just like Tarkovsky's lunatic, the wanderer, the vagrant 'is more prophet than dead weight, standing halfway between the material world and the spiritual world'.[7] He has tamed the rugged and windy coast, to the point that he made it his spiritual ally. Consequently, it becomes for him a living expanse, which he can call upon to find renewed energy and a kind of impetuous vitality.

Bruno Dumont thus celebrates the eternal sanctity of untamed nature, in a way that echoes Merleau-Ponty's definition of nature:

> Nature is primordial – that is, it is the non-constructed, the non-instituted; hence the idea of an eternity of nature (the eternal return), of a solidity. Nature is an enigmatic object, an object that is not an object at all; it is not really set out in front of us. It is our soil — not what is in front of us, but rather, that which carries us.'[8]

The farm and the hamlet accumulate traces of the past and of fatal mysteries, but in the tumultuous natural environment of the Opal Coast, by contrast, temporality is open-ended and perpetually changing. There is a radical break between the place and the environment, between culture and nature; the hamlet appears irremediably perverted by men. Bruno Dumont's tormented narrative goes back and forth, in a continuous series of ruptures, thus making the distinction between the two even clearer. The film is, in fact, a diptych, with two vastly different, even incompatible parts: one that celebrates the energy of life, of both the sacred and the spiritual, and another that shows only the abject and the defective, inertia and stagnation.

The long static shots intensify the farm's coarseness, roughness and decay. The odds and ends that are piled up everywhere constitute, in the words of François Dagognet, a 'trajectology'[9]:

> everywhere, throughout the world, there are myriads of traces and inscriptions; everything leaves behind some indication of its presence. We must read and interpret those 'residues'. The humblest kitchen implement (even completely broken down), the flimsiest ragged fabrics are marked, as if by a tattoo, by the way they were used and by the passage of time. When we take

that into consideration, we see that every abandoned object, every no-longer-useful tool can produce an inexhaustible testimony.[10]

Bruno Dumont, however, does not follow François Dagognet's restorative approach; he does not attempt to find value in the dirty clutter that dots the farm. Instead, he sees it as evidence of neglect and dereliction, in the farm but also, by extension, in the hamlet.

An Archaic Place Fighting the Forces of Evil

As the story progresses, Bruno Dumont's camera explores, through these hypnotic static shots, the large divide that separates the harmful life of the hamlet and the wild strength of the dunes. He uses cross-cut editing to show two ways of life that are in constant opposition to one another, while at the same time permeating each other. One day, a woman comes running. She asks the vagrant, who is lying down in the hollow of a dune, if he can come quickly to her house because her daughter is sick with a strange illness. In a bedroom of a house by the roadside, a young woman's body is lying on the bed. The intensity of the light shifts quickly up and down, perhaps as a reminder of Dumont's premise of a separation between the world of nature and the world of culture. In the sickly darkness, the vagrant sits next to the bed. All of a sudden, he pulls sharply on the covers, revealing the adolescent girl's bare legs. He then gets up and leaves.

Later, the vagrant is once again called upon by the mother to come and see the young girl. He walks in the dark bedroom and gives a fervent look. She is sitting on the floor, surrounded by pools of blood. A close-up shows the paleness of her youthful face; she moans, then throws herself at his feet. The mother exits the room, and the vagrant kisses the teenager forcefully on the mouth, as if to exorcise the evil that possesses her. As he comes out of the room, the mother, who has been waiting outside, kneels and thanks him. So, it appears that the vagrant commands a mysterious power, by which he can enter a room and cure possessed souls. Again, the hamlet seems evil-ridden, a place where dark, wicked forces determine the fate of the inhabitants. The way that Bruno Dumont relates the foul destiny of men to supernatural experiences can be linked to the works of Georges Bernanos, most notably *Under the Sun of Satan*. As Gaétan Picon wrote: 'The priest is Bernanos's hero, because he is the only character, in the modern world, who welcomes the silence and the solitude of the spiritual life that is otherwise drowned out by vanity and noise.'[11]

In *Hors Satan*, the hero is a mystagogue vagrant rather than a priest, a sorcerer–angel who exorcises and saves the hamlet from a malignant fever.

Yet, Bruno Dumont refuses to allow any Christian interpretation of his films. His spirituality is wild and divergent; it springs from an unspeakable source and aims to provide the profane world with a grace both holy and fierce. Bruno Dumont once said that he believed his job was to 'construct apparitions'[12]; in a way, he embraces the supernatural experience – or, as François Mauriac put it when talking about Georges Bernanos, he makes 'the supernatural natural'.[13]

Hors Satan's vagrant wanders about, looking to root out 'evil'. He does not pray for a temporary reprieve, as would a religious man. Traditionally, women have usually been the victims of demonic possessions, and even when they are not directly affected, they are made into scapegoats and persecuted. The character of the vagrant is frail-looking but he is granted powers of vision and healing: he is the defender, the protector, the exorcist healer. An enigmatic, ambiguous fervour possesses him when he kills the forest warden by beating him with a stick because he came too close to his protégée. He is a walking body with no roof over his head; he punishes perverted men by killing them and cleans the hamlet of its impurities. He lives in the margins and attacks obvious satanic figures, such as the man who abused his stepdaughter. But he also encounters mysterious and unknown illnesses, like the paralysis that afflicts the teenage girl. *Hors Satan* thus shows a contemporary countryside forced to confront the Devil.

Bruno Dumont's film represents the hamlet as an infected, cursed and diseased place, corrupted by sexual terror. This primitive, hidden violence finds its way into every shot, through the heavy, inhumane, pervasive silence. As Emmanuel Levinas wrote:

> One could easily forget that even if silence is the natural place of peace and of *Musica Universalis*, it is also a stagnant pond, under which lie hatred, deceitful intentions, resignation and cowardice. One forgets heavy, painful silences, the silences that burst forth from Pascal's terrifying 'infinite spaces'. One forgets the inhumanity of a silent world.[14]

This inhumane silence is made even 'louder' by the high volume of ambient sounds, the teenage girl's tears and moans, for instance, or the impact of the sounds of the various violent outbursts, the crack of the rifle, the shock of the wooden stick on the body of the young forest warden, the frenetic kiss that the vagrant plants on the teenage girl to exorcise the evil that possesses her. No artificial sounds are edited in; there are no complementary sound effects, no plethoric dialogue attempt to cover the furious motions of the vagrant or the loud gusts of wind. While the silence of the characters only seems to add to the despondency of the hamlet, it has quite the opposite effect outside of it: the landscape of the dunes represents freedom, and the wind is its solitary emissary. Like Robert Bresson before him, Bruno Dumont favours a 'reduction of speech, but not a complete disappearance of it'.[15] The various sound elements clash with one another, they surge and fill the screen, just like the incandescent cruelty rises and overwhelms the hamlet.

In all of Bruno Dumont's work, men must struggle with their own body's pathological urges, and their actions contaminate the rural surroundings in which they live. This is particularly true of *Hors Satan*: the hamlet's hideous shame and primitive, archaic depravity suffocate it. In fact, this archaic power is such that all futures are suspended, and the contemporary world falls back into a dark and grimy past. All rationality is forgotten, and in its stead rises an ontological, anachronic and crude brutality. 'What is archaic', writes Yves Vadé, 'is not what is past, but what is no longer possible, though one should immediately add that it is nevertheless *still present*.'[16] Because of its closeness to nature, the hamlet in *Hors Satan* is literally cut off from the rest of society, and the small, isolated rural community remains inert, a place where the irrational laws of bestiality and evil determine the lives of men.

In *Hors Satan*, the hamlet is characterised by a very vague topography, though it is strangely held in place by its curse. A single establishing shot allows the audience to get a glimpse of the general geography and see the various buildings that are part of it. Most of the time, Bruno Dumont simply alternates wide shots of the farm with medium shots of the small house where the sick teenage girl lives. The hamlet in *Hors Satan* turns out to be more an insoluble mystery than an identifiable place.

It is also in a hamlet located near a small village in the Boulonnais region of northern France that the film *P'tit Quinquin* takes place. Several farms are huddled together, and in one of them live P'tit Quinquin and his extended family: his grandparents, his parents and his uncle, who suffers from a mental illness that sometimes makes him dance odd pantomimes in the courtyard. In *P'tit Quinquin*, as in *Hors Satan*, the hamlet stands away from the rest of the world, by the roadside, far away from all institutional structures (town hall, post office and so on) and shops. But it is a self-sufficient place, whereas the hamlet in *Hors Satan* was fragmented and isolated.

In the various instalments of the four-episode series, Bruno Dumont's camera follows P'tit Quinquin's bicycle, usually with Ève perched on the back wheel; these camera movements help define the limits of the hamlet, as characters move about it. The road, in these dolly shots, represents a chance at freedom, which the children use to get away from overprotective families; it is a rallying point, a space where the community of children can get together. The road is also an escape, which can allow one to reach the social frenzy of the distant village, or the seaside, nearby. The road is, in the words of François-Bernard Huyghe, a way to tear yourself away from local things. If a territory is a barrier both physical and theoretical, then the road is its negation: an oriented space, an opening whose innovations contradict and complete the territory's protective familiarity. A road is the opposite of a village.[17]

The hamlet, in the *P'tit Quinquin* series, is particularly remote; it is neither close nor far from the village or the sea, standing at the halfway point between the world of civilisation and the world of nature. The hamlet is close to the village because of the road, yet it is geographically far. It stands away from everything, yet paradoxically it is attuned to all that is happening around it – in this particular case, a series of murders occurring throughout the region.

The Lebleu family farm, where P'tit Quinquin lives, is right next to another farm; there lives Ève, who plays the trumpet in the brass band of a nearby village. Every day, she comes to see her boyfriend, P'tit Quinquin. Together, the two preteens learn to deal with the strangeness of reality, the comedy and tragedy of life. Often shown from up close, the camera looking on with tact and affection, they play or sit together, walk around P'tit Quinquin's farm or the hamlet. On screen, the tiny locality appears quite extensive, a jumble of nearly identical structures – the farms. However, the houses and outbuildings are kept separate, in *P'tit Quinquin*, by very clear barriers, such as the gate of the farm, where Ève likes to play her trumpet while exchanging meaningful looks with her friend. That gate marks the beginning of the territory of the Lebleu farm. It is a threshold. 'A threshold is neither inside or outside,' writes Bernard Salignon, 'it is both, a subtle interaction between opening and closing, through which sensible forms and human practices can associate with one another without contradiction or encroachment.'[18] Bruno Dumont's geometric shots draw up a representation of the hamlet as a mosaic of private spaces, the farms, set in juxtaposition to each other.

But the hamlet is also a place of work, and Dumont regularly shows P'tit Quinquin's father going to the stables to mind the animals while lecturing his son. In *Hors Satan*, the hamlet was a mess of turmoil and perversions, but in *P'tit Quinquin*, the mischievousness and petulance of childhood are allowed to flourish, even as horrible crimes are committed in the hamlet itself or in its immediate vicinity. At the end of the fourth episode, Van Der Weyden, the officer in charge of investigating the heinous crimes, comes to the farm of P'tit Quinquin's family. Looking around, he says, in what is both a question and an affirmation: 'Things are OK around here, there's a good, earthy smell. But the soil is bitter, here. Be careful, this is the demon's land, you might be exterminated.'

In the first episode, P'tit Quinquin and his friends watch as a helicopter lands on the beach to remove a dead cow that has been found in a Second World War German bunker. The police officer and his assistant, Carpentier, listen to a medical examiner, who is saying that human blood was found inside the cow. Carpentier looks at the officer and says: 'What is this? The human beast, that's Zola, sir!' And Van Der Weyden answers: 'Now is not the time to be a philosopher, Carpentier!' Later, the two policemen, whose demeanour tends to be rather comedic, go to a warehouse where the cow is suspended from the ceiling. When the belly of the animal was opened, a headless human body was found inside, cut up in pieces. Each following episode adds to this murder, with a hyperbolic accumulation of horrifying and gruesome crimes. In the second episode, another body is found in the belly of a second cow. The investigators discover that these first two victims were lovers. In the third episode, the tragic excesses compete with a surfeit of comedy, as the body of a young woman, star of local radio talent show, is devoured by pigs. The two policemen go to the abattoir and learn that the dead cows were actually mad cows that ate human body parts. It seems as if, by ingesting human flesh, the domestic animals transgressed the natural order of things: their relationship to humans has been perverted. The herbivores eating human flesh acts as an inverse mirror, and the hamlet is cursed by an ever more unbearable, gruesome irrationality.

Both in *Hors Satan* and *P'tit Quinquin*, an uncanny, unfathomable forms of implausibility permeates everything and everyone in the hamlet with their foulness. These rural locales, isolated and forgotten, are besieged by regressive and transgressive forces that completely block out the future. They are, in effect, excluded from the world as if by quarantine. The hamlet is the place where the land will eventually bury you.

Figure 13.1 Hors Satan *(2011)*

Figure 13.2 Hors Satan *(2011)*

Figure 13.3 Hors Satan *(2011)*

Figure 13.4 Hors Satan *(2011)*

Figure 13.5 Hors Satan *(2011)*

Figure 13.6 P'tit Quinquin *(2014)*

Notes

1. 'Philippe Rouyer and Yann Tobin: Entretien avec Bruno Dumont', *Positif*, 608 (October 2011), p. 29.
2. Philippe Bonnin, 'Le Temps d'habiter', in Berque, de Biase and Bonnin (eds), *L'Habiter dans sa poétique première*, p. 23.
3. 'We shot the film in the nature reserve of the Dunes de la Slack, near Boulogne-sur-Mer. Access to it is forbidden, but after some long negotiations, a limited number of people were allowed to enter the reserve, no more than ten, we could not use any vehicles to get around, and we were not authorised to lay down tracks for dolly shots. We brought all the gear ourselves, using the lightest possible configuration. We used static shots, or panoramic shots, actors coming in and out of the frame' (Interview with Yves Cape, director of photography, by François Reumont. Available at: <http://www.afcinema.com/Entretien-avec-le-directeur-de-la-photographie-Yves-Cape-AFC-SBC-a-propos-dufilm-Hors-Satan-de-Bruno-Dumont.html> (last accessed 19 December 2016).
4. 'Bruno Dumont showed me images from Gabriel Figueroa, a Mexican director of photography, who shot among others the first Buñuel films. We drew quite a lot of inspiration from those shots where the horizon appears only in the top quarter of the frame, and not in the middle' (interview with Yves Cape, ibid.)
5. Michel Collot, *L'Horizon fabuleux*, vol. 1: *XIXe siècle*. Paris: José Corti, 1988, p. 21.
6. Antoine de Baecque, *Andrei Tarkovski*. Paris: Cahiers du cinéma, 1989, p. 60.
7. Ibid., p. 58.
8. Maurice Merleau-Ponty, *Nature: Course Notes from the Collège de France*, compiled and with notes by Dominique Séglard, trans. Robert Vallier. Evanston, IL: Northwestern University Press, 2003, p. 4.
9. François Dagognet, *Des détritus, des déchets, de l'abject: une philosphie écologique*. Le Plessis-Robinson: Institut Synthélabo pour le progrès de la connaissance, 1997, p. 13.
10. Ibid.

11. Gaétan Picon, *Bernanos: L'impatiente joie. Suivi de Lettres inédites de Georges Bernanos à Gaétan Picon*. Paris: Hachette Littératures, 1997, p. 44.
12. Rouyer and Tobin, 'Entretien avec Bruno Dumont', p. 31.
13. 'Georges Bernanos's unique talent is to make the supernatural natural.' François Mauriac, 'Journal d'un curé de campagne', *Gringoire*, 390 (24 April 1936).
14. Emmanuel Levinas, *Parole et silence et autres conférences inédites au Collège philosophique*, ed. Rodolphe Calin and Catherine Chalier. Paris: Bernard Grasset/Imec, 2009, p. 69.
15. Philippe Arnaud, *Robert Bresson*. Paris: Petite bibliothèque des Cahiers du cinéma, 2003, p. 83.
16. Yves Vadé, 'Retour du primitif, permanence de l'archaïque', *Modernités*, 7 (Bordeaux: PUB, 1996), p. 7.
17. François-Bernard Huyghe, 'Le Médium ambigu', *Les Cahiers de médiologie*, 2 (Paris: Gallimard, 1996), p. 57.
18. Bernard Salignon, *Qu'est-ce qu'habiter?* Paris: Éditions de la Villette, 2000, p. 102.

CHAPTER 14

Béla Tarr: Waiting behind Barricades

In films, waiting is usually a moment of inaction and growing exasperation, or else it is a short, insignificant instant that does not result in any introspection. Waiting is a brief pause, a respite that only exists contextually, until the action gets going again and the plot resumes its course. In other words, waiting is hollow, dead time, in the movies; it has no depth. It is just an interruption of motions and dialogues, and it must not last too long, so that active events can happen again, and so that time can become precious and impetuous again.

By contrast, in Béla Tarr's insistently protracted narrations, waiting implies both breaking-down and self-denial. To wait is to accept that what you expect will not come, that the passage of time is really just a 'suspended flow'. Tarr's first films focused on social criticism (*Family Nest*, *The Prefab People*, *Almanac of Fall*), on stories in which individual destinies interacted with general history and, more specifically, with communism's failed promises. But from *Damnation* on, the filmmaker used the towns and plains of Hungary to film 'situations' rather than 'stories'.[1] In his demonic trilogy (*Damnation* (1988), *Sátántangó* (1994), *Werckmeister Harmonies*), and in the follow-up film *The Turin Horse* (2011), waiting is represented as a disintegrating experience, as a confrontation with the indifferent and stolid power of places. As they wait, the characters are stuck and forced to remain 'nowhere'.

THE WINDOW SHOWS THE WORLD'S STAGNATION

Damnation begins in a vast, grey, muddy expanse. Several bins attached to a cable go endlessly back and forth between very high pylons, with a loud, continuous buzzing sound. As the camera moves very slowly away, it reveals a man, seen from the back, who is watching through a window the repetitive motions of the bins. Writes Andrea Del Lungo:

> A window looks on. According to the old metaphor, it is the eye of the house-body, that looks on the outside world even as it probes its own inner life. Through the window, humans begin the journey of personal understanding, by withdrawing into themselves, by observing the world melancholically or by analysing their own conscience.[2]

In this long, single take, Béla Tarr first turns his camera on the outside world, thus reversing the classical approach, which would suggest that one should begin by looking at the exterior landscape through the window frame, thus creating, as it were, a frame within a frame. But *Damnation* opens with an exterior shot, and a slow backward motion takes the camera inside the flat. The world outside matches the interior universe, even if it is enclosed by dark walls. The man, sitting with his back to the audience, observes life on the other side of the glass, but he has been relegated to the background. Béla Tarr focuses on the listless, indolent exterior scene. In most literary and cinematographic narratives, windows serve a specific function, both optically and spatially: they exist as a possibility – since the gaze can look for an escape – and they give inspiration to a daydream and help avoid, for a time, the difficulties of reality. But Béla Tarr follows the opposite trajectory and refuses to accept this consensus that windows lead to flights of fancy. On the contrary, going from outside to inside becomes almost like a form of reclusion. As *Damnation* begins, the horizon does not expand: the window makes it narrower. Life is represented as a muddy dead end, where time passes sluggishly, where every day is a monotonous, repetitive, mechanical grind. That is why the slow, backward dolly shot demonstrates that the window is not an opening that leads to dreams of other places, but a restriction, a *here* where one can do nothing but wait. Time is suspended, lethargic, and the window is a return from the world rather than an escape towards the future.

However, the man at the window is not just paralysed by a powerful, constant inertia. *Sátántangó*'s alcoholic doctor sits at his table every day, and he watches with sick joy the events occurring outside his window. The wandering gaze is replaced by a voyeuristic gaze. Since he cannot watch in person the abominable spectacle of human behaviour, the sclerotic spy simply observes obvious, mundane ugliness. Holding binoculars in his trembling hands, the doctor stares at his neighbours, Mr and Mrs Schmidt. At one point, Mrs Schmidt is visited by her lover, Futaki, while her husband is away. Futaki walks up to the window to make sure everything is fine. The watcher is now the one being watched; windows become the crux of intersecting suspicions, as the spy is himself spied upon. Every day, the doctor sits at his table in front of the window, and he establishes a daily inventory of all the objects near him: metal scraps, objects that are no longer useful, cracked walls, mud, stray dogs or wallowing pigs … This alcoholic, perverted character is actually a prism, from Béla Tarr's point of view, through which heterogenous things are bunched together in the gaze of the observer to create an appalling reality. The audience watches with the doctor, as the camera looks through the binoculars, and discovers as he does these degraded, dingy surroundings.

The insistent gaze of the voyeur, the moral and physical monstrosity of the doctor, form a fascinating, breath-taking accretion of hideousness, as the rhythmic motion of the binoculars observes and records the muddy paralysis of the outside world. What could have been considered dissimilar forms turns out to be, by their accretion and mutual attraction, similarities that must be incorporated.

Later, the doctor, still sitting at his table, puts down his binoculars and slowly pours himself a glass of palinka. The audience can finally see what the inside looks like: a filthy room, cigarette butts and piles of notebooks everywhere. He writes down everything he observes in those, down to the slightest action. 'Futaki is afraid of something … Early … morning … worried … He looks out of the window. Futaki is afraid of death.' The doctor's flat holds the archives of his paranoia, it is the place where he both writes and keeps the records of his suspicious investigations.

In both *Damnation* and *Sátántangó*, windows function paradoxically: they open the way yet block it at the same time; they transform the infinity of the outside world into a restrictive, archaic, miserable interior. Still, windows do let in, now and then, shards of the exterior that show that the dereliction is everywhere – thus, it can be said that windows also contribute to a reversal. To look out of the window, to lean on the sill represents a form of abdication, because it is an act that contributes to the general degradation of things rather than allowing one to stand apart from it. In all his films, Béla Tarr considers windows as the point where existential decay occurs. Looking out of the window is, in a way, a confirmation of one's own disintegration.

In Béla Tarr's latest film, *The Turin Horse*, windows resemble darkened mirrors, evoke a rush towards the exit. The narration is centred around five frugal meals – two boiled potatoes flavoured with a pinch of salt – shared by old Ohlsdorfer and his daughter, in their house in the Hungarian countryside. Tarr chose long single takes, using dollies or a Steadicam to depict the ritual, the formal repetitiveness of these meagre meals. Every gesture (setting the table, eating the potatoes) seems particularly intense and the attitude of the characters is restrained, expectant, impressively sober. The camera presents these fragments of rudimentary lives as natural acts that combine extreme simplicity (the gestures) and extreme poverty (the meals). Mundane motions create a rhythmic stability; looks, movements, objects are interdependent micro-events. Béla Tarr creates *circulatory images* that describe the endlessly repeated experience of extreme poverty; aesthetically, this is basically a kind of *formal petrification*.

In *The Turin Horse*, windows operate as a part in an incarceration mechanism. Many times, the old coachman or his daughter looks out fixedly, sitting on a stool, a blanket draped over their shoulders. The universe spreads outward from the window as if it was an unavoidable breach, forever battered by strong, loud winds that keep entering through cracks in the walls, thus reinforcing the feeling of captivity. The window looks out over a white, translucid expanse, a featureless space with no horizon, that the characters experience as a ghostly yet impassable partition. The outside is, in effect, unattainable.

Whenever the camera gets close to the window and shows life in the open air, dead leaves whirl about hypnotically, lifted up by the cruel, painful, powerful gusts of wind. In *The Turin Horse*, windows do not facilitate contact with others, nor do they give access to the outside world. Instead, they eternally shrink the universe until it is no more than a broken dead end. Wishing to flee this trapped, sequestered life, the father and his daughter hitch their old horse up and gather a few belongings. But the wind forces them to turn back. Standing outside the isolated house, the camera shows the face of the young girl in the window, watching fixedly the hostile exterior. In *The Turin Horse*, just as in *Damnation*, windows represent a place where one sits and waits, as if behind barricades; the gaze attempts to flee, but fails and gives up.

QUITTING, COLLAPSING

Characters watching or spying each other, wandering about, waiting around are recurring motifs in Béla Tarr's works. *Damnation*'s characters live outside as much as inside, but life for them is like a silent, hidden haemorrhage. 'For Béla Tarr,' writes Jacques Rancière, 'time is no longer simply the means by which the illusion of a story is unveiled, but rather the stuff, the fabric in which are created the expectations that become illusions.'[3]

In *Damnation*, Karrer, a lonely and aimless man, walks around in the rain, roams about the alleyways, and hides behind walls to spy on his lover's husband. She is a singer at a local bar, the Titanik. Karrer's erratic wanderings, the countless hours he spends watching the husband all contribute to his broken trajectory. Béla Tarr presents places and situations exactly as they are: an inertia that paralyses the characters' ability to act. The director frequently uses dolly shots to convey a sense of imprisonment, coming in waves: characters and islands of spatiality fuse together, forming fragile, strange aggregates; as the camera moves, it contains them, then releases them but only to keep circling around them, locking them up, sapping their vitality.[4]

Waiting, in these places, is therefore akin to Michael Edward's oxymoronic definition: 'to be motionless and yet constantly moving'.[5] In *Damnation*, waiting is a form of *tense renunciation*. As Nicolas Grimaldi points out, waiting 'is an experience of time both as delay and instability, as a real, incompressible interval and an eternal flow that brings or carries away all things'.[6] The instances of waiting in Béla Tarr's films vary according to the attitudes of the characters who decide to *stop*, and the places where they occur: waiting by the window or remaining outside in the rain both mean to stay in sclerotic places and to confront the paralysing flow of time.

Ever since the release of *Damnation* in 1988, Béla Tarr has presented places in his films as if they existed prior to the appearance of the characters on screen. But these localities are isolated from the rest of the world; these nowhere lands are not infinite, homogeneous spaces where the characters can freely roam, nor are they similar to the 'a-topias'[7] that are so important, for instance, in Wim Wenders's films. Places, in Tarr's works, are damaged by fissures, they are frozen, incongruous, corrupted amalgamations of decay. Places are noteworthy because of the defects, the powerlessness, the degradation they reveal – yet these negative elements, paradoxically, become a characteristic, a *quality* that makes them real. Béla Tarr's films display an incapacity to reach anything that is far away, or even to believe in the existence of somewhere else. Places for him are a purely material asthenia, and those living within them are stuck waiting hopelessly, as if life was nothing more than an interrupted analepsis.

Figure 14.1 Damnation *(1988)*

164 *The Sense of Place in Contemporary Cinema*

Figure 14.2 Damnation *(1988)*

Figure 14.3 Sátántangó *(1994)*

Figure 14.4 Sátántangó *(1994)*

Figure 14.5   The Turin Horse *(2011)*

Figure 14.6   The Turin Horse *(2011)*

Notes

1. In an interview with the newspaper *Libération* in May 1987 ('Pourquoi filmez-vous?'), Béla Tarr said: 'I hate stories because stories would like you to believe that something happened. But nothing ever happens: you go from one situation to another. These days, there's situations, and there's nothing else, and all stories are outmoded, they're all cliché, they've vanished. Only time remains. The only thing that's truly real, probably, is time.'
2. Andre Del Lungo, *La Fenêtre: sémiologie et histoire de la représentation littéraire*. Paris: Seuil, 2014, p. 8.

3. Jacques Rancière, 'Poétique et politique de la fiction', in Maury and Rollet (eds), *Béla Tarr: de la colère au tourment*, p. 140.
4. See Corinne Maury, 'Puissances d'enchaînement: de l'usage de la *dolly* et du Steadicam chez Béla Tarr', in Anthony Fiant, Roxane Hamery and Jean-Baptiste Massuet (eds), *Point de vue, point d'écoute au cinéma*. Rennes: PUR, 2017, p. 223.
5. Michael Edward, *Éloge de l'attente: T. S. Eliot et Samuel Beckett*. Paris: Belin, 1966, p. 77.
6. Nicolas Grimaldi, *Ontologie du temps: l'attente et la rupture*. Paris: PUF, 1993, p. 40.
7. Cf. Moure, *Vers une esthétique du vide au cinéma*, p. 169.

CHAPTER 15

Sharunas Bartas's Undergrounds

In his film *In the Memory of a Day Gone By*, made in 1990 when he was still a student, Sharunas Bartas used walking to weave together multiple urban scenes in the city of Vilnius. On a street, deaf children communicate playfully in sign language; people hurry along so as not to be late for religious services; maimed people wander about; in a building doorway, a child is playing hide-and-seek ... Vilnius is represented on screen as a rhythmic series of mundane micro-situations, each being unique enough, distinctive enough to stand on its own. Slowly, patiently, Bartas's camera walks by, barely grazing the surface of these moments, and the most banal, the most ordinary turn out to be unfathomable. In *Three Days* (1991) and *The Corridor* (1995), he applies this form of urban contemplation to remote, enclosed spaces: a cellar, a corridor, a bunker – places where solitary beings roam – or run-down buildings in Kaliningrad, where bodies worried by desire meet, in a sort of dance. In these two films, the filmmaker tells tales of lonely wanderings, of troubled, tormented people, of waiting. Long, immersive shots show broken, disconsolate lives, imprisoned in squalid locales.

Lives under the Ground

In *Three Days*, two young men go out of an isolated house in the country and take a train to the city of Kaliningrad. Once there, they walk towards the port and reach an empty, windy square. Three people, a man who is obviously drunk and two young women, enter the cinematographic frame and go and sit on a low wall. The two young men approach one of the women, who has been waiting by herself for a moment, the other having accompanied the drunkard somewhere off screen. As she comes back, she shouts: 'Who are you boys? Why aren't you saying anything?' The four of them start walking about aimlessly in the harbour. They wait, wander around, not saying anything, bathed in the glaring lights of the city. They seem reluctant to do anything, as if they refused to partake in any productive activity. Urban life and its constant bustle seem completely absent from this narrative. Once in a while, a wide shot shows the city and its harbour, but that is all. The audience learns nothing about the identity of these young men and women; they are seemingly forced to wander around and wait, as if indecision was, to them, a way of life. *Three Days* shows these young people drifting about marginal places around the city. It is a narrative based on a poetics of idleness – but it is not the languor of a pointless ennui, nor is it a pessimistic surrender: it is a withdrawal from the world, as if the soul had got lost. The attitudes of the bodies, the expressions on the faces are like territories, out of which emerge various emotions, shock or delight. But Sharunas Bartas never uses close shots to convey and magnify the feelings of his characters. On the contrary, faces and bodies are dependent on the places where they are situated. These people, with their fragile and diffident pauses, are filmed as if they were pure 'interior materialities', strongly connected to the places that they inhabit: city square, dimly lit room, dark cellar, underground bunker. In the bland room of a sleazy hotel, the dull light covers the face of the young woman as if it were a veil – making that chaste body seem even more fragile, in that gloomy place where she is temporarily staying.

Bartas tells the story of young people whose desires are never protected by/in a familiar place; rather, they are constantly pushed around by circumstances. Places need to be quietly tamed so that fleeting sexuality can blossom. Wandering, for the filmmaker, means not having a known trajectory. One is reminded of Sébastien Rongier's definition: 'To wander is to have no itinerary. It cannot be mapped, because its movements do not aim to reach any definite goal.'[1] In *Three Days*, wandering amounts to a sort of underground progression. Bartas does not copy the idealised image: the open road, the vast spaces to conquer. The young men and women of *Three Days* walk about listlessly, and their idleness and desires clash without ever creating stable relationships. This sort of imprisoned movement is also completely, insistently silent. The scarcity of dialogues reveals the hidden passion of untold desires, while shifting the focus on the places. There is not only one silence, there are many forms of silence, that whisper and glide between bodies.

According to José Moure, silence is,

> for some modern filmmakers who emphasise heterogeneity and rarefaction (Bergman, Antonioni, Godard, Resnais, Straub, Garrel ...), a *structural element* that cancels out time and empties spaces, opening gaps and establishing a link, in the cinematographic image, with the outside (or the reverse), thus revealing the absence, the lack, the unspoken, the irreducible that is always a part of it.[2]

In *Three Days*, the silence between two, three, four people highlights the anxious intensity of desire, accentuates the mute expressivity of places and the idleness of bodies.

The isolated house, which the two young men left to go wander around the city, is very small and remote. Using exterior long shots and interior medium shots, Bartas shows the isolation of the family home near a small river, and its dilapidated state. Like all other marginal and minor places in this film, the house exhibits the signs of injury and stress. A sense of isolation, of marginality, of decay permeates the whole narrative: there are no open spaces, there is no harmony or glory in these areas where people live or pass through. There are only neglected, disgraced places.

The two young men and the young woman ask for a room at a hotel, but the manager refuses to give them one, with a look of aggressive and judgemental contempt. They are only allowed to spend the night in the sordid cellar of the hotel, where rejects and outcasts sleep. In that filthy place, they use a wooden box as a table, and the bed is just a rank mattress set down on the floor. There is almost no light, rubbish is strewn about, stains darken the floor and walls, wires hang down from the ceiling. This is not an obscure space,[3] an accumulation of objects from the past, but a place of rejection, the last refuge of an errant, fragile, petulant, cursed youth. The cluttered, dirty mess offers resistance, however. It is a minor, cursed place, but people use it because it hides them and provides them with temporary shelter, a place where they can freely give in to their despair. As the story progresses, many such places appear – cheap hotels, cellars, empty city squares, bunkers) – degraded, neglected places. Bartas creates, within the fixed frame of the images, heterotopian spaces[4] where idle, marginal young people gather and meet. In other words, these remote, neglected places where the young men and women of *Three Days* interact are negative places, run-down lairs in which to conceal themselves.

When they come down the stairs and into the cellar, the young woman casually says: 'It's pretty cool, here!' The filth does not matter, only the ever-present possibility of staying or going, the unstable, sometimes painful feeling of being free. This minor, rejected space reinvents itself as a place of transgressive hospitality. Each character slips in and they share a furtive moment of vulnerability together. In effect, Sharunas Bartas reverses the philosopher Henri Maldiney's proposition, according to which 'it is the sacredness of a space that makes it into a place'.[5] These gloomy spaces that the young men and women visit are indeed cursed, yet they also offer protection. The cellar, in *Three Days*, seems like a dungeon: it imitates, under the ground, the disreputable acts going on on the upper floors of the hotel above.

When the trio breaks up, the woman and one of the young men go to the seaside, where they find an abandoned Second World War bunker, build a fire and huddle near it. Like a commemorative stela,[6] left at the mercy of time and the elements, the bunker has slowly become a sand-choked ruin and a shelter for passing travellers. 'Anachronistic in times of peace,' writes Paul Virilio, 'a bunker seems a little bit like a survival machine, like the wreck of a submarine washed up on shore.'[7] The concrete military fortifications still watch over the sea, but it has in time been converted to an ephemeral squat. The young man and woman warm themselves by the fire while making small talk in a low voice. In this cold concrete 'house', surrounded by all kinds of rubbish, they sit, wait, seek warmth and protection against the cruelty of the world.

INERTIAS AND SILENCES

In *The Corridor*, a teenager with longish blond hair sits on the floor. The audience can hear, off screen, the sound of water dripping and some kind of loud din. A man dressed in black sits on a bed and strokes gently the angelic, almost androgynous face of the tired-looking young man. The close-up shows the hands of the adult touching the dark circles under the boy's eyes, pulling the skin to inspect his eyes and to look under the eyelids. Soon, the adult appears on screen, with a sombre attitude and hands held tightly together. He wipes his hands wearily across his face. The teenager gets up, runs down a grey corridor, opens a door. A bright light bursts out of it, contrasting strongly with the dull corridor. Whether inside or outside, though, the loud noises remain. The young man stands and waits in front of a stone facade, then he goes down into a cellar, grabs a bottle of alcohol and drinks many times from it. The audience will never know the name of this teenager, nor will anything be told about his past; he is simply the symbol of the radical, hidden violence that permeates this exhausted place. Stuck in this gloomy microcosm, he tries to escape from this daily life weighed down by inertia and petrified by poverty. Having had his fill of alcohol, he goes on a drunken walk through fields that spread out near a river.

Many times, in *The Corridor*, Bartas uses static shots to show a dark and narrow passage where bodies stand and wait. That corridor is not a hall that opens on to other rooms or flats; it is a tunnel, a prison, so dark that one cannot even tell how long it is. The director deliberately uses weak lighting to create that feeling of being trapped in a constrictive space. The dark grey hues change the architectural purpose of the corridor: instead of being a *way towards others*, it has become a *barrier against oneself*. The second time the corridor appears, a man's tired face shows up in the foreground. The background becomes blurry and the whole space seems sluggish, torpid. It is a prison cell with no depth, a condemned space, impossible to escape. Those who are waiting, those who are standing around in this underground cavern seem imprisoned by a sort of purposeless anxiety. Even the constant, loud noises do nothing to diminish the feeling that the corridor is a gaol, a dark abyss.

In *The Corridor*, there is a particular kind of silence that weighs upon everything and creates a strange torpid inertia.[8] It is not quite paralysis but it resembles a permanent existential anxiety. In the same building, in the same corridor, we find people standing at the margins of society: alcoholic child, introverted teenage girl, expansive girl, pensive man. All share the same unwillingness to deal with the outside world. So Sharunas Bartas builds for them *interior worlds*, born in defiance of the *exterior systems*. However, it would be too restrictive to say that *The Corridor* is only a film about affliction and exhaustion: it goes further than that. The unbearable silences, the constant noise, the unrestrained and enthusiastic party – all contribute to an atmosphere of disillusionment that oscillates between discouragement and anxiety. It is not exactly a self-centred dejection, nor is it the so-called 'Slavic melancholy' that appears so frequently in movies or in novels. This disillusionment seems almost like a state of existential exhaustion: 'Anxiety robs us of speech,'[9] wrote Martin Heidegger somewhat peremptorily. The troubled silence that permeates Bartas's images summons a black anxiety, like 'a sort of suction pad on the soul'.[10] Lonely beings are put together within tightly confined spaces, where they wait, linger and think. Their faces appear meditative, but they remain absolutely silent, until frenzied sounds, coming from the corridor, the bedroom or the yard outside (bottles being broken, feet pounding the floor, voices grumbling or shouting confusedly) pull them out of these interior meanderings. The soundtrack adds an exuberant and chaotic presence; it is a buoyant, aggressive manifestation of the community, a tyrannical counterpoint to the meditative, lonely, silent faces. While the first part of *The Corridor* watches these confined, idle, adult and pubescent bodies, surrounded by the endless, uninterrupted noises, the second part focuses on the liberating virtue of music and dance, and their capacity to bring together the whole community.

All these bodies that, up until then, were only heard hitting things, breaking things, shouting, ranting and raving, assemble in one large room. There is very loud music, a recording of an accordion playing the tango[11]; a man with a bright smile and an open shirt is leaning against the window. He raises his arms and pretends, with clumsy enthusiasm, to be a conductor. A close-up shows the playful and energetic expression of his face. In a dark corner of the room, a man spills his drink very slowly in the cleavage of a woman who is hugging him. The camera then shows the old tape recorder. The music has changed to some pop tune.[12] Two dancers are monopolising the centre of the dance floor, with everybody watching them. The man is without a shirt, and the woman has an almost childish air. They improvise together, with both abandon and restraint, and the camera watches carefully as they come together, separate and come together, again and again. There is freedom and exuberance in this improvised duo; it is a dialogue, in which the two partners[13] manage just barely to remain in control; it is a struggle against the devastating force of a shapeless life.[14] Dancing is a form of liberation, an emancipation, for a few, brief moments, from a purposeless existence, but it is also a fulcrum, the point where introspection and cheerful excess meet. Dancing is an affirmation of life's sovereign primacy.

In *Three Days* and *The Corridor*, Sharunas Bartas looks very closely at things that are impossible to understand and, in some cases, quite vile, but he does so by using series of quick cinematographic glances that give places and people an equal treatment. Small, cruel, everyday events occur everywhere, but in these locales of little or no importance – the cellar, the bunker, the corridor – the young and marginal characters can look for that protection which they cannot find anywhere else; there, they can remove themselves from the clamour of the outside world. One of the aesthetic and political particularities of Sharunas Bartas's films lies precisely in the way he programs these underground meanderings and transforms them into silent, interior meditations. Silence, in these films, is not an affirmation, but a renunciation, yet it is never passive: it is part of the process of germination. Behind those recurring moments of interrupted dialogue, thought moves mysteriously and shines brightly.

Figure 15.1   Three Days *(1991)*

Figure 15.2 Three Days *(1991)*

Figure 15.3 Three Days *(1991)*

174 The Sense of Place in Contemporary Cinema

Figure 15.4 Three Days *(1991)*

Figure 15.5 The Corridor *(1995)*

Figure 15.6 The Corridor *(1995)*

Notes

1. Sébastien Rongier, 'L'Errance: épuisement du lieu et entrave du lien', in Dominique Berthet (ed.), *Figures de l'errance*. Paris: L'Harmattan, 2013, p. 183.
2. José Moure, 'Du silence au cinéma', *MEI Médiation et information*, 9 (1998), p. 37. Available at: <http://www.mei-info.com/wp-content/uploads/revue9/ilovepdf.com_split_3.pdf> (last accessed 28 October 2015).
3. Ibid., p. 35.
4. 'Heterotopias always presuppose a system of opening and closing that both isolates them and makes them penetrable.' Michel Foucault, *Of Other Spaces: Utopias and Heterotopias*, trans. Jay Miskowiec. Available at: <https://web.mit.edu/allanmc/www/foucault1.pdf> (last accessed 16 March 2022).
5. Henri Maldiney, 'L'Espace et le sacré', *Question de*, 70 (Paris: Albin Michel, 1987), p. 27.
6. Paul Virilio, *Bunker Archéologie*. Paris: Les Éditions du Demi-cercle, 1991, p. 39.
7. Ibid., p. 39.
8. The philosopher Umberto Galimberti states that 'inertia is a way for the body to get its matter back. It does not oppose by dissension but by meaninglessness. By developing its power of absorption, it protects the body from all production and expansion processes from which the social imagination gets its inspiration even as it attempts to destroy them.' Umberto Galimberti, *Les Raisons du corps*. Paris: Grasset, 1998, p. 303.

9. Martin Heidegger, 'What is Metaphysics?', in *Basic Writings*, New York: HarperCollins, 1977, p. 101.
10. Antonin Artaud, *L'Art et la mort*, in *Œuvres*. Paris: Gallimard, 2004, p. 187 (quoted by Évelyne Grossman, *L'Angoisse de penser*. Paris: Les Éditions de Minuit, 2015, p. 9).
11. Astor Piazzolla, *Adíos Nonino*, 1959.
12. *Porto Rico*, from the band *Vaya con Dios*.
13. Most of the actors in *The Corridor* are not professionals.
14. See Blanchot, *L'Entretien infini*, p. 357.

Epilogue

Because they bring together trace elements of daily life, because they focus on moments without qualities, because they claim an attraction to marginal places, because they unearth the vulnerabilities that are hidden there, the films I have discussed go beyond the ordinariness of spaces to create a true 'aesthetics of place'. Events both repetitive and inventive, both familiar and strange, can occur there: places are a parchment on which is inscribed our ever-moving contemporaneity. Many books allude to the 'spirit of place', or to the *'genius loci'*, to which are attributed mysterious qualities, allegorical values, but that amounts to taking away from places this fundamental trait: people live there. This is where concrete, quotidian gestures are structured and repeated. This is not the case for the places discussed in this book; they are ordinary homes, isolated areas, sometimes titanic, sometimes minor locales: they are dynamically connected with the inside and the outside, their echoes are heard near and far, here and everywhere.

In some of the films of Chantal Akerman, Avi Mograbi or Jean-Daniel Pollet, the houses the audience sees on screen belong to the filmmakers themselves: they give the viewers access to the centre of their subjective thought while paradoxically allowing themselves to step away from that centre. These houses are worlds unto themselves; they are wells to be dug, places where silent confessions and noisy disavowals fill the space, where thoughts about oneself and thoughts about others are shared and linked. What is considered private comes out of its shell, so to speak, and takes part in the experience of the world's tumult. These houses are not residences any more, they have become spaces where interior powers and exterior forces clash and collide. In them, speech becomes free, mobile, fragmentary, poetic and political, inventive and questioning. They may be turned into workshops, transformed into a temple, made simultaneously 'nomadic' and 'cloistered'. These houses form an archipelago of disparate poetic and political dwellings. *To dwell*, for these filmmakers, means to build fortresses, so that they may *reveal* (themselves) through whispers, angry revolts or provocations. But they still imply rather than explain, they prefer to include rather than exclude.

In Pedro Costa, Tariq Teguia or Pier Paolo Pasolini's 'real fictions', to live on the outskirts of the city does not just mean to occupy another space. It implies that bodies remain fixed in place and stay inside, while simultaneously walking about and living outside. Yet, they do not focus on the sorry state of the walls and facades, as that would be over-aestheticising. Rather, they attempt – quite successfully – to renew by their aesthetic and ethical positions the dynamic connections between places and those who live in them, those who arrive or those who leave. They create between these marginal places and their characters an unbreakable bond, an alliance – or misalliance. As Michel Deguy points out:

> to dwell somewhere means inventing the difference between the inside and the outside. It means clearing the way, experimenting, and building the sense, the value and the very possibility of coming in and out, of being inside or outside, of opening and closing, within a multivalent, fundamental process – the progressive creation of meaning by those who are there.[1]

The predictably negative images of architectural and urban disarray, in the films of these three directors, paradoxically tell stories of strength, memory and difference. The rhizomatic complexity of marginalised beings is illustrated poetically, in the images of cracked walls and ruins: the architectural anatomy, both interior and exterior, becomes a silent understanding, a tale of the individual and collective human experience.

By placing bodies in various postures (standing, walking, hitting, touching, shouting, listening), Danièle Huillet and Jean-Marie Straub, Philippe Grandrieux, Lisandro Alonso and Naomi Kawase go beyond forests' obvious symbolic function and grant them a sensory power, an existential dimension, an economic identity. For Huillet and Straub, bodies talk while firmly anchored in the ground of the woodlands; for Philippe Grandrieux or Lisandro Alonso, gestures are fluidly or nervously choreographed. In their films, the actors avoid clichés and create non-psychological incarnations, thus connecting human life to all the variety of living things. Forests are primordial places, as well as energy reserves threatened by eco-political games; they are dynamic laboratories of reconciliation between poetics and ethics, where dialogues and appeasement are possible, where tragedies can be avoided.

Filmmakers such as Bela Tarr, Bruno Dumont and Sharunas Bartas choose instead to restore the broken, chaotic, desolate places they depict. Those places are like suitcases, in which discarded objects accumulate. Their narratives present a *hyle*,[2] which in no way discredits or demeans the lives of the men who inhabits those 'nowheres'; they show how places shape their lives. The vitality of these abandoned spaces lies precisely in their accumulation of rubbish, junk and relics that fill the cinematographic screen with their obsolete, silent powers, give eloquent testimony of their precariousness and existential decline. However, the point for these filmmakers is not to make filth sacred, or to please the audience with images of impure and chaotic beauty; rather, they mean to show the dark side, the subterranean power of these inert, vile places. There, the disgraceful becomes grand, the archaic dominates the modern (Bruno Dumont), men hide and wait behind barricades (Bela Tarr), not to hide from others, but to seek refuge with others (Sharunas Bartas).

But it is obvious that this enquiry into the sense of place in contemporary cinema is by no means exhaustive. As Patrick Prado wrote: 'It would be useless to attempt a comprehensive typology of places, simply because it is the accumulation of qualities, of "adjectives", that determine and define them, and the possibilities are, therefore, infinite. *Places are the essential space of differentiation*.'[3] Welcoming nooks, remarkable fulcrums, havens for individuals and communities: places in cinema can be uncertain work sites or impregnable fortress, they are the mirror before which the self ('je') plays its little games ('jeu'). They are the spaces where one's fate is sealed and unsealed.

Notes

1. Michel Deguy, 'Que peut la pensée contre le géocide?', in Berque, de Biase and Bonnin (eds), *L'Habiter dans sa poétique première*, p. 209.
2. I am borrowing this word from Dagognet, *Des détritus, des déchets, de l'abject*, 1997, p. 11.
3. Prado, 'Lieux et délieux', p. 122.

Bibliography

Film

Agamben, Giorgio, 'Notes sur le geste', *Trafic*, 1 (Winter 1991).

Akerman, Chantal, *Chantal Akerman: The Pyjama Interview*, interview with Nicole Brenez. Useful Book #1, Vienna International Film Festival, 2011, quoted in Dominique Bax and Cyril Béghin (eds), *Chantal Akerman, Bande(s) à part*, vol. 25. Bobigny: Bande(s) à part Festival de Cinéma à Bobigny, Le Magic Cinema, 2014.

— 'Entretien avec Chantal Akerman réalisé par Blandine Jeanson et Martine Storti', *Libération*, 9 February 1976; reprinted in Dominique Bax and Cyril Béghin (eds), *Chantal Akerman, Bande(s) à part*, vol. 25. Bobigny: Bande(s) à part Festival de Cinéma à Bobigny, Le Magic Cinema, 2014.

— *No Home Movie* press kit, Zeugma Films Distribution, February 2016.

André, Emmanuelle and Dork Zabunyan, *L'Attrait du téléphone*. Crisnée: Yellow Now, 2013.

Arnaud, Diane, *Le Cinéma de Sokourov: figures d'enfermement*. Paris: L'Harmattan, 2005.

Arnaud, Philippe, *Robert Bresson*. Paris: Petite bibliothèque des Cahiers du cinéma, 2003.

Aumont, Jacques, *Du visage au cinéma*. Paris: Éditions de l'Étoile et Cahiers du cinéma, 1992.

Baecque Antoine de, *Andrei Tarkovski*. Paris: Cahiers du cinéma, 1989.

Bax, Dominique and Cyril Béghin (eds), *Chantal Akerman, Bande(s) à part*, vol. 25. Bobigny: Bande(s) à part Festival de Cinéma à Bobigny, Le Magic Cinema, 2014.

Béghin, Richard, 'L'Époque de la survivance: de la mémoire des ruines dans À l'ouest des rails de Wang Bing', *Cinémas: revue d'études cinématographiques/Cinémas: Journal of Film Studies*, 15: 2–3 (2005).

Benhaïm, Safia, 'L'Antre de Saturne', in Nicole Brenez (ed.), *La Vie nouvelle/Nouvelle Vision:* à propos d'un film de Philippe Grandrieux. Paris: Éditions Léo Scheer, 2005.

Blümlinger, Christa, 'Le Peuple qui manque: à propos des installations d'Avi Mograbi', in *Avi Mograbi: The Details*. Rennes: Éditions Galerie Art et Essai, 2011.

Bordwell, David, *Ozu and the Poetics of Cinema*. London and Princeton: British Film Institute and Princeton University Press, 1988.

Brenez, Nicole (ed.), *La Vie nouvelle/Nouvelle Vision*: à propos d'un film de Philippe Grandrieux. Paris: Éditions Léo Scheer, 2005.

— 'Insurrections de l'amour en contexte matérialiste', in Jérôme Game (ed.), *Images des corps/ Corps des images au cinéma*. Lyon: ENS Éditions, 2010.

Collet, Jean, 'Le Blanc et le noir', in *Pier Paolo Pasolini, Accattone*, vol. II: *Dossier*. Paris: Éditions Macula, 2015.

Comolli, Jean Louis and Vincent Sorrel, *Cinéma, mode d'emploi: de l'argentique au numérique*. Paris: Éditions Verdier, 2015.

Costa, Pedro, Interview by Jean-Sébastien Chauvin, *Colossal Youth* press kit, 2006.

— Interview by Emmanuel Burdeau and Thierry Lounas (4 December 2006), *Cahiers du cinéma*, 619 (January 2007).
— *Dans la chambre de Vanda: conversation avec Pedro Costa*. Nantes: Capricci, 2008.
Daney, Serge, *La Rampe*. Paris: Petite Bibliothèque des Cahiers du cinéma, 1996.
Darras, Matthieu, 'Routes à jamais perdues', *Positif*, 545–6 (July/August 2006).
Deleuze, Gilles, *Cinema 2. The Time-Image*, trans. Hugh Tomlinson and Robert Galeta. London: The Athlone Press, 1989.
Deshays, Daniel, *Entendre le cinéma*. Paris: Klincksieck, 2010.
Didi-Huberman, Georges, *Survivance des lucioles*. Paris: Les Éditions de Minuit, 2009.
— *Remontages du temps subi: l'œil de l'histoire 2*. Paris: Les Éditions de Minuit, 2010.
Dobbels, Daniel, 'L'Exergue', in Dominique Païni and Charles Tesson (eds), *Jean-Marie Straub, Danièle Huillet, Hölderlin/Cézanne*. Lédignan: Éditions Antigone, 1990.
Dumas, Robert, 'La Peinture de l'arbre à l'épreuve de la politique allemande', in Jean Mottet (ed.), *L'Arbre dans le paysage*. Seyssel: Champ Vallon, 2002.
Dumont, Bruno, 'Entretien avec le directeur de la photographie Yves Cape, Association française des directeurs de la photographie cinématographique, à propos du film *Hors Satan* de Bruno Dumont, 16 mai 2011', interview by François Reumont, <http://www.afcinema.com/Entretien-avec-le-directeur-de-la-photographie-Yves-Cape-AFC-SBC-a-propos-du-film-Hors-Satan-de-Bruno-Dumont.html> (last accessed 19 December 2016).
— 'Philippe Rouyer et Yann Tobin: entretien avec Bruno Dumont', *Positif*, 608 (October 2011).
Epstein, Jean, Écrits sur le cinéma. *Tome 1: 1921–1947*. Paris: Seghers, 1974.
Faure, Élie, *The Art of Cineplastics*, trans. Walter Pach. Boston: The Four Seas Company, 1923, p. 24.
Fitoussi, Jean-Charles, 'Le Temps d'un retour, notes de tournage de *Sicilia!*', *La Lettre du cinéma*, 8 (Winter 1999).
Foucher, Michel, 'Du désert, paysage de western', in Alain Roger (ed.), *La Théorie du paysage en France (1974–1994)*. Seyssel: Champ Vallon, 1995.
Frange, Pierre-Henri, Gilles Mouëllic and Christophe Viart (eds), *Filmer l'acte de création*. Rennes: PUR, 2009.
Gardies, André, *L'Espace au cinéma*. Paris: Méridiens Klincksieck, 1993.
— 'Le Paysage comme moment narratif', in Jean Mottet (ed.), *Les Paysages du cinéma*. Seyssel: Champ Vallon, 1999.
Gaudin, Antoine, *L'Image-espace: pour une géopoétique du cinéma*. PhD dissertation, Université de Paris-III, 2011.
Grandrieux, Philippe, 'Master Class', presented by André Habib. *24 Images*, 160, transcript from extras of *Un lac* DVD, Hors Champ, <https://horschamp.qc.ca/article/grandrieux-de-a-g> (last accessed 23 March 2022).
— Interview by Claire Vassé, 2008. *Un lac* press kit. Film Distributor: Shellac.
Guérin, Marie-Anne, 'Oh! Cette coulante liquidité de l'air', in *L'Internationale straubienne: à propos des films de Danièle Huillet et Jean-Marie Straub*. Paris: Éditions de l'œil/Centre Pompidou, 2016.
Habib, André, *L'Attrait de la ruine*. Crisnée: Yellow Now, 2011.
Houcke, Anne-Violaine, 'Le Retour de l'antique dans le cinéma italien moderne: de Warburg à Fellini et Pasolini', *Mise au point*, 3 (2011), online 30 August 2012, <http://map.revues.org/992> (last accessed 22 December 2015).
Joubert-Laurencin, Hervé, *Pasolini, portrait du poète en cinéaste*. Paris: Cahiers du cinéma, 1995.
Kràl, Petr, *Le Burlesque, ou la morale de la tarte à la crème* [1984]. Paris: Ramsay, 2007.
Kuyper, Éric de, 'Aux origines du cinéma: le film de famille', in Roger Odin (ed.), *Le Film de amille: usage privé, usage public*. Paris: Méridiens Klincksieck, 1995.

Lacoste, Yves, 'Westerns et géopolitique', in Jean Mottet (ed.), *Les Paysages du cinéma*. Seyssel: Champ Vallon, 1999.

Lafosse, Philippe, *L'Étrange Cas de Madame Huillet et Monsieur Straub: comédie policière avec Danièle Huillet, Jean-Marie Straub et le public*. Toulouse and Ivry-sur-Seine: Ombres/À propos, 2007.

Lavin, Mathias, 'Ici comme ailleurs? Intériorisation de frontières dans *Là-bas* de Chantal Akerman', in Corinne Maury and Philippe Ragel (eds), *Filmer les frontières*. Saint-Denis: PUV, 2016.

Leblanc, Gérard, *Scénarios du réel*, vol. 2. Paris: L'Harmattan, 1997.

— 'La Poétique Epsteinienne', in Jacques Aumont (ed.), *Jean Epstein, cinéaste, poète, philosophe*. Paris: La Cinémathèque française, 1998.

Leperchey, Sarah, *L'Esthétique de la maladresse au cinéma*. Paris: L'Harmattan, 2011.

Maury, Corinne, *L'Attrait de la pluie*. Crisnée: Yellow Now, 2014.

— 'Du sol refuge à la friche nourricière', in Caroline Renard, Isabelle Anselme and François Amy de La Bretèque (eds), *Wang Bing*. Aix-en-Provence: Presses Universitaires de Provence, 2014.

— 'Puissances d'enchaînements: de l'usage de la *dolly* et du *steadicam* chez Béla Tarr', in Anthony Fiant, Roxane Hamery and Jean-Baptiste Massuet (eds), *Point de vue, point d'écoute au cinéma*. Rennes: PUR, 2017.

— and Philippe Ragel (eds), *Filmer les frontières*. Saint-Denis: PUV, 2016.

— and Sylvie Rollet (eds), *Béla Tarr, de la colère au tourment*. Crisnée: Yellow Now, 2016.

Ménil, Alain, 'Entre utopie et hérésie: quelques remarques à propos de la notion d'essai', in Suzanne Liandrat-Guigues and Murielle Gagnebin (eds), *L'Essai et le cinéma*. Seyssel: Champ Vallon, 2004.

Mercier, Marc, 'Pour en finir avec l'art orthochromatique', in Nicole Brenez (ed.), *La Vie nouvelle/Nouvelle Vision: à propos d'un film de Philippe Grandrieux*. Paris: Éditions Léo Scheer, 2005.

Mograbi, Avi, *Mon occupation préférée*, interviews with Eugenio Renzi. Paris: Les Prairies Ordinaires, 2015.

Mons, Alain, 'Le Bruit-silence ou la plongée paysagère', in Jean Mottet (ed.), *Les Paysages du cinéma*. Seyssel: Champ Vallon, 1999.

Moravia, Alberto, 'Pasolini, Civil Poet', lecture given at Yale University, 1980.

Moser, Walter, 'Présentation. Le Road movie: un genre issu d'une constellation moderne de locomotion et de médiamotion', *Cinémas: revue d'études cinématographiques/Cinémas: Journal of Film Studies*, 18: 2–3 (Spring 2008).

Mottet, Jean (ed.), *L'Arbre dans le paysage*. Seyssel: Champ Vallon, 2002.

— 'Prologue', in Jean Mottet (ed.), *L'Herbe dans tous ses états*. Seyssel: Champ Vallon, 2011.

— 'Du paysage à l'expérience sensible du monde: présence de la forêt dans le cinéma japonais', in Claire Harpet, Philippe Billet and Jean-Philippe Pierron (eds), *À l'ombre des forêts: usages, images et imaginaires de la forêt*. Paris: L'Harmattan, 2014.

Moullet, Luc, 'La carte et le territoire', in *Luc Moullet, notre alpin quotidien: entretien avec Emmanuel Burdeau et Jean Narboni*. Nantes: Capricci, 2009.

Moure, José, *Vers une esthétique du vide au cinéma*. Paris: L'Harmattan, 1997.

— 'Du silence au cinéma', *MEI Médiation et information*, 9 (1998), <http://www.mei-info.com/wp-content/uploads/revue9/ilovepdf. com_split_3.pdf> (last accessed 28 October 2015).

Niney, François, 'Confondre l'ennemi sans se confondre avec lui', in *Images documentaires*, 23 (1995).

— *L'Épreuve du réel à l'écran: essai sur le principe de réalité documentaire*. Brussels: De Boeck, 2002.

Odin, Roger, *Le Film de famille: usage privé, usage public*. Paris: Méridiens Klincksieck, 1995.

Païni, Dominique, 'Le Front d'Empédocle', in *Jean-Marie Straub, Danièle Huillet/Hölderlin, Cézanne*. Lédignan: Antigone, 1990.
— *Le Cinéma, un art moderne*. Paris: Cahiers du cinéma, 1997.
Pasolini, Pier Paolo, *L'Inédit de New York*, interview with Giuseppe Cardillo, presented by Luigi Fontanella, trans. Anne Bourguignon. Paris: Arléa, 2008.
Rancière, Jacques, *Les Écarts du cinéma*. Paris: La Fabrique Éditions, 2011.
— 'Les Incertitudes de la dialectique', *Trafic*, 93 (Spring 2015).
— 'Poétique et politique de la fiction', in Corinne Maury and Sylvie Rollet (eds), *Béla Tarr: de la colère au tourment*. Crisnée: Yellow Now, 2016.
Rieupeyrout, Jean-Louis, *La Grande Aventure du western, 1894–1964*. Paris: Cerf, 1964.
Roger, Philippe, 'La Poétique sonore de Sokourov', in François Albera and Michel Estève (eds), *Alexandre Sokourov*. Condé-sur-Noireau: Éditions Charles Corlet, CinémaAction, 2009.
Rohmer, Éric, interview with Antoine de Baecque, 'Architecture-fiction: la vie en villes. Cergy-Pontoise', *Libération* (29 March 2002).
Sokourov, Alexandre, 'Interview d'Alexandre Sokourov donnée à Georges Nivat', in Murielle Gagnebin (ed.), *L'Ombre de l'image: de la falsification à l'infigurable*. Seyssel: Champ Vallon, 2002.
Straub, Jean-Marie, 'Après *Le Genou d'Artémide* et *Le Streghe*', *Le Portique*, 33 (2014), document 7, online 5 February 2016, <http://leportique.revues.org/2764> (last accessed 11 January 2017).
— and Danièle Huillet, *Quei loro incontri* press kit (2006), distributed by Pierre Grise Distribution, 2008, <http://www.gncr.fr/films-soutenus/ces-rencontres-avec-eux> (last accessed 2 February 2017).
— 'Rencontres avec Jean-Marie Straub et Danièle Huillet, École supérieure des beaux-arts du Mans, mars 1994', in Jean-Louis Raymond (ed.), *Rencontres avec Jean-Marie Straub et Danièle Huillet*. Paris and Le Mans: Les Éditions Beaux-arts de Paris /École supérieure des beaux-arts du Mans, 2008.
— 'Entretien avec Renato Berta', in *L'Internationale straubienne: à propos des films de Danièle Huillet et Jean-Marie Straub*. Paris: Éditions de l'œil/Centre Pompidou, 2016.
Teguia, Tariq, *Cinéaste au centre, discussion entre Tariq Teguia et Jacques Rancière*. Paris: Centre Georges-Pompidou, 8 March 2015, <https://www.centrepompidou.fr/cpv/resource/cdy6bG9/r5XgG78> (last accessed 16 March 2022).
— 'La Leçon de cinéma de Tariq Teguia', Festival des Films d'Afrique du Pays d'Apt, 2009, interview with Olivier Bardet, <http://www.africultures.com/php/?nav=articleetno=9014> (last accessed 23 September 2016).
David, Vasse, 'Le Dos et le sol: de quelques dos dans le cinéma de Danièle Huillet et Jean-Marie Straub', in Benjamin Thomas, *Tourner le dos au cinéma: sur l'envers du personnage au cinéma*. Saint-Denis: PUV, 2012.

ART HISTORY, IMAGE THEORY, PHOTOGRAPHY

Barthes, Roland, *Empire of Signs*, trans. Richard Howard. New York: The Noonday Press, 1982.
Saint Girons, Baldine, *Les Marges de la nuit: pour une autre histoire de la peinture*. Paris: Les Éditions de l'Amateur, 2006.

Philosophy

Agamben, Giorgio, 'What is the Contemporary?', in *What is an Apparatus and Other Essays*, trans. David Kishik and Stefan Pedatella. Stanford: Stanford University Press, 2009.

Aristotle, *Physics, The Complete Works of Aristotle, The Revised Oxford Translation*, vol. 1, ed. Jonathan Barnes. Princeton: Princeton University Press, 1991.

Bachelard, Gaston, *Poétique de l'espace* [1957]. Paris: PUF, 1961.

Bégout, Bruce, *La Découverte du quotidien*. Paris: Allia, 2005.

Besse, Jean-Marc, *Habiter un monde à mon image*. Paris: Flammarion, 2013.

Dagognet, François, 'Route, anti-route et méta-route', *Les Cahiers de médiologie*, 2 (1996).

— *Des détritus, des déchets, de l'abject: une philosophie écologique*. Le Plessis-Robinson: Institut Synthélabo pour le progrès de la connaissance, 1997.

Dastur, Françoise, *Hölderlin, le retournement natal*. Paris: Encre Marine, 1997.

Derrida, Jacques, *Speech and Phenomena, and Other Essays on Husserl's Theory of Signs*, trans. David B. Allison. Evanston, IL: Northwestern University Press, 1973.

— *Chaque fois unique, la fin du monde*. Paris: Galilée, 2003.

Foucault, Michel, 'Preface to Transgression', in *Language, Counter-Memory, Practice: Selected Essays and* Interviews, ed. Donald F. Bouchard, trans. Donald F. Bouchard and Sherry Simon. Ithaca, NY: Cornell University Press, 1977.

— *Of Other Spaces: Utopias and Heterotopias*, trans. Jay Miskowiec, <https://web.mit.edu/allanmc/www/foucault1.pdf> (last accessed 16 March 2022).

Galimberti, Umberto, *Les Raisons du corps*. Paris: Grasset, 1998.

Goetz, Benoît, *Théorie des maisons: l'habitation, la surprise*. Lagrasse: Verdier, 2011.

Grimaldi, Nicolas, *Ontologie du temps: l'attente et la rupture*. Paris: PUF, 1993.

Heidegger, Martin, *Essais et conférences*. Paris: Gallimard, 1958.

— 'Building Dwelling Thinking', in *Poetry, Language, Thought*, trans. Albert Hofstadter. New York: Harper Colophon Books, 1971.

— 'What is Metaphysics?', in *Basic Writings*, New York: HarperCollins, 1977.

Jankélévitch, Vladimir, *La Mort*. Paris: Flammarion, 1977.

Jouannais, Jean-Yves, *L'Idiotie*. Paris: Beaux-Arts Magazine/Livres, 2003.

Levinas, Emmanuel, *Totalité et infini, essai sur l'extériorité*. The Hague: M. Nijhoff, 1961.

— *Parole et silence et autres conférences inédites au Collège philosophique*, ed. Rodolphe Calin and Catherine Chalier. Paris: Bernard Grasset/Imec, 2009.

Margel, Serge, 'Au lieu de profondeur', in Catherine Malabou (ed.), *Plasticité*. Paris: Éditions Léo Scheer, 2000.

Merleau-Ponty, Maurice, *Phenomenology of Perception*, trans. Colin Smith. London: Routledge & Kegan Paul, 1962.

— *Nature: Course Notes from the Collège de France*, compiled and with notes by Dominique Séglard, trans. Robert Vallier. Evanston, IL: Northwestern University Press, 2003.

Nancy, Jean-Luc, 'L'Offrande sublime', in *Du sublime*. Paris: Belin, 1988.

— 'Image et violence', *Le Portique*, 6 (2000), online 24 March 2005. <http://leportique.revues.org/451> (last accessed 8 June 2016).

Nuselovici, Alexis (Nouss), *L'Exil comme expérience*. FMSH-WP-2013-43, 2013, <https://halshs.archives-ouvertes.fr/halshs-00861245> (last accessed 7 June 2016).

Rongier, Sébastien, 'L'Errance: épuisement du lieu et entrave du lien', in Dominique Berthet (ed.), *Figures de l'errance*. Paris: L'Harmattan, 2013.

Sansot, Pierre, *Du bon usage de la lenteur*. Paris: Payot et Rivages, 2000.

Schoentjes, Pierre, *Poétique de l'ironie*. Paris: Seuil, 2001.
Virilio, Paul, *Bunker Archéologie*. Paris: Les Éditions du Demi-Cercle, 1991.

GEOGRAPHY, ARCHITECTURE, ANTHROPOLOGY, HISTORY

Agier, Michel, *Le Couloir des exilés: être étranger dans un monde commun*. Bellecombe-en-Bauges: Éditions du Croquant, 2011.
Britannica, The Editors of Encyclopaedia. 'aliyah'. *Encyclopedia Britannica*, 30 July 2019, <https://www.britannica.com/topic/aliyah> (last accessed 23 March 2022).
Arnould, Paul, 'La Forêt: le sens et les sens', in Andrée Corvol, Paul Arnould and Micheline Hotyat (eds), *La Forêt: perceptions et représentations*. Paris: L'Harmattan, 1997.
Augé, Marc, *Non-places: Introduction to an Anthropology of Supermodernity*, trans. John Howe. London: Verso, 1995.
Balandier, Georges, *Le Pouvoir sur scène*. Paris: Fayard, 2006.
Berenstein-Jacques, Paola, Alain Guez and Antonella Tufano, 'Trialogue: lieu/mi-lieu/non-lieu', in Chris Younès and Michel Mangematin (eds), *Lieux contemporains*. Paris: Descartes & Cie, 1997.
Berque, Augustin, *Le Sauvage et l'artifice*. Paris: Gallimard, 1986.
— Alessia de Biase and Philippe Bonnin (eds), *L'Habiter dans sa poétique première: actes du colloque de Cerisy-la-Salle*. Paris: Éditions Donner lieu, 2008.
— and Maurice Sauzet, *Le Sens de l'espace au Japon: vivre, penser, bâtir*. Paris: Éditions Arguments, 2004.
Besse, Jean-Marc, 'Entre géographie et paysage', in Michel Collot (ed.), *Les Enjeux du paysage*. Brussels: Ousia, 1997.
— 'Cartographier les lieux de nulle part', *Notre histoire*, 233 (2005).
— 'Cartographie et pensée visuelle: réflexions sur la schématisation graphique', in Isabelle Laboulais (ed.), *Les Usages des cartes (xviie–xixe siècles): pour une approche pragmatique des productions cartographiques*. Strasbourg: PUS, 2008.
— *Habiter un monde à mon image*. Paris: Flammarion, 2013.
Bonnin, Philippe, 'Le temps d'habiter', in Augustin Berque, Alessia de Biase and Philippe Bonnin (eds), *L'Habiter dans sa poétique première: actes du colloque de Cerisy-la-Salle*. Paris: Éditions donner lieu, 2008.
Brochot, Aline and Martin de la Soudière (eds), 'Pourquoi le lieu', *Communications*, 87 (2010).
Cauquelin, Anne, *Le Site et le paysage*. Paris: PUF, 2002.
Certeau, Michel de, *L'Invention du quotidien. 1. Arts de faire*, ed. Luce Giard. Paris: Gallimard, 1990.
Charbonnel, Nanine, 'Homo Viator ou Les Dix Métaphores de la marche', *Les Cahiers de médiologie*, 2 (Paris: Gallimard, 1996).
Clément, Gilles, 'Le Tiers-Paysage', <http://www.gillesclement.com/cat-tierspaysage-tit-le-Tiers-Paysage> (last accessed 14 February 2017).
Collot, Michel (ed.), *Les Enjeux du paysage*. Brussels: Ousia, 1997.
Deguy, Michel, 'Que peut la pensée contre le géocide?', in Augustin Berque, Alessia de Biase and Philippe Bonnin (eds), *L'Habiter dans sa poétique première: actes du colloque de Cerisy-la-Salle*. Paris: Éditions Donner lieu, 2008.
Demangeot, Jean, *Les Milieux naturels du globe*. Paris: Armand Colin, 1996.
Foucher, Michel, *L'Obsession des frontières*. Paris: Perrin, 2007.
Godin, Christian and Laure Mühlethaler, *Édifier: l'architecture et le lieu*. Lagrasse: Verdier, 2005.

Goetz, Benoît, 'La Dislocation: critique des lieux', in Chris Younès and Michel Mangematin (eds), *Lieux contemporains*. Paris: Descartes & Cie, 1997.
Harrison, Robert, *Forests, the Shadow of Civilisation*. Chicago: University of Chicago Press, 1992.
Huyghe, François-Bernard, 'Le Médium ambigu', *Les Cahiers de médiologie*, 2 (Paris: Gallimard, 1996).
Illich, Ivan, *Dans le miroir du passé: conférences et discours, 1978–1990*. Paris: Éditions Descartes et Cie, 1994.
Lévy, Jacques and Michel Lussault (eds), *Dictionnaire de la géographie et de l'espace des sociétés*. Paris: Belin, 2013.
Maldiney Henri, 'L'Espace et le sacré', *Question de*, 70 (Paris: Albin Michel, 1987).
— 'Topos–Logos–Aisthèsis', in Michel Mangematin, Philippe Nys and Chris Younès (eds), *Le Sens du lieu*. Brussels: Ousia, 1996.
Mangematin, Michel, Philippe Nys and Chris Younès (eds), *Le Sens du lieu*. Brussels: Ousia, 1996.
Mons, Alain, 'L'Intervalle des lieux', *Le Portique*, 12 (2003), online 15 June 2006, <http://leportique.revues.org/578> (last accessed 8 September 2015).
Nora, Pierre (ed.), *Rethinking France: Les Lieux de mémoire*. Chicago: University of Chicago Press, 1999–2010.
Paquot, Thierry (ed.), *Banlieues/Une anthologie*. Lausanne: PPUR, 2008.
— 'Les Banlieues au cinéma: filmothèque', in Thierry Paquot (ed.), *Banlieues/Une anthologie*. Lausanne: PPUR, 2008.
Pezeu-Massabuau, Jacques, 'La Maison japonaise: standardisation de l'espace habité et harmonie sociale', *Annales ESC*, 4 (1977).
Piveteau Jean-Luc, 'Lieu et territoire: une consanguinité dialectique?', *Communications*, 87 (2010).
Prado, Patrick, 'Lieux et "délieux"', *Communications*, 87 (2010).
Roger, Alain (ed.), *La Théorie du paysage en France (1974–1994)*. Seyssel: Champ Vallon, 1995.
Saint Girons, Baldine, 'Jardins et paysages: une opposition catégorielle', in Jackie Pigeaud and Jean-Paul Barbe (eds), *Histoires de jardins: lieux et imaginaire*. Paris: PUF, 2001.
Salignon, Bernard, *Qu'est-ce qu'habiter?* Paris: Éditions de la Villette, 2000.
Tiberghien, Gilles A., 'Demeurer, habiter, transiter: une poétique de la cabane', in Augustin Berque, Alessia de Biase and Philippe Bonnin (eds), *L'Habiter dans sa poétique première: actes du colloque de Cerisy-la-Salle*. Paris: Éditions Donner lieu, 2008.
Vallat, Colette, 'Centre et habitat précaire, périphérie et habitat illégal. Quelle place pour les grands ensembles en Italie?', in Frédéric Dufaux and Annie Fourcault (eds), *Le Monde des grands ensembles*. Paris: Créaphis, 2004.
Wajcman, Gérard, *Fenêtre: chroniques du regard et de l'intime*. Lagrasse: Verdier, 2004.
Younès, Chris and Michel Mangematin (eds), *Lieux contemporains*. Paris: Descartes et Cie, 1997.

LITERATURE

Akerman, Chantal, *Ma mère rit*. Paris: Mercure de France, 2013.
Artaud, Antonin, *Œuvres*. Paris: Gallimard, 2004.
Bailly, Jean-Christophe, *Le Propre du langage: voyage au pays des noms communs*. Paris: Seuil, 1997.
Blanchot, Maurice, *L'Entretien infini*. Paris: Gallimard, 1969.
Butor, Michel, *Michel Butor par Michel Butor*. Paris: Seghers, 2003.
— *Le Génie du lieu* [1958]. Paris: Grasset, 2015.

Collot, Michel, *L'Horizon fabuleux*, vol. 1: *XIXe siècle*. Paris: José Corti, 1988.
— *La Matière-émotion*. Paris: PUF, 1997.
— 'Paysages en movement: l'image-émotion', *Vertigo*, 31 (2007).
— *La Pensée-paysage*. Arles: Actes Sud/ENSP, 2011.
Corbin, Alain, 'Conquérir la paresse', *Le Magazine littéraire*, 433 (July 2004).
Del Lungo, Andrea, *La Fenêtre: sémiologie et histoire de la représentation littéraire*. Paris: Seuil, 2014.
Edwards, Michael, *Éloge de l'attente: T. S. Eliot et Samuel Beckett*. Paris: Belin, 1966.
Genet, Jean, 'Quatre heures à Chatila', *Revue d'études palestiniennes*, 6 (Winter 1983), reprinted in *L'Ennemi déclaré: textes et entretiens*. Paris: Gallimard, 1991.
Grossman, Évelyne, *L'Angoisse de penser*. Paris: Éditions de Minuit, 2015.
Mauriac, François, 'Journal d'un curé de campagne', *Gringoire*, 390 (24 April 1936).
Oz, Amos, *A Tale of Love and Darkness*, trans. Nicholas de Lange: Boston: Houghton Mifflin Harcourt, 2004.
Perec, Georges, *Ellis Island*. Paris: POL, 1995.
— *Espèces d'espaces* [1974]. Paris: Galilée, 2000.
Picon, Gaétan, *Bernanos: L'impatiente joie. Suivi de Lettres inédites de Georges Bernanos à Gaétan Picon*. Paris: Hachette Littératures, 1997.
Ponge, Francis, *La Table*. Paris: Gallimard, 1991.
Starobinski, Jean, *Action et réaction: vie et aventure d'un couple*. Paris: Seuil, 1999.
Tanizaki, Junichirō, *In Praise of Shadows*, trans. Thomas J. Harper and Edward G. Seidensticker. Stony Creek: Leete's Island Books, 1977.
Vadé, Yves, 'Retour du primitif, permanence de l'archaïque', *Modernités*, 7 (Bordeaux: PUB, 1996).
Vittorini, Elio, 'Interview de Vittorini par D. Mascolo et E. Morin', *Lettres françaises*, 160 (June 1947).

Psychoanalysis

Lacan, Jacques, *Le Séminaire, livre V. Les Formations de l'inconscient (1957–1958)*. Paris: Seuil, 1998.
Mills, Jon, *L'Inconscient et son lieu: genèse de la réalité psychique*. Montreal: Liber, 2013.

Index

Note: n indicates note, italic indicates illustration

abandoned places, 178–9
absence, 117–18
Accattone, 115, 116, 119, 122–3n
action/reaction, 51–2
aesthetic plasticity, 2
aesthetics, topological, 125
'aesthetics of place', 177
Agamben, Giorgio, 118, 127
Akerman, Chantal, 17–44, 177
    Ma mère rit, 35–6
Akerman, Natalia, 29, 33, 35–40, 42n
Algeria, 134–43, 141n
Algiers, 134–43
Alonso, Lisandro, 103–13, 178
anachronism, 115–18
anaphoric places, 3
antiquity, 116–18, 122n
archaic place, 151–5
architecture, 4–5
'areolar spaces', 62
Argentina, 103
Aristotle, *The Physics*, 4
armchairs, 37–8
Arnould, Paul, 106
audience, 6–8
Augé, Marc, 3, 11n, 118
August: A Moment Before the Eruption (2002), 53, 55–8, *57*, 60n
Avatar (2009), 73
Avenge But One of My Two Eyes (2005), 53–4, *58*

Bachelard, Gaston, *The Poetics of Space*, 13, 24
Bailly, Jean-Christophe, 3
Balandier, Georges, 50

banlieue, 115–43
barricades, 159–66
Bartas, Sharunas, 145, 167–76, 178–9
Barthes, Roland, 63, 68
'becoming a place', 91–2
beds, 25–6, 28n
Bégin, Richard, 117–18, 138
Bégout, Bruce, 17–18, 119
Belmont, Yves, 104
belonging, 31–2
Benhaïm, Safia, 79
Benjamin, Walter, 51, 119
Bernanos, Georges, 152
    Under the Sun of Satan, 151
Berque, Augustin, 62, 84, 86
Berta, Renato, 91
Besse, Jean-Marc, 18, 34, 130, 137
Bing, Wang, 5, 104
Black Sin (1988), 97
Blanchot, Maurice, 17, 29
Blow Up My Town (1968), 17–21, *20*, 25–6, 33
blurry images, 76, 77, 170
bodies
    attached to places, 126–8, 178
    'embodied', 2
    march of, 83–9
    and natural elements, 86, 96
    as political philosophy, 46–7
    and space, 19–21, 22
Bonnin, Philippe, 148–9
borgate, 122n
Boulonnais region, France, 153–5
Boyfriends and Girlfriends (1987), 111–12
Brenez, Nicole, 40, 46, 59n
Bresson, Robert, 130, 153

Brussels, 29, 35–7
bunker, 169–70
burlesque idiocy, 55–8
'Buti films', 92–9
Buti ravine, 92–9
Butor, Michel, 3

Cabrera, Dominique, 112
Cameron, James, 73
Cape, Yves, 149, 157n
capitalism, 90–1
Carné, Marcel, 118
Cauquelin, Anne, 3–4, 6, 104
Cave of the Patriarchs, Hebron, 56, 60n
Certeau, Michel de, 3
Charbonnel, Nanine, 84
Château, Dominique, 7
chromatic intoxication, 79
Chroniques d'une banlieue ordinaire (1992), 112
CinemaScope, 149
circulatory images, 161–2
cities, 29–42
civil war, 136–7, 140
Clément, Gilles, 5
cloistered nomadism, 17–44
La Clôture (2003), 135–6, *141*, 141n
Clouzot, Henri-Georges, 59n
Collet, Jean, 119
Collot, Michel, 6, 105–6, 149
   La Matiere-emotion, 133n
colorimetry, 1
Colossal Youth (2006), 112–13, 124–33, *131*, *132*
community, 128–31
Comolli, Jean-Louis, 129
constructed degradation, 138
'constructed ruins', 138–9
contemporary ruins, 138–9
Corbin, Alain, 25
The Corridor (1995), 167, 170–2, *174*, *175*
Costa, Pedro, 46, 59n, 112–13, 124–33, 178
crafting, 66–9
cursed places, 147–58

Dagognet, François, 137, 150–1
daily chores, 17–19
daily life, 2, 17–21, 22–8
Damnation (1988), 1–2, 159–66, *163*, *164*

dancing, 172
Daney, Serge, 102n, 128
Dastur, Françoise, 98
The Death of Empedocles (1987), 91–2, 97, 98
Deguy, Michel, 178
Del Lungo, Andrea, 159
Deleuze, Gilles, 19, 90
demonic trilogy, 159–66
Derrida, Jacques, 83, 136
Deshays, Daniel, 78
Didi-Huberman, Georges, 51, 118
dilapidated fragility, 124–6
Dobbels, Daniel, 127–8
dogs, 1–2
domesticity
   cataclysm, 23
   daily chores, 17–19
   daily life, 2, 17–21, 22–8
   gestures, 66–9
   reversed, 17–18
   series of episodes, 56
doors, 35–6
Down There (2006), 21, 30–4, *39*
Drifting Clouds (1996), 1
Dumont, Bruno, 145, 147–58, 178–9
dwelling, 2, 4, 13, 43, 128, 177
   'undwelling', 24

École du Fresnoy, 46
editing, 6–7, 34–6, 46, 51
Edward, Michael, 162
Ellis Island, 31–2
emptiness, 61–3
Epstein, Jean, 77
everyday rowdiness, 17–21
evil, fighting the forces of, 151–5
exploitation site, 105–7

fabricated place, 128–31
Fabrika (2004), 104
Farocki, Harun, 51
Faure, Elie, 139
Ferrailles d'attente (1998), 134–5, 141n
Festival des Films d'Afrique du Pays d'Apt, 141n
Festival du nouveau cinéma, 81–2n
Figueroa, Gabriel, 157n

'film-parcours' (journey movies), 11n
fixed dynamic, 34
Fontainhas, Lisbon, 124–33, 132–3n
Ford, John, 7–8, 93
forests, 75–82, 105–7, 178
    dual, 103–13
    fleeting sacredness, 79–80
    from sensory environment to economic site, 75–113
formal petrification, 161–2
fortification, poetics of, 66–9
Foucault, Michel, 25
Frank, Robert, 141n
From the Clouds to the Resistance (1979), 92

Galimberti, Umberto, 175n
gardens, 63–4
Gardies, André, 7
Gaudin, Antoine, 11n
Genet, Jean, 52
'genius of place', 3, 177
Le Genou d'Artémide (2008), 93, 98–9, *100, 101*
geography, 5, 29, 91–2
geology, 91–2
globalisation, 5
Godard, Jean-Luc, 45
Goetz, Benoît, 4, 14, 43, 128, 139
    Theorie des maisons, 24
Goldstein, Baruch, 60n
Grandrieux, Philippe, 75–82, 178
'grieving memory', 138–9
Grimaldi, Nicolas, 163

Habib, André, 81–2n
habitus, 2
haikus, 68–9
halted flight, 137
hamlets, 147–58
harmoniousness, 94
Harrison, Robert, 73–4
healing restraint, 84–5
Heidegger, Martin, 4–5, 106, 171
Hölderlin, Friedrich, 92, 97, 98, 99
horizons, 6–8, 33–4, 83, 106, 121, 140, 149, 157n
Hors Champ magazine, 81–2n
Hors Satan (2011), 147–55, *155, 156*

Houcke, Anne-Violaine, 122n
'household films', 43
houses, 13–14, 177
    Japanese, 125
    as a place of declarations and meditations, 45–1
How I Learned to Overcome My Fear and Love Arik Sharon (1997), 47–52, 55, *58*
Huillet, Danièle, 46, 90–102, 127–8, 178
A Humble Life (1997), 61–71, *68, 69, 70*
Humiliated (2003), 93
Hungary, 1–2, 159–66
Huyghe, François-Bernard, 153–4

I, You, He, She (2018), 28n
I Don't Belong Anywhere: Le Cinéma de Chantal Akerman (2015), 19
Illich, Ivan, 129
illness, 14, 20–1, 33
immobility, 127–8
In the Memory of a Day Gone By, 167
In Vanda's Room (2000), 124, 126
incarcerated anchoring, 34
incipient places, 3
L'Inconsolable (2011), 93
indignant irony, 55–8
industrial sites, 104
inertia, 170–2, 175n
initiatory walk, 85–7
inner life, 22–3
interior worlds, 171
isolated places, 147–58
isolation, 168–9
Israel, 30–4
Israeli–Palestinian conflict, 45–58

Japan, 61–71, 83–9
Japanese house, 125
Jean-André, 115
Jeanne Dielman, 23, quai du commerce, 1080 Bruxelles (1975), 22–8, *26, 27*
Jouannais, Jean-Yves, 56
Joubert-Laurencin, Hervé, 115
journey movies, 11n

Kaliningrad, 167–70
Kaurismäki, Aki, 1
Kawase, Naomi, 83–9, 178

Kommunisten (2014), 90
Kràl, Petr, 17

La Madrague, 134, 136–41
Lacan, Jacques, 22
Lambert, Marianne, 19
landscape, 5–7, 33–4
  atmospheric, 6–8
  predatory, 105–7
  scrapped, 134–7
  'third', 5
'landscape dance', 77
Lebanon, 52
Leblanc, Gérard, 77
Levinas, Emmanuel, 152
Libération (newspaper), 111–12, 166n
La Libertad (2001), 103–113, *107*, *108*
Likud Party, 47–52
lives under the ground, 167–70
living room as 'confession box', 47–52
local change of scenery, 29–42
localization, 5
locus, 29
loneliness, 171
lonely wanderings, 167–76
loners, 1–2
loss, 83–9
low-angle shots, 33–4, 53, 105, 127, 129, 135
Loznitsa, Sergei, 104

Maldiney, Henri, 5, 169
Mamma Roma (1962), 113, 116–21, *120*, *121*
The Man with No Name (2009), 5
The Man Without a Past (2002), 1
Mangolte, Babette, 22–3
Margel, Serge, 77
marginal places, 178
Marxism, 90–1, 97
mature revolt, 18–19
Mauriac, François, 152
'meaning of meanings', 149
memory, grieving, 138–9
'memory space', 3
Ménil, Alain, 50
mental disorder, 22–3
Merleau-Ponty, 150
Mills, Jon, 19–20
The Mirror (1975), 66

Mograbi, Avi, 43, 45–60, 177
Mons, Alain, 34, 126
Monument Valley, 7–8
Mother and Sons (1997), 6
mothers, 14, 19–21, 23–5, 29–31, 35–40, 42n
Mottet, Jean, 89n
Moulley, Luc, 91
Mount Testaccio, 115
Moure, José, 7–8, 168
The Mourning Forest (2007), 83–9, *87*, *88*
moving inwardness, 61–71
moving margin, 106
Les Muertos (2004), 103–13
multisensory place, 75–82
music, 1, 96, 105, 127, 171–2
The Mystery of Picasso (1956), 59n

Nancy, Jean-Luc, 54, 65
nature, 5–6, 62–4, 68, 73–4, 83–7, 90–9, 103–7, 116–18, 150, 150–4, 157n
neurotic seclusion, 20–8
New York, 29, 36–7
News from Home (1976), 29, *38*
night, 79–80, 140
Niney, François, 52
  Images documentaires, 48–9
No Home Movie (2015), 20–1, 34–40, *40*
nomadism, 137
  cloistered, 17–44
  sedentary, 29
'non-place', 3, 11n
Nora, Pierre, 3
'nowheres', 145, 159–66
Nuselovici, Alexis, 31

'off centre', 2
Opal Coast, France, 147–58
Oriental Elegy (1996), 64–5
Orsi, Grazia, 97
Ossos (1997), 124
Other, 22, 55, 83
Ozu, Yasujirō, 125

Paquot, Thierry, 111
Paraná River, 105–7
Pasolini, Pier Paolo, 112–13, 115–23, 178
Pasolini l'enragé (1966), 115
pathos, 2, 33, 96, 98–9

Pavese, Cesare, 97, 98
    Dialogues with Leuco, 92, 94–5, 98–9
Perec, Georges, 31–2, 36
    Species of Spaces, 24
Pezeu-Massabuau, Jacques, 62
Picon, Gaétan, 151
Piveteau, Jean-Luc, 5
place, 2–9
    aesthetics of, 177
    becoming a, 91–2
    fabricated, 128–31
    genius of, 3, 177
    multisensory, 75–82
    as narrative agent, 3
    'non-place', 3, 11n
    plastic eurythmics of, 139–41
    practice of, 3
    spirit of, 177
places
    abandoned, 178–9
    anaphoric, 3
    archaic, 151–5
    cursed and isolated, 147–58
    for the displaced, 124–33
    incipient, 3
    marginal, 178
    referential, 3
    strangeness of, 147–76
    unique, 95
planned space, 128–31
plastic eurythmics of place, 139–41
poetics of fortification, 66–9
political workshop, 45–60
Pollet, Jean-Daniel, 177
Ponge, Francis, 37
Portrait d'une paresseuse (1996), 24–6
'potato shot', 23
poverty, 1, 115–16, 130–1
'practice of place', 3
Prado, Patrick, 4, 179
predatory landscape, 105–7
production site, 103–5
P'tit Quinquin (2014), 147, 153–5, *157*

Quei Loro Incontri (2006), 93, 94, 96–7

rain, 2
Rancière, Jacques, 97–8, 126, 162

'real fictions', 178
rebellious alterities, 118–21
referential places, 3
reversed domesticity, 17–18
'rhythmic space', 62, 67
Rohmer, Eric, 111–12
Rome, 115–21, 122–3n
Rome Rather Then You (2006), 113, 134, 136–41, *141, 142*
Rongier, Sébastien, 168
The Room (1972), 28n
rubbish, 1, 54, 148, 169–70, 178–9
ruins, 134–43
Russia, 66, 104

'sacred sobriety' of the undergrowth, 90–102
Saint-Girons, Baldine, 64, 79–80
    Les Marges de la nuit, 140
Salignon, Bernard, 154
sanitised apartment, 124–33
Sansot, Pierre, 67
Sátántangó (1994), 159, 160–1, *164*
scenery, 1–3, 8–9, 29–42, 99, 128
Schoentjes, Pierre, 55
scrapped landscape, 134–7
The Searchers (1956), 7–8
seclusion, neurotic, 20–8
sedentary nomadism, 29
semio-narratology, 3
set design as witness, 119
Seyrig, Delphine, 22
shadows, 66–7
Sharon, Ariel, 47–52, 55
Sicilia!, 46, 92, 102n
silence, 152–3, 168, 170–2, 179
site, 104
    economic, 75–113
    exploitation, 105–7
    industrial, 104
    production, 103–5
slums, 124–33
Sokurov, Alexander, 6, 43, 61–71
solitude of men, 145–76
Sombre, 76
sophisticated dereliction, 1
sound, 19, 33–4, 61–7, 75–9, 83, 91, 94, 97–9, 105–6, 134, 152–3, 159, 170–1

space, 2
　planned, 128–31
　rhythmic, 62, 67
　third, 104
spaces
　areolar, 62
　of thought, 43
spectators, 6–8
spirituality, 6, 117–18, 150–5
　of the Japanese house, 61–6
　'spirit of place', 177
　spiritual journey, 83–9
'staple', 128
Starobinski, Jean, 51
strangeness of places, 146–76
Straub, Jean-Marie, 46, 59n, 90–102, 127–8, 178
Straubs, 90–102, 127–8, 178
Le Streghe (2009), 93
studios, 45–7
suicide, 30–1, 41n

Tanizaki, Junichiro, *In Praise of Shadows*, 67
Tarkovsky, Andrei, 66, 150
Tarr, Béla, 1–2, 145, 159–66, 178–9
'teenage' films, 18–19
Teguia, Tariq, 112–13, 134–43, 178
telephone, 53–5
temporality, 18
territory, 2, 5
third space, 104
'third-landscape', 5
Three Days (1991), 167–70, 172, *172*, *174*
thresholds, 130, 154
Tiberghien, Gilles, 104
topography, 5, 13, 62, 65, 79, 94, 117, 136, 139, 141, 153
'topological aesthetics', 125

topos, 2, 4–5, 53
trajectory, 90, 150–1, 160, 162, 168
The Turin Horse (2011), 159, 161–2, *165*

Un Lac (2008), 75–80, *80*, *81*, 82n
undergrounds, 167–76
undergrowth, 'sacred sobriety' of the, 90–102
'undwelling', 24
unique places, 95
'unremarkable heritage', 148–9
utopia, 115–18, 134–7

Vadé, Yves, 153
Vassé, Claire, 82n
La Vie nouvelle, 79
Vilnius, 167
Virilio, Paul, 170
Vittorini, Elio, 90, 94, 97, 98, 102n
　Women of Messina, 95–6

Wacjman, Gérard, 32
waiting, 159–66, 166n, 167–76
walking, 84–7, 89n, 91–2
walls, 29–41, 53–5
Wasteland (1960), 118
wastelands, 115–23
Wenders, Wim, 163
Werckmeister Harmonies (2000), 159
West of the Tracks (2004), 104
Where Does Your Hidden Smile Lie? (2001), 46, 59n
windows, 32–3, 43, 159–62
women, 18–19, 30, 76, 102n, 142n, 152
Workers, Peasants (2001), 93–8, *99*, *100*
workshop
　political, 45–60
　as stage, 55–8